Theory and Research
in Conflict
Management

Theory and Research in Conflict Management

Edited by **M. Afzalur Rahim**

New York
Westport, Connecticut
London

Library of Congress Cataloging-in-Publication Data

Theory and research in conflict management / edited by M. Afzalur
  Rahim.
          p.   cm.
     Includes bibliographical references.
     ISBN 0-275-93173-0 (alk. paper)
     1. Conflict management. I. Rahim, M. Afzalur.
  HD42.T53   1990
  658.4—dc20   90-31212

Library of Congress Catalog Card Number: 90-31212
ISBN: 0-275-93173-0

First published in 1990

Praeger Publishers, One Madison Avenue, New York, NY 10010
An imprint of Greenwood Publishing Group, Inc.

Printed in the United States of America

The paper used in this book complies with the Permanent
Paper Standard issued by the National Information Standards
Organization (Z39.48--1984).

10 9 8 7 6 5 4 3 2 1

Contents

Preface

M. Afzalur Rahim

In recent years, there have been renewed interest and significant changes in the study of conflict in social and organizational contexts. The formation of the International Association for Conflict Management to encourage research, teaching, and training and development on managing social and organizational conflicts and the publication of the *International Journal of Conflict Management* attest to this renewed interest.

In our previous publication, *Managing Conflict: An Interdisciplinary Approach,* we tried to present conflict management as an interdisciplinary field of study. The present work is designed to discuss theory and research in conflict management. This work is organized around six sections: organizational conflict, communication and conflict, negotiation and bargaining, mediation and arbitration, conflict in the public sector, and international conflict. This work retains the interdisciplinary approach to the study of conflict and conflict management used in the previous book. It is expected that this will help social system leaders to improve their conflict management skills.

This book contains 12 competitive papers presented at the Second Biannual Conference of the International Association for Conflict Management. These papers were selected on the basis of their reviewers' comments and recommendations of their respective chapter editors. Each paper and chapter introduction was revised or rewritten according to my comments, to maintain consistency and quality. We have strictly followed the APA style guide to prepare each paper and chapter introduction.

I am grateful to the authors for their creative and expeditious responses to my editorial comments. Their cooperation made my work as editor-in-chief easier and more enjoyable than I was led to believe it would be. My special thanks are due to the chapter editors Robert Baron, Tricia Jones, James Dworkin, Gabriel Buntzman, Thomas Pavlak, and Roderick Kramer who devoted many hours to preparing their respective chapters. My thanks are also due to Jim Dunton, senior editor of Praeger Publishers, who encouraged me to complete the book. I have enjoyed the opportunity to work with the authors on this project. The chapter editors and I worked hard to prepare a high quality book. Time will show to what extent we succeeded in attaining our objectives.

I Organizational Conflict

INTRODUCTION

Robert A. Baron

Conflict is a serious problem in modern organizations. In many cases, it wastes precious human resources that would be better directed to other activities, including the primary work of the organization. Indeed, surveys of practicing managers suggest that they spend more than 20% of their time dealing with conflict or its aftermath (Thomas, in press; Thomas & Schmidt, 1976).

Although conflict often produces negative effects, it is now widely recognized that it can yield major benefits as well (Thomas, in press). For example, conflict between individuals or groups within an organization often helps uncover persistent problems so that they can undergo careful scrutiny. In this manner, conflict sometimes serves as the impetus for effective, needed change. Similarly, conflict sometimes has the effect of increasing communication between the opposing sides. And communication, of course, is essential to enhanced coordination and related, beneficial outcomes.

The central task with respect to organizational conflict, then, is that of managing this process — doing everything in our power to ensure that its positive effects are maximized while its negative and potentially disruptive effects are minimized. Such management of conflict, in turn, requires a full and sophisticated grasp of major elements in the conflict process. Individual causes and determinants of conflict, such as faulty attributions, poor styles of communication, and personal traits or characteristics that contribute to interpersonal friction, all play a role in this regard and must be taken into account (e.g., Baron, 1988; Tjosvold, 1986b). Similarly, organization-based factors, such as competition for scarce resources, ambiguity over responsibility or jurisdiction, growing internal complexity, and faulty or inadequate forms of communication, must also be considered.

The two chapters in this section fully reflect our growing sophistication with respect to conflict and our increasing knowledge of its causes, patterns, and effects. In the first, Rahim explores the effects of a number of important factors, including conflict and stress, on several important organizational outcomes (e.g., burnout, and job performance). In addition, and clearly reflective of the multifaceted approach described above, Rahim also includes two potential moderators of such relationships — hardiness and social support — in his research. These previously have been described as potential moderators of the impact of stress upon job performance and job burnout (Kobasa, Maddi, & Kahn, 1982; Kirmeyer & Dougherty, 1988), and their potential role in this respect is assessed by Rahim. The results of this intriguing study indicate that both stress and conflict do indeed exert important effects upon organizational behavior. High levels of stress are associated with decreased job performance and job burnout. Similarly, high levels of conflict are also associated with job burnout. In contrast to previous findings, however, neither hardiness nor social support appeared to moderate the relationships of conflict and stress to the key dependent measures.

In the second chapter, Tjosvold examines the impact of two important variables — goal interdependence and communication skills — on modes of conflict management. Key findings indicate that when individuals hold shared, cooperative goals, conflict is managed much more effectively than when they hold competitive or independent ones. Specifically, individuals reported they had more positive expectations for conflict resolution and they engaged in more effective actions to manage actual conflicts when they held cooperative goals than when they held independent or competitive ones. In addition, effective communication also contributed to effective conflict management. Such skills as expressing one's views clearly, trying to understand the other's perspective, and combining the best of the ideas expressed influenced conflict resolution in a beneficial manner. Taken as a whole, Tjosvold's results suggest that the development of shared, cooperative goals, plus training in specific communication skills, can be important steps toward the effective management of a wide range of organizational conflicts.

Together, the chapters by Rahim and Tjosvold underscore the breadth and value of recent advances in our understanding of organizational conflict. Such carefully conducted investigations add appreciably to our knowledge of conflict, and so, too, to our ability to intervene constructively when the negative effects of this process threaten to overwhelm its potential benefits.

1 Moderating Effects of Hardiness and Social Support on the Relationships of Conflict and Stress to Job Burnout and Performance

A number of studies have shown the pernicious effects of job stress on individual effectiveness. A significant area of research concerns the identification of factors that aid as moderators (buffers) against the adverse effects of job stress. Two variables that have been empirically identified as potentially important moderators of the effects of job stress are personality characteristics and social support. The objective of the study was to investigate the main and moderating relationships presented in Figure 1.1. The main relationships investigated were of conflict, stress, hardiness, and social support to job burnout and performance and of hardiness and social support to conflict and stress. The principal objective of this study was to test the moderating effect of hardiness personality and social support on the relationships of conflict and stress to job burnout and performance.

A number of studies have used the indices of role conflict and ambiguity developed by Kahn, Wolfe, Quin, Snoek, and Rosenthal (1964) and Rizzo, House, and Lirtzman (1970) to measure stress. These are the measures of stressors rather than stress. In the present study a measure of stress developed by the author and his colleagues and measures of stressors developed by Rahim (1983), such as intrapersonal (role), intragroup, and intergroup conflicts, were used.

A large number of studies on stress reported data that had potentially fatal problems of common method variance. This resulted from the

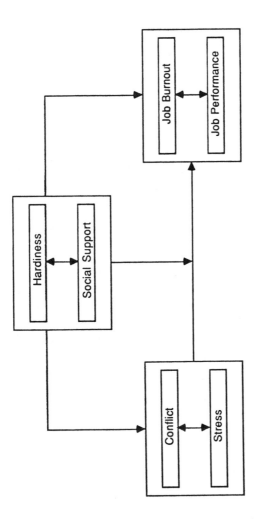

FIGURE 1.1 — Hardiness and Social Support as Moderators of the Relationships of Conflict and Stress to Job Burnout and Performance

collection of all data from a single self-report questionnaire. Methodologically speaking, researchers on stress should address a number of issues. First and foremost among these is the lack of independence between criterion and predictor variables. A subject assesses his or her own stress or stressors and then reports his or her reactions, such as job burnout or satisfaction. Without objective measures of stress (or the effects of stress), or at least independent measures, the results may simply reflect some intrasubject consistency between perceptions of one's own stress and report of one's own responses. In the present study self-report measures of organizational conflict, job stress, and job burnout (emotional exhaustion, depersonalization, and personal accomplishment) were collected from employees. Measures of overall job performance (performance, conformance, dependability, and personal adjustment) were collected from the employees' supervisors.

Kobasa (1979) and Kobasa, Maddi, and Kahn (1982) found support for the hypothesis that hardiness personality dispositions mitigate (moderate) the insidious effect of stress. Evidence also indicates that hardiness personality may also have main effects on stress (Kobasa, Maddi, & Courington, 1981; Kobasa, Maddi, & Kahn, 1982). This indicates that persons who are high on hardiness experience less stress than persons who are low on hardiness. Hardy personality has three characteristics: commitment, control, and challenge. Commitment reflects a sense of purpose and meaningfulness, which is expressed as a tendency to become actively involved in whatever one is trying to accomplish. Control refers to the belief that one can influence life events rather than feel helpless. "This does not imply the naive expectation of complete determination of events and outcomes but rather implies the perception of oneself as having a definite influence through the exercise of imagination, knowledge, skill, and choice" (Kobasa, Maddi, & Kahn, 1982, p. 169). Challenge refers to the belief that change rather than stability is perceived not as burdensome but as a normal part of life that provides an opportunity for learning and growth. Kobasa, Maddi, and Courington (1981) stressed that the three dimensions of hardiness are highly interrelated and can be summed to create a composite measure of hardiness.

Funk and Houston (1987) criticized the studies that reported the moderating effects of hardiness on the stress-illness relationship. They indicated that hardiness research contains significant drawbacks including little empirical evidence to indicate that hardiness in fact buffers the effects of stress on illness, failure to provide evidence that the three dimensions of hardiness are factorially independent, and frequent use of inappropriate statistical techniques to test the buffering effects. Their study and the study by Hull, Van Treuren, and Virnelli (1987) provided justifications for these criticisms.

To overcome these limitations, in the present study new items were selected to measure the three factorially independent dimensions of hardiness. We tested the buffering effects of hardiness and social support through hierarchical multiple regression analyses with interaction terms (Cohen & Cohen, 1983).

Social support can be broadly defined as the availability of help in times of need from supervisors, coworkers, family members, and friends. Social support is hypothesized to interact with stress such that when a person has low levels of social support, the correlation between stress and strain is stronger than when a person has high levels of social support.

Social support may have main effects on conflict, stress, and job burnout. For example, a good relationship with one's supervisor and coworkers may make work situations less stressful. A study by House (1981) with factory workers found that social support has positive effects on the physical and mental health of workers. Studies with other occupational groups such as nurses (Constable & Russell, 1986), teachers (Russell, Altmaier, & Van Velzen, 1987), and employees from police and fire departments (Fusilier, Ganster, & Mayes, 1987) found similar results. Social support can also directly reduce job burnout by adding positive need-fulfilling elements into one's life (Kanner, Kafry, & Pines, 1978).

Like hardiness the findings on the buffering effect of social support on the stress-illness relationship have been inconsistent. Some studies have found evidence of buffering effects (Abdel-Halim, 1982; Etzion, 1984; Kobasa & Puccetti, 1983; Seers, McGee, Serey, & Graen, 1983; Fusilier, Ganster, & Mayes, 1987; Kirmeyer & Dougherty, 1988) whereas other studies have not (Fisher, 1985; Ganster, Mayes, & Fusilier, 1986). Kaufmann and Beer (1986) found social support to strengthen the positive relationship between stressors and strains, which contradicted most theories and models of job stress and social support.

The studies reported above have considered the buffering effects of hardiness and social support independently. A study by Ganellen and Blaney (1984) found commitment and challenge dimensions to be significantly correlated with social support. They discussed the possibility that the studies that found social support to be a moderator of life stress may have indirectly measured hardiness. It is possible that the hardy type may be more active in seeking social support, particularly under stressful conditions. It may also be that other persons respond more favorably to the purposefulness and optimism the hardy person conveys.

The term *burnout* was coined by Freudenberger (1974), a clinical psychologist who examined burnout among social agency staff working outside conventional helping organizations such as free clinics and halfway houses. Burnout is defined here as a state of emotional exhaustion, depersonalization, and feelings of low personal accomplishment (Maslach & Jackson, 1981a). Emotional exhaustion is caused by excessive psychological and emotional demands made on people helping people. Depersonalization refers to treating people like objects and is often reflected in the use of object labels (e.g., kidney in room 301) rather than personal names when referring to clients. Low personal accomplishment results when employees no longer believe their actions can and do make a difference. Several studies have found a positive relationship between stress and job burnout (Etzion, 1984; Russell, Altmaier, & Van Velzen, 1987).

A number of field studies have found a negative relationship between job stress and job performance (Schuler, 1975; Jamal, 1985). A study by Motowidlo, Packard, and Manning (1986) with nurses reported negative correlations between job stress and interpersonal aspects of job performance, such as sensitivity, warmth, consideration, and tolerance. It should be pointed out that Cohen's (1980) review of experimental studies found an inverted-U relationship between stress and performance. This hypothesis has rarely been tested in real work settings.

METHOD

Measurement

Conflict

Intrapersonal, intragroup, and intergroup conflicts were measured with the Rahim Organizational Conflict Inventory-I (Rahim, 1983a). This

21-item instrument uses a 5-point Likert scale to measure the perceptions of the three types of conflict. A higher score indicates a greater amount of one type of conflict. Rahim (1983b) has provided evidence of construct and criterion-related validities, internal consistency (ranging between .79 and .82) and retest reliabilities (ranging between .77 and .85) for the three subscales.

Stress

Perceptions of stress were measured with the 13 items developed by the first author and his colleagues (e.g., "There is a lot of tension in my job"; "At times I feel nervous on my job."). Each item was cast on a 5-point Likert scale. A higher score indicates a greater amount of stress experienced by a subject. The scale was constructed by factor analysis of data collected from 275 faculty members of a university. Internal consistency reliability of the scale was .81.

Hardiness

The control dimension of hardiness was measured with five items from the internal locus of control developed by Levenson (1973). Commitment and challenge dimensions were measured with eight and seven items, respectively, developed by the author and his colleagues (e.g., "I like to set high standards of accomplishment for myself" [commitment]; "I like to work on something challenging" [challenge]). The three subscales were factorially independent. The internal consistency reliability coefficients for the subscales were above .75. In the present study the items were cast on a 5-point Likert scale. A higher score indicates perceptions of greater hardiness by a subject.

Social Support

Social support from supervisor, coworkers, and family members was measured with the Social Support scale designed by Caplan, Cobb, French, Harrison, and Pinneau (1975). Each of the three subscales consists of four items cast on a 5-point Likert scale. A number of studies have reported satisfactory internal consistency reliability and criterion-related validity of the scale.

Job Burnout

Job burnout was measured with Maslach Burnout Inventory (Maslach & Jackson, 1981a). The MBI measures emotional exhaustion, depersonalization, and personal accomplishment with 22 items. Each item is rated on both an intensity and frequency dimension. In the present study the respondents rated each item on the frequency dimension. Previous studies have indicated that the intensity and frequency ratings are highly correlated (Constable & Russell, 1986; Maslach & Jackson, 1981b). The instrument appears to have sufficient construct and criterion-related validities and reliability ranging from .71 to .90 for the three subscales (Maslach & Jackson, 1981a).

Job Performance

Job performance was measured with the Minnesota Satisfactoriness Scales (Gibson, Weiss, Davis, & Lofquist, 1970). The MSS is a 28-item questionnaire designed to be completed by an employee's supervisor. The items are cast on a 3-point Likert scale. The four subscales of the MSS are performance, conformance, dependability, and personal adjustment. The performance subscale measures the subordinate's promotability and the quality and quantity of work. The conformance subscale measures how well the subordinate gets along with the supervisor and coworkers as well as the observance of rules and regulations. The dependability subscale measures the frequency of disciplinary problems created by the subordinate. The personal adjustment subscale measures the subordinate's emotional health or well-being. The four subscales together measure overall performance of a subordinate. Factor analysis of the MSS items found support for these four independent dimensions. The MSS was developed from supervisor ratings of 2,373 workers. The median internal consistency reliability of the subscales was .87 and median retest reliability for several job groups over a two-year interval was .50.

The stress scale and the subscales for the above measures were constructed by averaging the Ss' responses to their respective items. This resulted in the creation of 1 continuous scale and 16 continuous subscales.

Sample

A stratified random sampling was used to select 57 of the 115 employees of a manufacturing plant in Kentucky. These employees and their nine supervisors were asked by their manager to participate in a study sponsored by a local university. Fifty-five employees filled out the above questionnaires. The MSS was completed by 9 supervisors for the 55 employees in separate rooms of the plant during company time. Before the questionnaires were distributed, the first author assured the respondents that only the researchers would have access to their individual questionnaire data. Only the summarized data would be provided to the management of the plant. After the questionnaires were completed, the questionnaires for each superior-subordinate dyad were matched. Two of the 57 dyads could not participate in the study because of their absence during the two days of data collection. The response rate was over 96%.

Analysis

To simplify data analysis and interpretation, composite hardiness, social support, conflict, burnout, and performance scales were constructed by adding their respective subscale scores. Two stepwise multiple regression analyses were performed to test the main effects of hardiness and social support on conflict and stress. Eight hierarchical regression analyses were computed to investigate the main effects of conflict, stress, hardiness, and social support and the moderating effects of hardiness and social support on job burnout and performance. In each analysis, one of the independent variables (e.g., conflict) was entered in the regression equation in Step 1; in Step 2 one of the moderating variables (e.g., hardiness) was entered in the equation; and in Step 3 the interaction of the independent and moderating variables (e.g., Conflict x Hardiness) was entered in the equation (Cohen & Cohen, 1983, Chap. 8). The entry criterion for the independent and moderating variables was set at .05 level, but for interaction terms it was set at .10 level (Cohen & Edwards, 1989, p. 244).

RESULTS

Table 1.1 shows the descriptive statistics for the independent, moderating, and dependent variables. The correlations were in the

TABLE 1.1
Variables, Number of Items, Means, Standard Deviations, Zero-order Correlations, and Internal Consistency Reliability Coefficients

Variables	No. of Items	Mean	SD	Correlations					
				1	2	3	4	5	6
1. Conflict	21	8.18	1.54	(.84)	.45	-.19	-.20	.39	-.16
2. Stress	13	2.98	.68		(.86)	-.18	-.34	.67	-.37
3. Hardiness	20	11.60	1.12			(.79)	.27	-.13	.11
4. Social Support	12	10.99	1.83				(.80)	-.13	.13
5. Job Burnout	22	7.29	2.79					(.83)	-.36
6. Job Performance	28	10.61	1.80						(.93)

$r \geq .26$ $p < .05$ (two-tailed test)

expected directions. The internal consistency reliability coefficients as assessed by Cronbach alpha, which are shown in the diagonal of the correlational matrix, were satisfactory (Nunnally, 1978).

Results from the two stepwise multiple regression analyses showed that the main effect of social support on stress was significant [$Beta = -.3359$, $t(53) = -2.60$, $p < .05$; $R^2 = .11$, $F(1,52) = 6.74$, $p < .05$]. The main effects of hardiness and social support on conflict and of hardiness on stress were nonsignificant.

Results for the first two hierarchical regression analyses show that conflict was positively associated with job burnout [$Beta = .3902$, $t(53) = 3.06$, $p < .005$; $R^2 = .15$, $F(1,52) = 9.34$, $p < .005$]. The main and moderating effects of social support and hardiness on job burnout were nonsignificant. Results from the next two regression analyses show that the main effects of conflict, social support, and hardiness, and the moderating effects of social support and hardiness on job performance were not significant.

Results from fifth and sixth regression analyses show that the main effect of stress on job burnout was significant [$Beta = .6695$, $p < .0001$;

$R^2 = .45$, $F(1,52) = 42.25$, $p < .0001$]. The main and moderating effects of hardiness and social support on job burnout were not significant.

Results from the remaining two regression analyses show that the main effect of stress on job performance was significant [*Beta* $= -.3640$, $t(53) = -2.82$, $p < .01$; $R^2 = .13$, $F(1,52) = p < .01$]. The main and moderating effects of social support and hardiness on job performance were nonsignificant.

DISCUSSION

This study failed to confirm the ameliorating effects of hardiness personality and social support on the relationships of conflict and stress to job burnout and overall performance of employees in a manufacturing plant. The study did not find support for the main effects of hardiness on conflict and stress and of social support on conflict. Only the main effect of social support on stress was significant. This is consistent with House's (1981) study of factory workers. This possibly indicates that employees who receive a high degree of social support perceive a smaller amount of stress. The study failed to confirm the main effects of hardiness and social support on job burnout as suggested by the literature. Although zero-order correlations between them were significant, the relationships became nonsignificant after the common variance between conflict and job burnout and between stress and job burnout were removed. It should be noted that the zero-order correlation between job burnout and job performance was significant [$r(54) = -.36$, $p < .01$].

The study found significant positive relationships of conflict to job burnout but not to job burnout. As predicted stress was positively related to job burnout and negatively related to job performance.

The results discussed above cast doubt on the findings of previous studies that indicated the mitigating effects of hardiness on the relationship between stress and individual effectiveness as measured by job burnout and job performance. It provided further support to the studies by Funk and Houston (1987) and Hull, Van Treuren, and Virnelli (1987) that criticized the buffering effect. The results also found no support for the mitigating effects of social support on the stress-strain relationship. Schilling's (1987) review of social support literature indicated that it is a complex phenomenon and that "current knowledge suggests that social support remains a vague and inadequately defined concept" (p. 28). This indicates that our conceptualization of social support must improve before empirical research can proceed effectively.

Miner (1982) indicated that "theories have suffered badly from measurement failure that remain to this day" (p. 444). This is particularly true of the existing measures of stress and hardiness personality. We developed the measures for stress and the two dimensions of hardiness, such as commitment and challenge. Studies are needed to investigate the psychometric adequacies of these and existing measures used in the studies on conflict and stress.

One of the limitations of this study is that the relationships discussed were correlational and not causal. Field and laboratory experiments are needed to investigate causal links presented in Figure 1.1. Future studies should also investigate the relationships of conflict and stress to individual and organizational outcomes using techniques, such as simultaneous equations (Namboodiri, Carter, & Blalock, 1975). Researchers have found it appropriate to use this technique when each of the dependent variables are correlated with some or all of the remaining dependent variables. Another probable limitation is the sample size, but it would be remembered that a random sample of 55 dyads with a response rate of over 96% is better than a large sample with a response rate of about 30%.

2 The Goal Interdependence Approach to Communication in Conflict: An Organizational Study

Dean Tjosvold

To work, manage, and live in an organization is to be in conflict. People in organizations conflict about vague assignments, the refusal to accept feedback, unfair distribution of work, incompatible goals, downgrading coworkers, and personalities (Bergmann & Volkema, 1989). Conflicts, contemporary researchers argue, are potentially constructive, but they must be well handled (Deutsch, 1973; Pruitt & Syna, 1984; Rahim, 1986a). How people communicate and treat each other is considered critical in determining how conflicts will be managed and whether they will be productive or destructive. This study examines conflict management in a diversified social services organization through the concepts of goal interdependence.

Communication is a central issue in conflict research (Putnam & Jones, 1982). Researchers have used a variety of approaches to identify the kind of communication and interaction that contributes to conflict management. Experimental studies have tried to document the impact of particular strategies, such as promises, concessions, and threats. Observational studies have coded messages and related them to the outcomes of the conflict. These schemes include such strategies as threats, information seeking and giving, problem solving, and procedural statements (Bales, 1950; Donohue, 1981; Morley & Stephenson, 1977). Much organizational conflict has built upon Blake and Mouton's (1964) work that postulates five conflict styles of integrating, obliging, dominating, avoiding, and compromising (Rahim, 1983b).

Important problems interfere with research progress on communication and interaction during conflict. People can threaten, promise, shout, cry, demand, plead, aggress, and use many other strategies in conflict. These strategies can be accompanied by warmth, coldness, anger, and other nonverbal messages (Johnson, 1971). Research is further complicated because the impact of any strategy depends, in part, on the context in which it occurs. How people respond to a threat depends upon other messages sent with the threat (Tjosvold, 1974). Relatedly, observation schemes are difficult to compare and can become quite complex (Putnam & Jones, 1982).

These problems are reflected in the difficulties of developing highly consistent findings on the effects of strategies. Threats, for example, are generally considered to escalate conflict (Deutsch & Krauss, 1962), but experimental and observational studies also show that they can aid conflict management (Kelley, 1965; Putnam & Wilson, 1989; Tjosvold, 1974).

The goal interdependence approach used in this study attempts to identify the general context and communication patterns of conflict. According to Deutsch (1949, 1973), whether people believe their goals are cooperative, competitive, or independent very much affects the dynamics and outcomes of conflict. Tjosvold (1986b, 1989) recently developed an approach to organizational interdependence and conflict based on Deutsch's theory. In cooperative interdependence, employees use a shared vision and mission, common tasks, and complementary roles to conclude that their goals are positively related. They understand that their goal attainment helps others reach their goals; they can be successful together. Task force members committed to make a good recommendation to their boss are in cooperation; they recognize that one member's good ideas helps them all achieve their goal of an effective recommendation. Cooperative interdependence is theorized to induce effective communication and constructive conflict.

In competition, employees use a mistrustful climate and win-lose rewards to believe their goals are negatively related; success by one makes the goal attainment of others less likely (Tjosvold, 1986a, 1989). Task force members committed to appearing to be the brightest to their boss are frustrated when one member develops good ideas because they fear the boss will see that person as the most competent. They are expected to have difficulty communicating and managing conflict. The third alternative is independence. Here employees use interpersonal distance and individual tasks and rewards to conclude their goals are unrelated. They see little need to communicate and manage conflict.

From the goal interdependence perspective, conflicts occur in cooperative as well as competitive situations. Conflict is defined as incompatible activities where people at least temporarily interfere with and obstruct each other's behavior (Deutsch, 1973). Task force members committed to appear to be the brightest often argue against each other's views to show that they are the most competent. However, task force members with cooperative goals can also disagree about how they should proceed and the nature of the recommendation they should make.

In addition to considerable experimental research that supports the major propositions of the theory (Deutsch, 1949, 1973, 1980; Johnson, Johnson, & Maruyama, 1983; Johnson, Maruyama, Johnson, Nelson, & Skon, 1981; Tjosvold, 1984), studies have documented that goal interdependence alters the course and consequences of conflict (Tjosvold, 1985). People who argued opposing positions with cooperative goals were found to take each other's perspective, ask each other questions, demonstrate understanding of the opponent's arguments, and create superior solutions that integrated their ideas and information (Tjosvold & Johnson, 1977, 1978; Tjosvold & Deemer, 1980; Tjosvold, 1982). People in competition, however, were found to be closed-minded to their opponent's views. They either failed to reach an agreement or found a solution that reflected only one point of view.

This research suggests that cooperative goals very much contribute to conflict management. In addition, cooperators communicate they are working for mutual benefit, express their views, understand each other, and try to integrate their ideas. Communication skills appear to complement cooperative goals for productive conflict management.

However, important limitations make the interdependence approach to conflict management less useful than desirable. Research has been primarily experimental in social psychological laboratories. Studies are needed to test the generalizability of the findings to work and other settings.

A related research need is to describe more specifically how people actually communicate and behave toward each other when they deal with problems cooperatively and competitively. There has been little work on identifying the behaviors in cooperation and competition in actual conflict situations.

Previous research has concentrated on the effects of goal interdependence, and research is needed on the antecedents of cooperation, competition, and independence. Deutsch (1973) proposed that the consequences of goal interdependence are also the conditions that create the interdependence. Tasks, rewards, and attitudes are likely to affect conclusions about goal interdependence (Tjosvold, 1986a). Common tasks and shared rewards of the organization's structure and positive interpersonal attitudes are expected to induce cooperative goals.

The major hypothesis of this study is that to the extent that employees in conflict believe their goals are cooperative rather than competitive and independent they are more likely to communicate their ideas and information, open-mindedly consider opposing views, use each other's ideas to complete their tasks efficiently and productively, and develop confidence that they can work together in the future.

METHOD

Participants and Organization

A social service agency was interested in how its employees handled conflicts with each other. The agency has five programs of family counseling and training, a residence for adolescents, treatment of troubled elementary students, child care workers, and enterprises, including a thrift store and recycling. At the time of the study, it had approximately 50 full-time employees. From all the groups 32 employees were selected and agreed to be interviewed for the study. Each was asked to describe two conflicts; they gave a total of 57 incidents.

Interviewees were assured that their responses would be held confidentially by the research team. Results were given to the organization, but only general findings and incidents whose source could not be identified were used in the feedback.

Interview Schedule

The critical incident method was used to develop the interview schedule (Flanagan, 1954). Respondents were asked to describe in detail a recent, significant incident in which they had a problem involving other employees. Previous discussion with the organization revealed central issues that generated considerable conflict. Employees were asked to discuss an incident in which they had opposing views, had difficulty getting support from their supervisor, confronted a change in the work place, were developing an innovation, or engaged in team decision making. To give a variety of ways conflict was managed, they were to select a conflict that was handled relatively well and one that was handled less effectively. Interviewees first described the setting, what occurred, and the consequences. Then they answered specific questions to code the incident.

They identified their goals and the other's goals in the interaction. Cooperative, competitive, and independent goal interdependencies were described, and respondents distributed ten points over them, giving the most points to the one that was most descriptive of the situation. Interviewees then gave their reasoning for this distribution. The number of points assigned each interdependence was used as its measure. To identify antecedents of goal interdependence and behaviors within them, situations were sorted into cooperation, competition, and independence on the basis of which one was given the most points. The six situations in which respondents gave two goal interdependencies the same number of points were not used in these analyses.

Interviewees responded to a series of questions using 7-point scales to code their expectations and the communication that occurred in the incident. First the interviewees indicated their expectations by rating the extent they had been confident they could manage the conflict successfully. To code the communication, they rated the extent they expressed their own views, tried to understand the other, worked for mutual benefit, put together the best of the ideas expressed, felt accepted, tried to influence the other, and tried to dominate (reversed). This self-communicate scale had a Cronbach alpha reliability of .72. Then the respondents rated the other person on these same dimensions. This other-communicate scale had a reliability of .79.

The respondents were asked to indicate their responses to the interaction after they had a chance to evaluate it. They indicated on 7-point scales the extent that they made progress on the task, worked efficiently on it, and became more confident they could work with the other in the future.

Coding Descriptions

In addition to the responses to specific, Likert-type questions, the interviews yielded descriptive information. Shortly after the completion of the interview, the interviewers wrote short paragraphs to describe the interaction.

Rather than rely on a priori categories, the categories for behavior were developed empirically. Six raters independently studied the interactions and developed categories for them. Then they formed three two-person subgroups that worked independently to agree upon the categories and the interactions that belonged to these categories. The subgroups later met to develop the categories and sorted the incidents into these agreed upon categories. The subgroups had an inter-rater agreement of 84% on this sorting of incidents. They met to resolve their differences, and these agreed upon classifications are reported. In a similar fashion, the raters coded the reasons employees had for their goal interdependence. They were able to agree 92% of the time; their agreed upon ratings are reported.

Interviewers

Five undergraduates were trained to be interviewers. In 15 hours of training they practiced interviewing and received feedback so that they would interview in a standard, nonsuggestive manner. They were trained to have the person describe the conflict and then to code it through the respondent's answers to specific questions. They were not told the theory being tested nor the hypotheses. They pledged to protect the confidentiality of the respondents.

RESULTS

Interdependence Dynamics and Outcomes

The zero-order correlations (Table 2.1) support the major hypothesis that cooperative goals, in contrast to competitive and independent ones, contribute to productive conflict management. In conflicts regarding cooperative goals, employees were confident they could handle them well, communicated effectively, made progress on the task at hand, used their time and resources efficiently, and developed confidence they could

TABLE 2.1
Correlations Among Variables

	1	2	3	4	5	6	7	8	9	10
1. Cooperation	—									
2. Competition	-.71**	—								
3. Independence	-.54**	-.22*	—							
4. Expectations	.50*	-.45**		—						
5. Power	.07	-.04	-.05	.12	—					
6. Self-communicate	.77*	-.59**	-.35**	.50**	.13	—				
7. Other-communicate	.78**	-.64**	-.30**	.54**	.17	.91**	—			
8. Task Progress	.70**	-.58**	-.27*	.46**	-.00	.73**	.72**	—		
9. Efficiency	.75**	-.61**	-.30**	.63**	.15	.80**	.80**	.78**	—	
10. Confidence	.69**	-.70**	-.10	.53**	.05	.67**	.67**	.73**	.78**	—

$*p < .05$; $**p < .01$

TABLE 2.2

Hierarchical Regression Analyses for Progress, Confidence, Efficiency, and Outcome

Independent Variables	Dependent Variables								
	Progress			Confidence			Efficiency		
	b	R^2	ΔR^2	b	R^2	ΔR^2	b	R^2	ΔR^2
Interdependence:									
Cooperative	.40			.39			.40		
Independent	.09	.50	.47*	.25	.66	.64*	.07	.64	.61*
Confident of Success	.12			.43			.34		
Communication:									
Personal Style	.58	.57	.53*	.36	.67	.63*	.68	.73	.70*
Other's Style	.24			-.09			.26		
Net Contribution of Communication Variables		.06*			-.01			*.09*	

*$p \le .01$

work together in the future. In comparison, employees who had competitive goals lacked confidence they could work together, thought they communicated ineffectively, worked inefficiently, made little progress, and thought they would work less effectively in the future. Independence was negatively associated with communication, progress, and efficiency.

Cooperative goals were expected to contribute to constructive conflict by promoting effective communication. To test this implication, hierarchical regression analyses were completed. For each of the dependent variables of progress on the task, confidence in the relationship, and efficient use of resources, the variables of cooperative, competitive, and independent goals and expectations were first allowed to enter the regression analysis. Then the interaction variables of self-communicate and other-communicate were allowed to enter. Results confirm that cooperative goals are powerful antecedents of skillful communication and productive conflict. The interdependence scores and expectations were found to account for between 47% and 64%. Allowing the communication variables to enter the regression analysis increased the amount of variance accounted to between 53% and 70%.

TABLE 2.3

Reasons for Goal Interdependence

	Cooperative	Competitive	Independent
Group Task	22	0	1
Shared Purpose	11	0	0
Common Rewards	9	2	0
Complementary Roles	4	0	0
Independent Roles	0	1	3
Negative Emotions	0	1	0
Win-Lose Rewards	0	7	0
Incompatible Task	0	1	1
Value of Outdoing	0	1	0
Independent Task	1	0	8
Value of Doing it Alone	1	0	0

Note: Multiple responses based on 51 incidences.

TABLE 2.4

Behaviors in Goal Interdependence

	Cooperative	Competitive	Independent
Provided assistance and support	7	0	1
Discussed issues to try and solve problem	4	2	1
Brainstormed and integrated ideas	12	0	0
Unable to reach an agreement	1	4	2
Made decision without consultation	2	1	0
Unable to find solution due to external circumstances	2	0	2
Avoided discussion	1	3	1
Was unwilling to assist	2	1	2

Note: There were 31 cooperative, 11 competitive, and 9 independent situations.

Reasons for Goal Interdependence

Results suggest the conditions that affect employee conclusions about goal interdependence. After the interviewees indicated the goal interdependence, they were asked to describe their reasoning that led them to make these conclusions. The distribution of the coded reasons (Table 2.3) was found to depend on the goal interdependence, $\chi^2(18) = 98.14$, $p < .01$. Important reasons given for cooperative goals were that they had been assigned a group task, they shared a sense of purpose in attaining broad organizational goals, they would share rewards if they were successful, and that their roles stipulated that they should assist each other. Rewards for winning and not losing, tasks that were incompatible, personal hostility, and the value of trying to outdo others were given for competitive goals. The assignment of an independent task and being rewarded for completing that task were given as reasons for independent goals.

The behaviors were coded and were found to depend upon the goal interdependence, $X^2(14) = 28.45$, $p < .01$. Cooperators were found to brainstorm and integrate ideas, provide assistance and support, and discuss issues to solve the problem. They also at times made decisions without consultation and were unable to reach an agreement. Despite asking for effective and ineffective incidents, few of the situations were identified as competitive or independent. Results that were obtained suggest that employees with competitive goals avoided discussions and failed to reach agreement. Employees with independent goals were unwilling to assist others and were unable to find solutions and reach agreements.

DISCUSSION

Results suggest goal interdependence is a useful way to identify the context and communication patterns that contribute to conflict management. Cooperative goals and skillful communication were found to be important antecedents for productive conflict. People in conflict who believed that their goals and aspirations were cooperative were able to express their views, show they were trying to understand each other, and put their ideas together. They then completed their tasks productively and efficiently and developed confidence they could work with each other in the future.

Cooperative goals explained a great deal of the variance on the measures of communication and conflict productivity. Yet skillful communication was able to account for a significant additional amount of variance on the measures of progress, efficiency, and confidence. Findings support the idea that communication skills complement cooperative goals for productive conflict management.

This study and previous research (Tjosvold, 1985) identify the general patterns of communication and interaction that accompany cooperative goals. However, the particular strategies and ways that people use to communicate in cooperative situations will vary depending on conditions. To specify these behaviors in the organization studied, the interactions were coded and sorted into incidents that were predominately cooperative, competitive, or independent. Employees with cooperative goals were found to provide assistance and support, discuss a specific problem to solve it, brainstorm, and integrate ideas. In competition, people were unwilling to make the effort to assist another, offered little support, made decisions without consultation, and were unable to reach an agreement. Additional research is needed to indicate the extent these behaviors characterize goal interdependence in other situations and samples.

Results suggest the conditions that led people to conclude their goals were primarily cooperative, competitive, or independent. Group tasks, common rewards, shared purpose, and complementary roles were cited as reasons for cooperative goals. Win-lose rewards were the major reason for competitive goals, and independent tasks for independent goals. These results are consistent with the argument that both an organization's structure and its culture affect conclusions about employees' goal interdependence (Tjosvold, 1986a, 1986b, 1989).

Conflict research has been criticized as relying too much on cooperation and competition as dependent measures in gaming situations (Putnam & Jones, 1982b). The goal interdependence approach uses cooperation, competition, and independence as predictors of the dynamics and outcomes of conflict. Goal interdependence, as antecedent, may help to develop more consistent findings on the effects of strategies. Future studies can induce strategies and goal interdependence independently. For example, promises in cooperation can be compared with those in competition. These studies can suggest the relative impact of goal interdependence and strategies on conflict dynamics and outcomes.

Researchers have recently argued that open communication is neither always appropriate nor useful in organizations (Eisenberg & Witten, 1987; Putnam & Pacanowsky, 1983). Results of this study indicate that employees are reluctant to communicate their ideas openly to the extent they believe their goals are competitive or independent. It should be noted that the effective communication identified in this study as an antecedent for productive conflict is more than openness. It includes showing that one is trying to understand the other, conveying a desire to work for mutual benefit, and integrating ideas.

This study's results are, of course, limited by its operations and sample. The data are correlational, and causal links must be drawn cautiously. Moreover, measures were self-reported by employees and these may be biased. However, respondents reported on specific events that should be less distorted and less subject to the problems of self-report than questions that ask for generalizations (Lord, 1985; Podsakoff & Organ, 1986). Recent studies indicate that people often accurately perceive themselves and their social environment (Funder and Dobroth, 1987; Shrauger & Osborne, 1981). Recent evidence also suggests that common method variance is not as much of an alternative explanation of results as commonly assumed (Spector, 1987). In addition, perceptions are very important in understanding conflict. Cooperation theory postulates that it is people's beliefs about how their goals are related that affects their conflict management. The limitations of the study should be considered in the context of previous studies that provide experimental support with behavioral measures for the major findings of this study.

Despite limitations, results, if successfully replicated and extended, have important practical implications. They suggest that, in addition to training in specific communication skills, managers and others should know how to develop strong cooperative goals. Conflict management can begin before the conflict occurs. To the extent that employees have cooperative goals through group tasks, a sense of shared purpose, and common rewards, they may be able to communicate effectively and make their conflicts productive.

Results support previous research that believes that are goals cooperative and skilled communication contributes to making conflict useful. Cooperative goals, especially when coupled with the skillful communication of opposing views, are important antecedents for managing conflict productively. More generally, goal interdependence appears useful for understanding the dynamics and outcomes of conflict in organizations. The impact of communication and strategies may depend significantly upon the goal interdependence in which they are used.

ACKNOWLEDGMENTS

The author thanks the Social Sciences and Humanities Research Council of Canada for its financial assistance and Choy Wong and other members of the research team for their able assistance.

II Communication Conflict

INTRODUCTION

Tricia S. Jones

Communication is widely recognized as an integral component of conflict management. As Hocker and Wilmot (1985) argue, communication can create, reflect, and remediate conflict situations. In a situation of conflict, the efficacy of dispute orientations and strategies depends upon the ability of interactants to enact those strategies using appropriate communicative interventions. Communication research in conflict contributes significantly to our understanding of effective conflict management processes, either from a basic or applied perspective. Recently, research from various fields, such as management, psychology, and social psychology, has emphasized the investigation of communication strategies associated with conflict outcomes as related to critical situational and personal variables. The need to understand the manifestation of resolution behaviors is implicit in this work. The combined contribution of these substantive research areas is a growing awareness of the complex interrelation of behavioral, social, and psychological variables that determine the formation and resolution of conflict episodes.

Contemporary communication research in conflict management has focused on examining the types of communication behaviors and strategies occurring in negotiation (Donohue, 1981a; Putnam & Jones, 1982a) and mediation (Donohue, Allen & Burrell, 1988; Jones, 1985).

While most of the communication research has been basic rather than applied, the significance of the knowledge gained depends upon the ability of practitioners to find useful and effective prescriptions for dealing with conflict situations. Indeed, some may argue that the provision of prescriptive advice is one of the most, if not the most, important contributions from the communication field. Both of the chapters in this section add to the growing awareness of the importance of applied research from a communication perspective.

Deanna Womack, in her chapter, directly addresses the need for more extensive applied communication research in negotiation. Her chapter presents a review of applied communication research in a variety of negotiation contexts, drawing from literature in intercultural negotiation, legal negotiation, interpersonal negotiation, and labor-management negotiation. Her review synthesizes two lines of research: research concerning messages and message patterns in negotiation, and research examining other variables that influence how messages are sent or interpreted in a negotiation interaction. These areas of research are further delineated by an examination of negotiation goals, either distributive or integrative, and the corresponding prescriptions available to negotiations from this literature.

Her chapter is particularly helpful because she includes summaries of effective communication behaviors for different negotiation goals and negotiation contexts. The result is an integration of information from applied communication research that suggests prescriptive advice for practitioners and calls for continued emphasis on applied studies from communication researchers.

While Womack's chapter deals exclusively with communication research in negotiation, Nancy Burrell's chapter investigates the use and effect of mediator communication behaviors. Burrell reports on a study in which she trained student mediators in a control-based model of mediation and had those mediators engage in simulated roommate conflict mediations. Mediation interactions were content analyzed in terms of the structure and function of mediator behaviors and the compliant or noncompliant nature of disputant responses.

Burrell's investigation concentrates on mediator's questioning behaviors and disputants' responses to questions throughout phases of mediation. Her research provides interesting insights to an often underinvestigated behavior, questioning tactics. Although mediation researchers have theorized about the importance of information-gathering tactics, researchers have seldom examined the specific effect of such tactics on the process or outcome of mediation. As such, Burrell's work extends the research program in the area of mediator communicative competence. Furthermore, her interest in the different uses of mediator tactics through phases of mediation adds to the recognition that mediation research is most useful when the focus is the ongoing process of the mediation rather than the simple frequency of tactics occurring in an interaction. Burrell's work may be described as primarily basic in orientation, but the results of her study suggest useful advice for mediators in the application of questioning behaviors.

Both chapters in this section reflect a growing concern among communication researchers that the fruits of their labor enable practitioners to deal more effectively with dispute resolution situations. Womack and Burrell have supplied valuable information for negotiators and mediators and have provided an impetus for further applied research in both areas.

Both papers suggest some promising directions for further communication research from an applied perspective. One such direction is the investigation of the efficacy of training disputants to use effective behaviors. Thus far, the majority of research has concentrated on the description of communication strategies and the identification of disputant characteristics that are related to the use of certain strategies. Underlying this research is a largely untested assumption that disputants can be taught to adapt their communicative interventions in a manner favorable to resolution. Serious investigation of the validity of this assumption and the conditions under which it applies could significantly improve the social relevance of this body of work. Additionally, as both Womack and Burrell demonstrate, there is a growing impetus for a macro-oriented understanding of the impact of conflict contexts on the selection and instrumentality of communication strategies. Particularly in conflicts involving cultural differences between disputants, such research is limited. This area provides fertile ground for applied communication research, especially for practitioners faced with a growing awareness of and preponderance of cross-cultural disputes. Additionally, investigations that emphasize the achievement of satisfactory resolution often adopt an immediate rather than long-term definition of satisfaction. Applied researchers can contribute important insights with research that adopts longitudinal definitions of satisfactory outcomes. It would be valuable to assess whether the communication strategies that are suggested for obtaining resolution produce settlements that stand the test of time.

3 Applied Communications Research in Negotiation: Implications for Practitioners

Deanna F. Womack

In the past 15 years (since Miller & Simons, 1974), negotiation has become a major topic of organizational communication research. Yet applied communication research in negotiation is rare according to Smith's (1988) description: "[Applied research] explores theoretical relationships for the purpose of understanding and solving problems related to everyday communicative actions and interactions" (p. 182). Applied researchers in areas other than negotiation communication often conduct studies in field settings and use research methods that allow them to develop prescriptive rules of effective communication. Applied research is contrasted with basic research, which "explores theoretical relationships with little regard for the practical implications of research findings" (Smith, 1988, p. 182). In negotiation communication, for example, basic research is not concerned with prescribing how to negotiate effectively but with describing the communication variables and patterns that affect negotiations. Basic researchers may discover relationships that lead to particular outcomes, but such discoveries are secondary to the purpose of the research, which is primarily to describe or to explore, not to prescribe.

As the study of communication in negotiation is relatively recent, it is not surprising that the vast majority of studies represent basic research. Few researchers have attempted to make practical generalizations or to find implications for communicating effectively during negotiations. The observation of Lewicki, Weiss, and Lewin (1988) about negotiation research is also true for communication studies: "Conspicuous in their absence . . . are models that have a solid empirical/conceptual footing in theory and empirical research but which can be extended to provide concrete prescriptions for managers" (p. 80). While a comprehensive model of negotiation communication still seems premature, the research is sufficiently advanced to draw implications for effectiveness from some basic communication research. It is also useful to integrate communication findings with communication implications developed by scholars studying negotiation in professional contexts through applied research. Although several excellent surveys of the negotiation literature have recently been published (Putnam 1985; Putnam & Jones, 1982b; Putnam & Poole, 1987), none explicitly deals with applied research or implications for practitioners. Thus, it is appropriate to integrate findings to recommend effective communication strategies and practices for negotiators. If, as Kurt Lewin has said (cited in Thayer, 1982, p. 21), "There is nothing so practical as a good theory," what practical applications have developed from communication research in the field of negotiation?

Negotiation as a method of managing organizational conflict usually involves interdependent parties who trade proposals for a settlement (e.g., an out-of-court agreement to settle a lawsuit, a business contract, or a collective bargaining contract). Most organizational negotiations involve a mixture of cooperative and competitive motives that influence the proposals and counterproposals negotiators exchange. Negotiation communication concerns the messages that negotiators send and receive and by which they come to share meaning during the process. Negotiation and bargaining are used here as equivalent terms.

Lewicki, Weiss and Lewin (1988) claim that research and theory in negotiation have developed along two parallel lines, regardless of academic discipline. Descriptive models "take a scientifically 'detached' position and attempt simply to describe and to predict actual conflict dynamics, while [normative models] prescribe actions for individuals and historically have reflected an evaluation of conflict as fundamentally bad and destructive" (p. 7). Most normative models indicate negotiators should use collaborative or "win-win" strategies (e.g., Fisher & Ury, 1981); few have an explicit communication focus (Hocker & Wilmot, 1985, does). For negotiation communication studies, the descriptive-normative distinction does not distinguish the research methods used. Interpretive communication research based on transcripts, observations, or interviews of negotiators has led to scientific, descriptive models rather than to normative ones (e.g., Bullis & Putnam, 1985; Putnam, Wilson, Waltman, & Turner, 1986). In addition, work by practitioners comparing perceptions or communication patterns used by effective and ineffective negotiators fails to meet the criteria for normative research because it is based on empirical research by relatively detached observers. Unlike authors of the "popular press" models illustrative of normative research, these practitioners do not appear to assume that conflict has primarily negative consequences, nor do most of them favor a particular approach without providing empirical evidence of its effectiveness (e.g., Rackham & Carlisle, 1978a, 1978b; Williams, 1983). Instead, the differences in approach taken in the communication literature are better expressed as differences between basic and applied research. Although much of the basic communication research consists of laboratory experiments, both basic and applied researchers have used interpretive, observational methods.

This chapter synthesizes two lines of research: research concerning messages and message patterns and research involving psychological or other variables that may influence how messages are sent or interpreted. First, an overview of the nature of negotiation communication is presented. Then, following Walton and McKersie (1965), distributive (emphasizing outcomes for oneself) or integrative (emphasizing outcomes for all parties) goals are used as the primary contextual feature for classifying the studies. This is an artificial distinction because most actual negotiations involve both distributive and integrative bargaining goals. Yet this organizing scheme appears to be best for several reasons. Organizing the research by professional context or even context characteristics results in chains of findings based on one or two studies because the applied research consists of investigations in different professional fields (e.g., legal or business negotiations) and because applied authors rarely discuss key contextual features or motives. Yet few findings appear to hold true regardless of context (Weingart, Thompson, Bazerman, & Carroll, 1988). The research is organized in three categories: studies involving primarily distributive negotiations, studies involving primarily integrative negotiations, and general findings. The studies are classified according to the intent of the researchers and their emphasis on discovery (basic research) or application (applied research). Research describing communication characteristics of each context is presented first, followed by recommendations from basic and applied research. Finally, effective communication behaviors are summarized.

THE NATURE OF COMMUNICATION
IN NEGOTIATION

As a joint decision-making process (Pruitt, 1981), negotiation is governed by shared formal and informal rules negotiated by the bargainers. After the rules have been determined, the bargainers cooperate within those rules in order to achieve some goal, often to gain a competitive advantage over the other bargainer (Schelling, 1960). As a conflict management process, negotiation emphasizes the exchange of proposals by parties in order to reach a joint settlement (Putnam & Poole, 1987). Communication during negotiation may also involve tacit bargaining (Schelling, 1960; Walton & McKersie, 1965). Verbal and nonverbal communication constitutes the fabric of negotiations.

> More specifically, communication undergirds the setting and reframing of goals; the defining and narrowing of conflict issues; the developing of relationships between disputants and among constituents; the selecting and implementing of strategies and tactics; the generating, attacking, and defending of alternative solutions; and the reaching and confirming of agreements (Putnam & Poole, 1987, p. 550).

Communication, then, is central to the bargaining process, whether bargaining occurs as an institutionalized form of conflict management, such as collective bargaining, or whether it involves negotiating marketing agreements on legal contracts and settlements or managing inter- and intragroup or interpersonal disputes.

The motivation behind the early negotiation research was practical: to predict settlement points and to identify strategies and tactics that allow parties to achieve their goals. Game theory (Luce & Raiffa, 1957) was designed to predict just such outcomes, but early game theory experiments usually preclude communication or investigated it as the absence or presence and use of communication channels (Deutsch & Krauss, 1960, 1962; Krauss & Deutsch, 1966; Siegel & Fouraker, 1960). In fact, the Deutsch and Krauss (1960, 1962; Krauss & Deutsch, 1966) trucking game studies demonstrated that "the mere availability of communication channels provides no guarantee that they will be used or used effectively" (Rubin & Brown, 1975, p. 92). Even when the opportunity for communication was present, bargainers communicated infrequently and used communication not to cooperate, but to threaten or intimidate each other (Deutsch & Krauss, 1962). The rather discouraging results of Deutsch and Krauss (1962) and the recent focus of communication scholars on conflict and negotiation have led to attempts to overcome the dysfunctional aspects of negotiation communication identified by Deutsch (1969):

> Communication between the conflicting parties is unreliable and impoverished. The available communication channels and opportunities are not utilized or they are used in an attempt to mislead or intimidate the other. Little confidence is placed in information that is obtained directly from the other; espionage and other circuitous means of obtaining information are relied upon. The poor communication enhances the possibility of error and misinformation of the sort which is likely to reinforce the pre-existing orientations and expectations toward the other (p. 12).

Deutsch notes that the competitive nature of many negotiation situations constrains open and effective communication.

Several difficulties are inherent in drawing conclusions about negotiation effectiveness from the early research. First, messages serve multiple functions and are generated in response to a particular context. Messages are simultaneous attempts to convey information and to influence the other party's interpretations and future actions (Donohue, Diez, & Stahle, 1983). Thus, message strategies are interdependent and should be studied as such. However, messages have typically been treated as independent variables (Putnam & Jones, 1982b). In addition, some types of negotiation serve a ritual function (i.e., collective bargaining; Bullis & Putnam, 1985); bargainers may use the negotiation process merely to inform the other side about offers or to posture (Colosi, 1983). Another complication revealed by empirical research is that negotiators may base their responses more on directives from their constituents than on their counterparts' bargaining strategies (Roloff & Campion, 1987; Tjosvold, 1977). Particular negotiation outcomes such as impasse can become a bargaining strategy designed to influence future negotiations (Theye & Seiler, 1979). Perhaps the major difficulty in studying negotiation communication is that the same utterance may perform multiple functions and lead toward multiple goals simultaneously (Putnam & Poole, 1987).

It seems evident that negotiation effectiveness can be determined only contextually, with regard to a goal, and that it differs with different perspectives. What one party deems effective, the other might not because the payoff structure of many negotiations precludes both parties' completely accomplishing their goals. In some contexts, for example, international relations, the goal might be merely to find some settlement acceptable to both sides. The goal of environmental negotiations may be the public welfare. Effectiveness may mean reaching some long-term settlement or settling without involving a mediator or arbitrator. Maintaining satisfactory interpersonal or business relationships between the negotiating parties, regardless of outcome, is another measure of effectiveness. In distributive negotiations, effectiveness involves maximizing profits or outcomes for one side. Maximizing the parties' joint payoff is a goal of integrative negotiations. From the radical humanist perspective, effectiveness consists of "the degree of freedom rather than constraint imposed on the actors by the reified structures which result from their own social construction of reality" (Bullis & Putnam, 1985, p. 19). Bullis and Putnam (1985) report a negotiation between teachers and school board in which teachers were quite satisfied with the negotiation outcome, yet they could have obtained higher payoffs. Thus, satisfaction may result from a situation in which negotiators underestimate their ability to achieve the majority of their goals. For this reason, multiple indications of effectiveness should be used.

COMMUNICATION RESEARCH IN DISTRIBUTIVE NEGOTIATIONS

Distributive negotiations are lengthy and typically involve deceptive arguments and few concessions (Gruder, 1971). Negotiators mask their true intents and needs by using linguistic codes, by exaggerating emotions and demands, and by exhibiting conflicting verbal and nonverbal cues (Lewicki & Litterer, 1985). Threats, putdowns, irrelevant arguments, commitments, demands, blaming statements, and bluffs are common in distributive negotiation (Lewicki, 1983; Putnam & Jones, 1982b; Walton & McKersie, 1965). Distributive negotiators use threats, rejections, requests for information, and attacking arguments as offensive maneuvers; defensive maneuvers include demands, retractions, commitments, and self-bolstering arguments (Donohue 1981a, 1981b; Putnam & Jones, 1982a). While attacking, negotiators use linguistic behaviors such as disclaimers, hedging, omissions, and vague language to project an image of strength. Negotiators defend against attacks by using language forms such as retractions, corrections, qualifiers, and warnings (Borah, 1963; Brown, 1977).

Experimental research involving marketing negotiations among Americans, Brazilians, and Japanese experienced in business revealed stylistic differences in negotiation (Graham, 1983, 1985). Graham's research is presented under the distributive heading even though he discusses some integrative bargaining goals because the dependent variable in his research was individual payoffs rather than joint outcomes (Graham, 1983, p. 48). Thus, it was likely that individuals sought to maximize individual gains and that bargaining communication primarily followed a distributive pattern. The Brazilian negotiating style differed most from the Japanese and U.S. styles. Brazilian bargainers made more extreme opening offers and larger initial concessions and used more touch and eye gazes than U.S. or Japanese bargainers. Brazilians also made fewer promises and commitments, gave more commands, and used the word "no" much more frequently (Graham, 1985). In addition, Brazilians interrupted more than twice as often as the other negotiators and tended to talk simultaneously for extended periods of time. Brazilians and Americans tended to make commands in the later negotiation stages (Graham, 1985). Graham found little support for Van Zandt's (1970) normative propositions about U.S. and Japanese bargaining differences. Americans tended to make more moderate initial offers and larger concessions than Japanese. Americans used aggressive persuasive strategies (e.g., commands) less frequently, but at an earlier stage, than Japanese. Japanese buyers (but not sellers) used aggressive persuasive strategies in later negotiation stages after other strategies had proven ineffective (Graham, 1985). Periods of silence were more characteristic of Japanese than of Brazilian or U.S. negotiations (Graham, 1985). Despite the equal power structure of the experimental game, the buyer or seller role was the strongest predictor of Japanese payoffs, with the buyer having the upper hand (Graham, 1983). Graham's (1983) findings also indicate the importance of accurate impression-formation and interpersonal communication skills, such as putting the opponent at ease for Japanese negotiations.

Effective Communication in Distributive Negotiations

Findings from Basic Research

Basic experimental research in communication has primarily investigated negotiation tactics and settlement outcomes. Inexperienced negotiators who used tactics with greater attacking power, who made high initial offers and refused to concede (Donohue, 1981a), and who used greater firmness more consistently had higher payoffs than opponents who did not use such tactics (Donohue, 1981b). Game theory research concerning the effect of concession patterns on negotiator payoff supports this finding (Pruitt, 1981; Rubin & Brown, 1975). Donohue (1981a) concluded that settling a distributive negotiation requires a more complementary style of interaction in which one negotiator submits to the other's attacks. Thus, if any settlement at all is more valuable than reaching an impasse, a negotiator may need to concede when the balance of power favors the opponent or when the opponent does not need the settlement as much as the negotiator. This suggestion is consistent with several studies that indicate settlements are more likely when negotiators respond to offensive tactics by using defensive tactics or integrative behaviors (Donohue, 1981b; Donohue, Diez, & Hamilton, 1984; Putnam & Jones, 1982a). Communication research using observational methods has investigated the development of issues in negotiation. Bargainers develop distributive issues by adding facts and accentuating their positions (Putnam & Bullis, 1984). Using questions to elicit information from the other party is more effective than demanding information because of the implied obligation to answer the question (Donohue & Diez, 1983; Putnam & Poole, 1987). Greenhalgh, Gilkey, and Pufahl (1984) indicate that distributive goals are most appropriate for negotiations in which the parties are relatively independent of each other. There is little need to maintain an ongoing relationship and little cost in damaging interpersonal relations.

Findings from Applied Research

Williams (1983) has investigated effective communication in legal negotiations in order to draw implications for training attorneys. Using interviews, surveys, and videotaped simulated negotiations, Williams identified three clusters of traits related to effective negotiators. The negotiators were divided into those using cooperative (65%) and aggressive styles (24%); the 11% of attorneys who did not cluster into cooperative or aggressive styles exhibited no particular pattern of traits. Then negotiators exhibiting each of the two styles were subdivided into groups reflecting three levels of effectiveness: ineffective, average, and effective. Descriptions of goals for aggressive attorneys were consistent with those identified above for distributive negotiations. Effective aggressive attorneys were described as dominating, forceful, attacking, rigid, and uncooperative. They used threats, took initial positions described as unrealistic by their counterparts, and were willing to stretch the facts. They also carefully observed their opponents, planned their timing and strategies, and revealed information gradually. In twice as many cases as effective cooperative attorneys, effective aggressive attorneys were forced to go to court to settle cases they had tried to resolve through negotiations, indicating that the aggressive style may more often lead to impasse.

Ineffective Communication in Distributive Negotiations

Findings from Basic Research

Basic research indicates that bluffs are an effective but risky distributive tactic. Bluffs may increase a negotiator's payoffs, but they can also cause the opponent to "lose face." If bluffs embarrass the opponent, they can escalate conflict and cause the opponent to be more unyielding, thus resulting in lower payoffs for the bluffer than might have been achieved without the bluff (Lewicki, 1983). Bluffs are especially likely to escalate conflicts concerned with value issues (Lewis & Pruitt, 1971; Pruitt & Lewis, 1975). Increasing face-to-face oral communication between negotiators reduces their tendencies to bluff (Crott, Kayser, & Lamm, 1980). Thus, negotiators who wish to bluff should limit face-to-face encounters; negotiators who wish to minimize bluffs should maximize the use of face-to-face negotiating sessions.

Some strategies and tactics have been identified as dysfunctional in basic studies of distributive negotiations. Making a high number of concessions (regardless of relative advantage) leads to lower payoffs (Donohue, 1981a). Because both Japanese and Americans who felt their opponents were interpersonally attractive had lower profits (Graham, 1983), negotiators from these cultures should avoid being attracted to their counterparts. Other kinds of dysfunctional behavior, such as reciprocating aggressive with aggressive strategies, may provoke a conflict spiral leading to impasse (Donohue, Diez, & Hamilton, 1984; Putnam & Jones, 1982a). Intense emotional tone affects the interpretation of verbal and nonverbal behaviors. Negotiators who wish to avoid impasse must make sure that their nonverbal behavior is interpreted by the opponent in ways that will facilitate agreement, especially if their behavior appears aggressive. Putnam and Jones (1982a) conclude from their research that "escalating conflicts appear to evolve from the *mismanagement of distributive communication*" (p. 191). From the point of view of achieving a settlement and avoiding impasse, the most effective means of managing conversation is to avoid reciprocal patterns of offensive tactics.

Findings from Applied Research

Williams' (1983) applied research indicated that ineffective aggressive negotiators were perceived as irritating and frequent complainers. They were unsure of the value of the case, used bluffs and threats, were unwilling to share information, refused to move from their positions, and exhibited socially undesirable behavior. These attorneys showed no concern for how the other negotiator might look in the eyes of the client. They were rude, emotional, quarrelsome, hostile, obstructive, and uninterested in the needs of the opposing client and attorney. Their counterparts perceived their goals to be maximizing profit for themselves or outmaneuvering the other attorney. Ineffective and effective aggressive attorneys shared only one characteristic: egotism.

COMMUNICATION DESIGNED TO ACHIEVE INTEGRATIVE GOALS

Communication behaviors associated with achieving integrative goals generally appear in sharp contrast to those designed to lead to distributive settlements. Problem-solving is generally the recommended approach for achieving an integrative settlement (Lewicki, Weiss, & Lewin, 1988). Multiple formal and informal communication channels are used (Lewicki & Litterer, 1985; Walton & McKersie, 1965). Negotiators attempt to redefine problems, analyze the causes of settlement difficulties, and explore a wide range of mutually acceptable, alternative solutions through maximum sharing of information and disclosure of each party's needs and interests (Fisher & Ury, 1981; Lewicki & Litterer, 1985). Integrative strategies result in negotiations characterized by more reactions from opponents, more offers near the time of settlement, generation of more alternative solutions, and more reference to self and others than to the constituency they represent, compared to distributive negotiations (Putnam & Jones, 1982a).

On the level of group-wide and organization-wide communication, Putnam and VanHoeven (1986) have examined the role of stories and rituals in integrative bargaining. Fantasy themes promoted the uniting of the teachers and school board against outsiders, whom both perceived as enemies and villains. Interpretive themes allowed both sides to use their perceptions to find a "scapegoat" to take blame for impasses. Blaming some consensually validated perception of the other party as the reason for negotiation difficulties allowed each side to be tolerant of the other's tactics and to maintain an integrative atmosphere rather than become angry with the other's intransigence. Using external rather than internal attributions allowed both sides to excuse, forgive, and transcend the other's dysfunctional behavior instead of allowing it to bring negotiations to an impasse or to damage the relationship.

Effective Communication in Integrative Negotiations

Findings from Basic Research

Descriptions of effective integrative communication drawn from the basic research literature primarily involve message-centered behavior. Negotiators can reduce the use of distributive tactics by increasing the parties' mutual dependence (Bacharach & Lawler, 1980) or by verbally emphasizing it in negotiations (Beisecker, 1970). Weingart, Thompson, Bazerman, and Carroll (1988) found that negotiations with a high number of offers and counteroffers were less effective in achieving integrative outcomes; they believe the frequency of offers substitutes for perspective-taking and information exchange. They conclude that revealing information about one's interests and engaging in longer question-response chains may lead to higher joint payoffs in integrative negotiations. Graham (1983) also suggests that U.S. bargainers ought to reveal more information about themselves to maximize joint payoffs. Americans whose opponents gave more information about themselves achieved higher payoffs than those with nondisclosive opponents (Graham, 1983). Listening is an important integrative communication skill. Effective integrative negotiators listen for both cognitive and emotional content; they drop defensive barriers, which hinder effective listening (Lewicki &

Litterer, 1985). Verbal communica-tion involves exploratory problem-solving, arguments that support the other, and acceptances of the other's analysis and proposals (Putnam & Jones, 1982a). Negotiations using face-to-face, rather than audio or audio-video, channels provide the highest joint outcomes (Turnbull, Strickland, & Shaver, 1976). One of the key components of integrative bargaining is generating alternative proposals. Creative proposals are developed when negotiators drop, simplify, and package issues (Gulliver, 1979). Separating and prioritizing subissues allows negotiators to clarify and simplify points of dispute (Bullis & Putnam, 1985). Putnam and Geist (1985) found that changing the type of claim initially argued (i.e., fact, value, definition, or policy) and adding qualifiers to proposals facilitated the formation of new proposals. Putnam, Wilson, Waltman, and Turner (1986) discovered that a longer search process eventually led to the development of creative solutions. In a teachers' collective bargaining negotiation, disagreements over definitions and causes of an issue led to harm and disadvantage statements, which were associated with a longer search process than other types of statements (Putnam, Wilson, Waltman, & Turner, 1986). Negotiations between parties who are relatively dependent on each other and who will continue to do business with each other in the future usually involve integrative goals (Greenhalgh, Gilkey, & Pufahl, 1984).

Findings from Applied Research

In Williams' (1983) research, cooperative attorneys had goals consistent with integrative negotiations. Effective cooperative negotiators were described as courteous, tactful, sincere, and trustworthy. They were fair-minded, adopted "realistic" opening positions, were willing to share information, and probed the opponent's position. They avoided the use of threats. Williams believes that the majority of effective attorneys adopt a cooperative style.

Ineffective Communication in Integrative Negotiations

Findings from Basic Research

Through basic research, Bullis and Putnam (1985) found that, although stories and rituals maintained integrative goals, the stories and rituals could also be ineffective. They constrained the teachers' thinking about possibilities for behavior and led to the teachers' failure to win outcomes that management had been willing to concede. Thus, from the authors' radical humanist perspective, the teachers' trust both in their chief negotiator and in their stories and rituals was dysfunctional because the stories and rituals severely curtailed the teachers' freedom to explore a wider range of negotiation tactics and strategies. The chief negotiator's interpretation of reality was enacted with few challenges. These findings underscore the role of conflict in generating alternative solutions and avoiding groupthink (Janis, 1972).

Findings from Applied Research

Applied research revealed that, although both effective and ineffective cooperative attorneys were described as experienced, fair, personable, trustworthy, and ethical, ineffective cooperative attorneys tended to be "milquetoasts" (Williams, 1983, p. 41). Ineffective cooperative attorneys apparently lacked confidence and vacillated between being patient and forgiving or demanding and argumentative. They were described as idealistic, a characterization that Williams (1983) believes indicates their "lack of versatility, adaptability, creativity, and wisdom" (p. 35).

GENERAL NEGOTIATION FINDINGS

The category of general negotiation findings may appear to represent conclusions that hold true for both distributive and integrative contexts. In fact, this is seldom the case. For example, Weingart, Thompson, Bazerman, and Carroll (1988) found no tactics that were effective across different negotiations. They argue, "Negotiators' tactical behavior should be flexible and based upon the information obtained during the negotiation" (p. 23). This section is included because much of the normative research does not specify whether distributive or integrative motives are primary; some studies investigate perceived effectiveness over a variety of negotiation contexts (e.g., distributive and integrative; collective bargaining, business contracts, and interpersonal conflicts in organizations). Thus, most findings presented here are drawn from studies that cannot clearly be classified as distributive or integrative.

Effective Communication

Findings from Basic Research

Lewis and Fry (1977) examined verbal and nonverbal behavior associated with negotiation settlements in both distributive and integrative negotiations. They found that dyads who reached impasse engaged in nonverbal behaviors similar to those of dyads who achieved a settlement, but that those behaviors were perceived differently (Putnam & Jones, 1982a). "For the impasse groups, the type of negotiation influenced the display and meaning of cues in bargaining interaction" (Putnam & Jones, 1982a, p. 273). Dyads who reached agreement were similar regardless of whether the negotiation was designed to be integrative or distributive. Agreement dyads offered proposals even after one acceptable settlement had been discovered. They avoided disruptive negotiation tactics, initiated many proposals designed to provide the same payoff before lowering their aspirations, and elicited their counterparts' reactions to statements. Important nonverbal behavior differences consisted of nonthreatening behaviors such as avoiding direct eye gaze and maintaining physical distance (Lewis & Fry, 1977; Putnam & Jones, 1982a).

Findings from Applied Research

Two teams of applied researchers have investigated the differences in effective and ineffective negotiators' communication without regard to a specific form of business negotiation. Salem and Berrios (1987) surveyed foreign operations officers of U.S. and Latin American companies operating in the other culture. Effective negotiators were those who had recently bargained with participants in a settlement with mutually beneficial outcomes; ineffective negotiators were parties to an agreement that participants later regretted. Participants described effective and ineffective counterparts through critical incidents and questionnaires. Effective negotiators were perceived as more empathic, friendly, attentive, relaxed, and open, and less dominant and contentious than ineffective negotiators. Empathy emerged from discriminant analysis as the primary characteristic distinguishing effective from ineffective negotiators. The authors conclude that, "When situations are high in uncertainty, other directed behaviors (i.e., empathic, friendly, and attentive communication) are more important to perceptions of effectiveness than alternative behaviors" (Salem & Berrios, 1987, p. 20).

Rackham and Carlisle (1978a,b) conducted research involving negotiators in labor, contract, and other types of organizational disputes. Their methods consisted of interviews and content analysis of observational interactions; the specific details of recording and assessing interaction data are not thoroughly described. Effective negotiators were judged proficient by both sides and had a consistent track record of reaching settlements that could be effectively implemented (e.g., collective bargaining contracts). During the planning stage, effective negotiators considered more options, concentrated more on common ground areas, considered more long-range aspects, and were more likely to set upper and lower limits (e.g., target and resistance points; see Walton & McKersie, 1965) compared to "average" (less effective) negotiators. They also tended to plan each individual issue independent of sequence; less effective negotiators tied together issues in a planned sequence (Rackham & Carlisle, 1978b). Compared to their "average" counterparts, effective negotiators "tended to advance single reasons insistently, only moving to subsidiary reasons if the main reason was clearly losing ground" (Rackham & Carlisle, 1978a, p. 8). Other types of communication that distinguish effective from less effective negotiators are behavior labeling (i.e., precueing statements such as, "If I could just make a suggestion"; Rackham & Carlisle, 1978a, p. 8), more testing and summarizing of assumptions and interpretations through the use of reflective statements (e.g., mirror questions), and giving more information about one's own feelings about how the negotiations are proceeding. This kind of personal revelation gives others a feeling of security because the negotiator's motives appear to be transparent; such statements were often substituted for direct disagreement (e.g., "I'm very worried that we seem so far apart on this particular point"; Rackham & Carlisle, 1978a, p. 11). However, effective negotiators avoid labeling disagreements, presenting reasons first so that their intent to disagree is not immediately apparent. The researchers view this tactic as a method of saving face; the counterpart appears to concede to a neutral, rather than a hostile, suggestion. Because effective negotiators are more concerned with successful implementation after an agreement has been reached, they are not afraid to probe areas of misunderstanding through perception-checking and summarizing the other's position. They also seek more information by asking questions, which, the authors note, serve three purposes. Questions give control of the conversation to the questioner and are more acceptable than direct disagreement. They also pressure the other party to respond actively, reducing counterparts' thinking time while giving the questioner more time to consider (Rackham & Carlisle, 1978a).

Williams (1983) found six characteristics common to effective negotiators. Both effective aggressive and effective cooperative negotiators were prepared on the facts and on the law, were effective trial attorneys (i.e., had a real threat potential if the case went to court), and took satisfaction in using their legal skills. In addition, both groups were self-controlled and observed legal etiquette and courtesies. Both were viewed as trustworthy, honest and ethical, although these characteristics rank in the top ten descriptors in terms of priority for cooperative negotiators but in the bottom ten for competitive negotiators. In comparing the two groups, Williams comments on their experience and the limitations imposed by their realism, rationality, and analytical skills. "They mean more than the idea of 'thinking like a lawyer'; they impose limits on how far a negotiator may credibly go in such things as interpretation of facts, claims about damages and other economic demands, and levels of emotional involvement in the case" (Williams, 1983, p. 28). Williams identifies perceptive reading of the opponent's cues as perhaps the most important common characteristic (See also Lewicki & Litterer, 1985).

Ineffective Communication

Basic research findings are limited to conclusions about ineffective communication in distributive or integrative contexts. The applied research suggests that ineffective negotiators are perceived to be less empathic and more dominant and contentious than their more effective counterparts (Salem & Berrios, 1987). Rackham and Carlisle's (1978a) "average" negotiators use "irritators," behavior such as labeling one's own proposal "fair," thereby implying the other is unfair and thus antagonizing rather than persuading the counterpart. Less effective negotiators are more likely to make immediate counterproposals and to become involved in attack-defend spirals. This result confirms the finding from basic research concerning distributive negotiations: countering aggressive with aggressive tactics is likely to lead to impasse (Donohue, Diez, & Hamilton, 1984; Putnam & Jones, 1982a). When arguing for proposals, ineffective negotiators dilute their arguments by giving many reasons, thus allowing opponents "a choice of which to dispute" (Rackham & Carlisle, 1978a, p. 8). They label disagreements (e.g., "We disagree because. . . ."), making the other defensive and less likely to hear the reasons following the label.

CHARACTERISTICS OF EFFECTIVE NEGOTIATORS

Descriptions of effective negotiators from the early research have tended to be confirmed through applied investigations. Research on both integrative and distributive negotiations with Americans suggests several types of communication related to negotiating success. For example, Reiches and Harral observe, "Successful negotiators may exhibit an awareness of an interactive, rather than a linear, view of the communication process" (1974, p. 43). Williams' (1983) applied research in legal negotiations indicates that one of the most important characteristics shared by effective negotiators of different styles is skill "in reading their opponent's cues. This refers not only to the ability to judge an opponent's reactions in negotiating situations, but to affirmatively learn from the opponent" (p. 29). Furthermore, effective negotiators communicate in ways that make clear their own feelings and reflect a sensitivity to the opponent's concerns. They also ask more questions, thus receiving more information about the other, and they check their perceptions for accuracy. They are better prepared to negotiate because they consider a wider range of alternatives and are more aware of long-term implications. Effective negotiators typically reveal information, resulting in higher joint payoffs. Face-to-face channels are recommended. Stories and rituals surrounding negotiations have the potential both to facilitate negotiations and to constrain the parties' flexibility in viewing the situation from many perspectives. It seems reasonable to conclude that sensitivity to the opponent's needs, to the needs of the opponent's constituents, to the power balances involved, and to the parameters of the situation are related to effectiveness for all types of bargainers. This description resembles Rubin and Brown's (1955) concept of high interpersonal orientation.

It is important to note that effective bargaining behaviors are culturally bounded. Recommendations from experimental research in international marketing include the following. Brazilians with high bargaining power who use deceptive bargaining strategies are likely to have higher payoffs.

Representatives of firms negotiating in Brazil should establish trusting relationships before negotiating so that deceptive strategies will be identified or inhibited. A more aggressive style may be most effective with Brazilians (Graham, 1985). To maximize individual profits, Americans should encourage their opponents to reveal task-related information. Americans are more likely to receive higher payoffs when bargaining against younger, less experienced opponents who are extroverts (Graham, 1983).

The research on sequences of bargaining behavior is less conclusive. Results from case studies of bargaining patterns need to be replicated or investigated through laboratory experiments. Apparently inconsistent results that relate integrative effectiveness to packaging issues but separating subissues, need further exploration. Some conclusions can be drawn with a reasonable degree of confidence. Research reveals that both effective distributive and integrative negotiators create a pattern of questions followed by brief responses through which their opponents reveal information. Weingart, Thompson, Bazerman, and Carroll (1988) found a similar pattern for effective integrative negotiations. Longer question-response chains may be effective in achieving distributive goals because they provide information about the other's needs and constraints and in achieving integrative goals when used to explore interests and develop a wide range of alternative solutions. Spiraling cycles of aggressive tactics countered with aggressive responses should be avoided because they tend to lead to impasse.

Although threats are effective in achieving distributive goals, negotiators who use them must have superior perspective-taking skills to determine when the threats might become counterproductive and lead to impasse. They must be sensitive to the needs of the other as well as to their own. Similarly, bluffs may be effective but may also promote impasse. Patterns of communication interaction ineffective for achieving distributive goals are making multiple concessions, which result in lower payoffs, and countering aggressive strategies with aggressive responses, a pattern that may lead to impasse.

Integrative strategies are generally less risky than distributive ones because they lead to higher joint outcomes and to fewer impasses. Generating large numbers of creative alternative proposals is a key component of effectiveness in integrative bargaining and is generally characteristic of effective negotiators. Taken as a whole, the research confirms that the effective characteristics of integrative bargainers are more generalizable than those of effective distributive bargainers. Williams' (1983) final recommendation is that negotiators analyze their own personalities and bargaining habits to identify their typical bargaining style (aggressive or cooperative) then modify them to conform to the characteristics of effective aggressive or cooperative negotiators. Until more research exploring negotiation communication from a process perspective has been conducted, this advice appears reasonable.

RECOMMENDATIONS FOR
COMMUNICATION RESEARCH

Several major recommendations may be made for future research. First, there is a need to integrate the research findings to develop models of negotiation communication. As the many disparate research findings indicate, there are few comprehensive models of communication in negotiations. The most inclusive of these is normative and remains to be tested (i.e., Hocker & Wilmot, 1985). Although communication scholars have developed models of communication styles or situational approaches (e.g., Putnam & Wilson, 1982; Riggs, 1983; Ross & DeWine, 1987, 1988) or to communication strategies and tactics in negotiation (Donohue, 1978; 1981b), these models do not integrate intents or particular types of messages into a comprehensive negotiation framework. The general descriptive models of intercultural (Nadler, Broome, & Nadler, 1985) and gender-related (Nadler & Nadler, 1987) negotiation communication most resemble typologies of variables. For the most part, they have not been tested. This problem is similar to that noted by Lewicki, Weiss, and Lewin (1988), except that there are only a few communication models and no complete, systematic investigations of their variables and relationships. Furthermore, there is a need to develop and test descriptive as well as normative theories. Whereas general descriptive negotiation models "have tended to 'build down' from theories of human behavior" (Lewicki, Weiss, & Lewin, 1988, p. 80), much negotiation communication research reflects the fragmentation and lack of integration typical of variable analytic approaches to communication research. Studies have been conducted, but few communication models have been built, either "downward" from broad theories of communication or "up" from combinations of research findings. Donohue's (1978; 1981b) model and research point the way to the kind of testing and theory-building needed. Recent summaries of communication research provide a starting point to identify and organize basic research findings. Many of the needs in communication mirror the suggestions of Lewicki, Weiss, and Lewin (1988) for general negotiation research: applied research needs to be integrated with basic research to form theories relating communication behavior to effective outcomes. As negotiation studies from other disciplines either involve communication variables or have direct communication implications, the ideal negotiation model is interdisciplinary. Before communication researchers can contribute, they must first develop mid-level and broader theories.

Much more applied research in negotiation communication is needed. Theorists might more clearly specify relationships in the Hocker and Wilmot (1985) model so that it can be tested. Investigators should continue to use experienced organizational negotiators as participants in experimental and observational studies and to avoid the current bias toward cooperation and win-win in normative models. They should avoid the problems identified in current applied research. For example, Rackham & Carlisle (1978a,b) do not describe their coding methods in sufficient detail for others to replicate theirs studies. Scholars should beware of generalizing from intercultural studies. To illustrate, Graham implicitly assumes that the tactics effectively used by someone from one's native culture will be equally effective if used by someone from another culture (Graham, 1983); that is, Americans bargaining with Brazilians will be effective if they use the tactics recommended for use by another Brazilian bargainer. Surprisingly, this crucial assumption remains untested. Both basic and applied researchers should recognize, make explicit, and test their assumptions.

For quantitative researchers, designs emphasizing a processual approach and allowing for causal associations between communication variables and bargaining outcomes are needed. Studies should involve observations rather than self-reports of communication behavior. In order for communication behaviors to be related to negotiation effectiveness, they must first be identified in actual use, not merely through self-reports, and a wider range of behavior should be studied over time and different contexts. Investigating questions, techniques, and objectives is likely to be profitable. Nonverbal behavior provides an important set of negotiation cues, especially in intercultural negotiations, yet this area of negotiation research is in its infancy. Communication scholars have long recognized effective listening as important, yet despite early research, no one has studied the impact of specific attending behaviors on negotiation effectiveness. In all types of studies suggested, effectiveness should be carefully and explicitly defined, and multiple indications of effectiveness should be used.

Content analysis of transcripts and/or videotapes captures the very rich data provided in actual negotiations. If taping actual negotiations is impossible, laboratory experiments involving experienced negotiators participating in naturalistic settings are acceptable; care should be taken to maximize external validity. The work of Putnam and her colleagues provides an example of interpretive research approaches investigating stories, rituals, and argument in bargaining. Traditional communication studies of argument should be pursued even more vigorously by connecting arguments, stories, and bargaining rituals with effectiveness. One profitable way to investigate competent communication is to identify effective and ineffective negotiators independently and then explore differences and similarities in their communication, a method used in most of the applied research presented here.

Finally, communication researchers should investigate effectiveness in a wider variety of negotiation contexts. The basic research in marketing negotiations and the applied work in law and business represent steps in this direction. Researchers might conduct applied studies involving advertising, insurance, public relations, real estate, or right-of-way professionals. Practitioners in these fields have long been trained by communication scholars, yet no empirical research has explored effective communication in these professions. The variety of negotiation contexts that provide new and fertile ground for researchers is almost without limit. Because there is general agreement in the field that effectiveness is situationally determined, exploring this new territory is essential in order to develop a comprehensive theory. To date, the limited research available, both basic and applied, is difficult to integrate; so few contexts and contextual elements have been investigated that commonalities between studies are hard to find. Researchers should explore characteristics that bridge a variety of negotiations, e.g., negotiations involving parties with a previous long-term relationship (collective bargaining or a business contract) or "one-shot" negotiations unlikely to create future relationships (buying a used car). If investigators can relate effectiveness to many different contextual elements, they may present a clear picture of what it means to be a competent communicator in negotiations. Given the importance of communication in negotiation, conducting more applied research and developing more basic and applied theories is vital for the communication discipline. The development of more communication theory and research about negotiating will increase understanding, make for vital teaching and sound practice, and enhance the lives of people from a variety of professions.

4   To Probe or Not to Probe: Evaluating Mediators' Question-Asking Behaviors

Nancy A. Burrell

In many ways mediation is a true test of a communicator's skills. Mediation is the process of using a neutral third party to help disputants resolve a conflict. A mediator has no formal or institutional authority to resolve the conflict. Participants must voluntarily agree to any resolution of the conflict. A mediator contributes to the process by offering advice, ideas, and structure to the interaction that allows participants to discuss with each other the nature of the dispute and the possible solutions to that conflict (Folberg & Taylor, 1984; Moore, 1986).

A critical skill for a communicatively competent mediator is to gather information about the conflict and those individuals who are involved directly and tangentially (Folberg & Taylor, 1984; Keltner, 1987). An efficient strategy for gathering information is question-asking (Berger & Kellermann, 1983). Researchers have looked at question-asking in a variety of communicative contexts such as employment interviews (Jablin & McComb, 1984; Tengler & Jablin, 1983), initial interactions (Berger, 1973; Calabrese, 1975), and parent/child discourse (Ervin-Tripp, 1976; Mishler, 1975a), but there has been little research examining how specific types of questions function in the context of mediation. Not only are mediators' questioning behaviors important; in addition, researchers need to focus on issues of gender and timing of their interventions (Burrell, Donohue, & Allen, 1988; Jones, 1987). One significant threat to a mediator's perceived neutrality and ability to build cooperative contexts is gender bias. The purpose of this investigation is to examine whether gender differences occur in mediators' question-asking behaviors based on form, function, and timing issues.

Questions play essential communicative functions in the context of mediation. In a global sense, questions enable participants to experience sensible discourse. In other words, through a series of questions a mediator is able to identify the conflict, sort out critical issues, and determine disputants' positions (Folberg & Taylor, 1984). Questions are used to control the introduction of topics and the cueing of their relevance (Donohue, Allen, & Burrell, 1985). For example, a mediator can ask participants for their proposed solutions or ask how a specific proposal could be enacted. Questions are used to clarify and/or verify information, impressions, and/or perceptions (Moore, 1986). Finally, questions trigger additional information based on an earlier answer (Mishler, 1975a,b; Stewart & Cash, 1988; Street, 1986). In short, appropriately framed questions facilitate the mediation process for all participants.

Effective mediation requires both appropriately framed questions and good listening skills. However, there is a great deal of variety in how questions are asked and the degree of mediator directiveness (Folberg & Taylor, 1984; Keltner, 1987; Moore, 1986). Questions generally are of two types: open and closed-ended (Kearsley, 1976; Moore, 1986; Quirk, Greenbaum, Leech, & Svartvik, 1972; Robinson & Rackstraw, 1972). Although there are numerous listings of types and subtypes of questions (Stewart & Cash, 1988), this investigation chose to focus on those question forms that were present in the mediation literature (Folberg & Taylor, 1984; Moore, 1986).

Open questions are described as general, often specifying only a topic. Open-ended questions allow the respondent considerable freedom in determining the amount and kind of information to disclose (Folberg & Taylor, 1984; Moore, 1986; Stewart & Cash, 1988). Some questions are highly open (e.g., "Tell me about yourself") whereas other questions can be moderately open with some restrictions (e.g., "Tell me about your most recent problem/conflict"). Closed-ended questions are restrictive and may supply possible answers (Folberg & Taylor, 1984; Moore, 1986; Stewart & Cash, 1988). Similar to open questions, some closed questions are moderately closed (e.g., "How long have you been living in the area?") whereas other questions are highly closed (e.g., "Do you live in the Chicago area?") because all that is required of a respondent is a simple yes or no. Question forms are important to the mediation process in that mediators must constantly monitor the quantity and quality of disputants' responses based on the timing, structure, and function of their questions.

Furthermore, a mediator's question-asking style is influenced by several factors. In some sessions, disputants answer questions in great detail whereas the same set of questions in another session may generate minimal information. In other words, the appropriateness of question forms in mediation is affected by the nature of disputants' loquacity. Similarly, a mediator may be pressed for time and, based on these time constraints, may alter his or her question forms. Also, a mediator's question forms may be influenced by his or her knowledge about the dispute (e.g., has identified critical issues at an earlier session). To summarize, numerous factors impact on the appropriateness of question forms.

As suggested earlier, a mediator's use of questions is an important mechanism in the information-gathering process. Keltner (1987) points out that the use of questions is an important tool for gathering information about disputants, the nature of the conflict, relevant and irrelevant issues, and about disputants' opinions and their perceptions of each other's opinions. The implication is that in order to facilitate the mediation process, a mediator should be knowledgeable about the framing of questions (e.g., their structure and function) as the session unfolds. However, there is no further discussion about the specific question-asking behaviors of mediators. Moreover, in many of the current self-help books for practitioners (Bienenfeld, 1983; Coulson, 1983; Fisher & Ury, 1981; Keltner, 1987; Moore, 1986), a mediator's skill at interviewing clients is characterized as "critical," but there has been little empirical research examining specific question-asking behaviors of mediators.

Whereas Keltner promotes question-asking as an important tool for mediators, Folberg and Taylor (1984) caution professional mediators about relying too heavily on questions to gain information during a mediation session. "If questions are used to the exclusion of other techniques, the conversation will cease to be an exchange and will become an unsatisfactory form of verbal ping-pong or interrogation," (Folberg & Taylor, 1984, p. 109). These scholars acknowledge the importance for practitioners to understand the various types of questions in order to have them serve the proper function. Folberg and Taylor point out that although open-ended questions are preferable, they can be so open or nondirective that they fail to produce the necessary information.

Second, closed-ended questions can suppress the true answer by leading disputants into believing that the only acceptable answer is the one referenced in the question.

To summarize, Folberg and Taylor (1984) suggest that the type of questions professional mediators use is dependent upon specific goals, in addition to how the session is unfolding. Mediators are advised to begin sessions with more open-ended questions to identify specifics. Although these mediation scholars seem to be making quite useful and pragmatic suggestions for professionals to follow, no empirical research is cited to support their suggestions. Two lines of research in the context of divorce mediation, however, begin to address the importance of mediator's question-asking behaviors, in addition to gender and timing issues.

Donohue, Allen, and Burrell (1985) examined 20 (10 agreement and 10 nonagreement) child custody disputes. These researchers proposed three general categories for mediator interventions. Questions were involved in two of the categories: reframing and expanding the information resource. The reframing category included interventions aimed at soliciting information from disputants to use in problem-solving. For example, a mediator's intervention could create an alternative proposal (e.g., "Wouldn't it be better if you began the visitation?") by reframing a disputant's earlier proposal. Expanding the information resource are requesting tactics which are used frequently at the beginning of mediation enabling mediators to identify underlying issues of disputes (e.g., "What do you mean by that?" or "What do you have in mind for the children?"). Donohue and his associates report that agreement mediators differ from nonagreement mediators in their use of reframing interventions. Agreement mediators were more likely to interrupt attacks by creating alternative proposals or reframing the utterance as a proposal. These results point to the importance of questions as appropriate intervention strategies.

Jones (1989) examined 36 (18 successful and 18 unsuccessful) divorce mediation sessions. Results of a lag sequential analysis showed that both successful and unsuccessful mediators obtained information by requesting information or clarification. However, successful mediators guided disputants to talk about themselves rather than to talk for their spouse, used summarization behaviors, avoided reciprocal disagreement cycles with disputants, and encouraged reciprocal problem-solving behaviors. The importance of mediators' question-asking behaviors are suggested in these results.

In another study examining gender differences in successful and unsuccessful divorce mediations, Jones (1987) reports that husbands engaged more actively in discussions of procedural matters (e.g., asked more questions or made agenda suggestions). However, wives provided more information to the mediator's questions. This information centered on details about themselves, children, spouse, and others involved in the dispute. Husbands' responses did not disclose information about themselves unless prompted by the mediator. Additional gender differences focused on mediators' behaviors toward husbands versus wives. Specifically, mediators adopted a more confrontive stance with wives while giving more credence to solutions and nonspecific solution talk of husbands. These results suggest researchers need to focus on issues of gender and timing and that mediators' questioning behaviors are important.

Furthermore, gender research in mediation is important because participants may respond to gender stereotypes and may punish out-of-role behavior. According to Jones (1987), implicit in the mediation context is an increasing propensity for expectations and reactions based on previous conflict histories/patterns and assumptions regarding gender roles. Gender bias is a potential threat to a mediator's perceived neutrality and ability to build cooperation. In a recent study, Hanisch and Carnevale (1988) report that disputants attributed bias to mediators based on their gender. Not only may disputants perceive mediators to act differently toward them; mediators may, in fact, behave differently toward disputants based on gender (Burrell, Donohue, & Allen, 1988). Conrad (1985) suggests that males and females respond differently to conflict situations in his review of over 100 studies on conflict gender differences. Thus, gender differences in the context of mediation is an important issue to explore.

Another important issue that researchers have begun to explore in the context of mediation is the timing of interventions. Jones (1988) points out that most scholars agree that effective mediation/negotiation proceeds through identifiable phases. Also, there is little empirical research that mediation is progressive in nature. In an investigation of agreement and nonagreement divorce mediations, agreement mediation progressed from differentiation to integration through information exchange, problem-solving, and finally resolution behaviors (Jones, 1988). However, nonagreement mediation continued to emphasize information exchange throughout the mediation and tended to deemphasize problem-solving and resolution behaviors. The results of this study provide empirical evidence for phase theories of mediation/negotiation. At a pragmatic level, these results suggest that the timing of interventions is an important consideration for mediators.

Because asking questions is important to the process of mediation and seems to be a part of a communicatively competent mediator's repertoire, the following research questions are forwarded:

RQ 1: Which question forms do mediators use more frequently?

RQ 2: What differences occur in male versus female mediators' use of question forms?

RQ 3: What relationship exists between male versus female mediators' use of question functions and disputants' responses?

RQ 4: How does the use of question functions change across phases of mediation?

RQ 5: What differences occur in male versus female mediators' use of question functions across phases of mediation?

RQ 6: What relationship exists between mediators' question functions and forms and disputants' responses to questions?

METHOD

The purpose of this study was to examine the question-asking behaviors of mediators trained according to the interventionist mediation model. This model is control-based and assumes that a key function of a mediator is to manage the interaction.

Participants

Forty-eight participants (25 male and 23 female) were selected from an upper-level communication course at a large midwestern university to enact the role of a mediator. From this group, 23 (13 male and 10 female) participated in the mediator training program. In addition, 48 same-sex dyads were selected from several introductory communication classes to be used as disputants and were randomly assigned to 1 of the 48 mediators. All participants engaged in the same dispute and experimental procedures.

Identifying a Conflict Situation

Before the study, a pilot test on roommate conflicts was conducted based on Sillars' (1980, 1981) research indicating that such conflicts are appropriate for examining the interventionist model of mediation. Roommate conflicts can escalate into dysfunctional conflict spirals because dissatisfied roommates tend to externalize blame by attributing the problem to one another, to utilize distributive and avoidance strategies in addressing the problem, and to reciprocate distributive acts (Sillars, 1980, 1981). Residence hall assistants frequently deal with very intense roommate disputes on such topics as considerateness and/or theft.

The goal of the pilot test was to identify a conflict situation with which individuals were familiar and had experience. Given the housing situation among undergraduates (the sample), roommate disputes were considered a primary area for experience with conflict. The pilot test sought to identify which particular issue(s) were most frequently experienced in roommate conflicts. The conflict rated as occurring most frequently, using a scale of 1 (not at all) to 7 (very frequent), centered on how the room should be kept and overall cleanliness of the room ($M = 5.53$, $SD = 1.21$, $N = 24$). Thus, the orderliness/cleanliness of the room was chosen to be the conflict situation in this investigation.

Mediator Training

Twenty-three participants were trained to mediate roommate conflicts according to the interventionist mediation model (Burrell, 1987; Burrell, Donohue, & Allen, 1988). The mediator training program centered on eliciting three specific behaviors: interrupting disputants as soon as they begin attacking each other, maintaining control of the interaction by enforcing the rules of the session, and encouraging disputants to formulate proposals. Detailed descriptions of the training program can be found in either Burrell (1987) or Burrell, Donohue, and Allen (1988). Briefly, participants viewed several videotapes of mediations, took part in discussions stressing intervention strategies, practiced several mediations through simulations of roommate conflicts and focused on active listening skills. Mediator training sessions lasted approximately four hours.

Conflict Interaction Procedures

Ninety-six participants (paired into 48 dyads) served as disputants in simulations of roommate conflicts about the orderliness/cleanliness of the room. Disputants were randomly assigned a neat or a sloppy role. Neat role disputants were instructed to prefer a room that is extremely neat and orderly to the point where disarray makes them nervous; that conditions in the room had become so bad that studying in the room was impossible because of the extreme mess created by the sloppy roommate; that their roommate had been reminded nicely about how they felt but the reminders had had *no* impact; that they were tired of being taken advantage of, ignored, and in general, "living like a pig!"; and that such messiness *must stop*.

By contrast, sloppy role disputants were instructed that they were extremely sloppy to the point that neatness makes them nervous; that conditions in the room had become so bad that spending time in the room was distasteful because their roommate kept cleaning up after them; that they had asked their roommate *not* to clean up after them; that they were extremely tired of being yelled at, being treated like a child, and feeling guilty because they did not hang up their clothes; and that such behavior *must stop*.

To ensure that the training program was effective, a control group (25 participants) was utilized. Mediators in the control group received the following instructions: a mediator is a neutral third party who helps people resolve their problems. Your role is to mediate (intervene) in a roommate conflict. Before the mediation session, think about possible strategies that you will use to get these two roommates to deal with their problems.

Participants enacting roommate roles reported to a different room to receive their instruction sets than those participants assigned mediator roles. Research assistants were present in the rooms to distribute directions and to ensure that those assigned roommate roles did not talk to each other. After reading the instructions describing neat or sloppy roles, "disputatious" roommates were given ten minutes to generate possible arguments that would further their positions during their mediations. They then were taken to an experimental room where the mediation of the dispute occurred. Because neat or sloppy roles were randomly assigned, participants were allotted time in case they were assigned to enact a role contrary to their usual behavior. All roommate conflicts were videotaped.

After the videotaping, participants who were enacting roommate roles completed a 15-item questionnaire (see Table 4.1) that focused on the perceived skills of the mediator. Items were designed to tap mediator competence in fairness, control, and effectiveness. Participants were asked to rate the mediator's performance on a scale of 1 (never) to 7 (always).

Finally, subjects participating in the mediator training program completed several open-ended questions assessing the training program. Participants were asked what aspects of the training program were most helpful, in addition to what elements in the training program should be excluded. All the participants enacting mediator roles (trained and untrained) were asked questions about how well they functioned as a mediator, how confident they felt in the mediator role, and how successful they were in helping disputants resolve their conflicts.

TABLE 4.1

Items for Perceptual Assessment Instrument

Fairness

  1. How fair was the mediator to the other person?
  2. How fair was the mediator to you?
  3. Did the mediator interrupt each participant equally?

Control

  4. Did the mediator seem to be listening to you?
  5. Did the mediator seem too controlling during the session?

Performance

  6. Did the mediator establish rules for conduct at the session's opening?
  7. Did the mediator seem to know what he or she was doing?
  8. Did the mediator encourage you to make suggestions about how to solve the problem?
  9. Did the mediator summarize each person's solution to the confict?
10. Did the mediator seem prepared?
11. Did the mediator keep you on track in dealing with the relevant issues?
12. Did the mediator seem to be listening to you?
13. Did the mediator clarify each person's position?
14. Did the mediator interrupt you at appropriate times?
15. Did the mediator represent your position accurately?

Interaction Indices

Because the purpose of this study was to examine the question-asking behaviors of mediators, transcripts of the 23 roommate mediations were constructed from the videotapes. Coders were instructed to record sequences of simple questions (N = 346) posed by mediators and disputants' answers (N = 346) to those questions. A question was operationally defined as having interrogative force, obligating the other party to respond, usually being followed by a brief, but noticeable pause and upward intonation, and typically containing question words (e.g., who, what, or when). An answer was operationalized as an utterance providing only the information requested in a previous question and an utterance that remained on the same topic or issue as that in the previous question.

In order to assess the reliability of segmenting the questions and answers examined in this research, two coders segmented the first two, middle two, and the final two mediations (6 of the 23 mediations or 38% of the data). These coders were selected from an upper-division communication course based on their interest in interaction analysis. Two training sessions were conducted to familiarize judges with the coding scheme and to practice coding transcripts from an earlier study. All intercoder reliabilities were computed using percentage of agreement between coders. Of the 88 question/answer speech acts identified by either coder, 84 of the 88 were identically segmented, yielding an overall reliability of 95%. Two question/answer segments were not identified in the first two mediations, and one question/answer sequence was deleted from both the middle and the last mediations.

Disputants' answers to mediators' questions were coded as agreement/compliance, neutrality/ambiguity, and disagreement/ noncompliance. These three moves represented varying levels of intensity of disputants' behaviors with disagreement being the most intense and agreement being the least intense. For example, a noncompliant response challenged the mediator's authority or obstructed the flow of the session (e.g., "I don't like your suggestion," or "No — I'm too busy to pick up my half of the room"). A response that was neutral or ambiguous could be a disputant's strategy for stringing out the interaction because he or she was indecisive about a particular issue, or this neutral tactic might be taken because the disputant was afraid and/or unable to express his or her true feelings (e.g., "I guess maybe I could think about taking the time to sort of pick up my stuff," or "I don't know — well, maybe my stuff sort of spreads out"). Finally, a response that agreed or complied with the mediator's question supported the mediator's attempts to gather information about the conflict or to identify specific proposals, and, overall, contributed positively to the interaction (e.g., "I see the problem as more like the 'Odd Couple' — I'm Oscar and he's Felix!" or "I agree that this can be worked out if we could just be honest with each other"). Disagreement responses were less frequent (N = 41) than neutral/ambiguous moves (N = 48), which, in turn were less frequent than agreement responses (N = 257). Two coders assigned the disputants' acts to categories from the six mediations segmented for the purposes of reliability. The two coders agreed 94% of the time on the functions of disputants' moves.

Mediators' questions were content coded according to their structure (either open or closed) and their function (informational, restatements, probing, social control, and evaluative). As noted earlier, open questions are typically identified by "wh" words. Closed-ended questions are identified by such words as have/has, is/are, and do. Closed-ended questions (N = 205) occurred almost twice as frequently as open-ended questions (N = 126). An "other" category was added because an additional 15 questions contained none of the identifying words (e.g., who/what or have/had) for categorizing open and closed questions structurally but were answered by disputants. The utterances were intended as questions by mediators (there was a rising intonation in the voice) and were used to direct or manage the interaction. These mediator utterances were responded to/answered as questions. For example, a disputant commented, "She never lifted a finger to help. I do everything!" The mediator responded, "She agreed to help?" The disputant replied, "Yes — sure — but wait til we get home." Clearly, the mediator's comment was seeking information and perhaps was directive — to point out that the roommate would be cooperative in the future, but it was interpreted as a closed question. Two coders agreed 98% of the time on the structure of mediator questions in the six mediations that were coded for purposes of reliability.

Mediators' questions were also categorized as serving five functions:

1. Seeking information (e.g., "What is your position?"),
2. Restating previous utterances or positions (e.g., "Did you say that your roommate will never change and that this is a waste of your time?"),

3. Probing for additional information (e.g., "Would you explain what you mean?" or "Can you tell me more about your roommate's poor housekeeping habits?"),
4. Socially controlling — a series of three or more questions in the same utterance (e.g., "Is this a problem with schedules that you can't keep the room clean, or is it more than an issue that she's neat and you're messy? Is there a solution we can figure out to this? How about if we start with you?"), and
5. Asking disputants to evaluate feelings, issues, or solutions/proposals (e.g., "Would you consider yourself somewhat of a perfectionist?" or "Do you think that this is something you could agree on?").

Questions seeking information (N = 148) and evaluations (N = 105) occurred most frequently followed by questions functioning as restatements (N = 57), social control (N = 21), and probes (N = 15) respectively. Using six mediations, coders agreed 98% of the time on questions seeking information, 96% on probing questions, 100% on restatements, 100% on social control questions, and 94% on questions serving an evaluative function for reliability purposes.

ANALYSIS AND RESULTS

Manipulation Checks

Two manipulation checks were performed in this study. The first manipulation check examined whether participants within the interaction rated trained mediators as performing their roles more competently than those mediators who did not receive training. If the training program standardized mediators' behaviors, both male and female mediators would be rated at comparable competency levels. Standardization is important because any evidence pointing to gender differences would not be attributed to mediator competence. An ANOVA was conducted with independent variables of gender of the mediator and amount of training, and a dependent variable of perceived role-performance. For perceived role-performance, a main effect for training occurred, $F(1, 46)$ = 36.87, p < .001; no significant effect was found for gender of the mediator, $F(1, 46)$ = 1.23, p = ns. Trained mediators (M = 86.71, SD = 9.45, N = 23) performed their roles with more proficiency than untrained mediators (M = 64.30, SD - 15.73, N = 25). No significant interaction was observed.

The second manipulation check asked two independent judges outside the interaction to rate mediators on whether they seemed trained or untrained. After viewing each of the 48 mediations, judges were asked to rate the mediator's performance based on the following behaviors: maintaining control of the interaction, establishing rules, enforcing the rules, clarifying disputants' positions, and guiding disputants toward a solution. On a scale of 1 (behaviors not exhibited) to 7 (behaviors exhibited) significant differences between the untrained group ($M = 2.60$, $SD = 1.08$, $N = 25$) and the trained group ($M = 6.10$, $SD = 1.12$, $N = 23$) were found $t(46) = 11.05$, $p < .05$. These results of the two manipulation checks indicate that easily identifiable differences exist in how competently mediators performed when rated by both participants within the mediation sessions and outside observers.

Research Question 1

Which question forms do mediators use more frequently? Mediators utilized closed-ended questions 59% of the time ($N = 205$) and used open-ended questions 36% of the time ($N = 126$). In addition, 15 questions in the "other" category were used 4% of the time by mediators.

Also, of interest was the distribution of question form by function. A comparison of distributions demonstrated that open and closed questions were not equally distributed among the five functions (Chi-square = 57.61, $DF = 4$, $p < .001$). Most open questions ($N = 86$) served the information function 68% of the time; closed questions functioned as both restatements ($N = 43$) and evaluations ($N = 83$) 21% and 40% of the time respectively. See Table 4.2 for the distribution of question form by function.

Research Question 2

What differences occur in male versus female mediators' use of question forms? Both male and female mediators used approximately the same number of open-ended questions ($N = 66$ for males, $N = 60$ for females). However, males used 122 closed-ended questions whereas females used 83 closed forms. A test of these question form distributions showed no gender differences when using open and/or closed-ended questions (Chi-square = 4.88, $DF = 2$, $p > .05$). In short, male and

TABLE 4.2
Distribution of Question Form by Question Function

Function	Form		
	Other	Open	Closed
Information	7	86	57
Restatements	3	11	43
Probes	0	5	10
Social Control	0	7	14
Evaluative	5	17	83

female mediators used the same proportion of open and closed question forms.

Research Question 3

What relationship exists between male versus female mediators' use of question functions and disputants' responses? To address this question a series of Pearson correlations were computed examining the relationship between question functions (information, restate, probe, social control, and evaluate) used by male versus female mediators and disputants' responses (agree, neutral, or disagree). The use of correlations to represent the proposed relationships are the same as a lag sequential analysis at lag one because the z-scores produced by a lag analysis are mathematically transformable to a correlation (Rosenthal, 1984). Positive correlations indicate male mediators receiving more disagreement from disputants than female mediators. By contrast, negative correlations indicate female mediators receiving more disagreement from participants than males. Insignificant correlations indicate no gender differences in question functions and disputants' responses.

Results of the Pearson correlations indicate three significant correlations. Female mediators received more disagreement from disputants when their questions functioned as informational $r(174) = -.15, p < .05$ and evaluative $r(115) = -.19, p < .05$. Males received more disagreement from disputants when their questions functioned as socially controlling $r(20) = .44, p < .05$. There were no gender differences when mediators' questions functioned as restatements $r(53) = .06$, $p = $ ns and probes $r(19) = .28$, $p = $ ns.

Research Question 4

How does the use of question functions change across phases of mediation? To address this question, the 23 mediations were divided into thirds. Specifically, the total number of question and answer utterances were divided by three in each of the 23 mediations. Based on a review of the mediation literature, it was suggested that questions function as seeking information in the opening phase of mediation, (T1), as restatements, probes, and social controls in the middle phase (T2), and as seeking evaluations in the closing phase of mediation (T3) (Folberg & Taylor, 1984; Moore, 1986). Therefore, question functions were recoded as informational = 1, restatements, probes, and social controls = 2, and evaluative = 3 to represent what has been suggested in the phase literature. To summarize, the predicted relationships are that mediators' informational questions should decrease over time while mediators' evaluative questions should increase over time. A curvilinear relationship should exist between mediators' restatements, probes, and social controls over time.

Results show that mediators used informational questions 79% in T1, 35% in T2, and 27% in T3 (a decrease as predicted). Mediators utilized restatements, probes, and social controls 19% in T1, 33% in T2, and 23% in T3 (a curvilinear relationship). Also, mediators' evaluative questions were used 7% in T1, 32% in T2, and 49% in T3 (an increase as predicted). Finally, a Pearson correlation was computed to examine the relationship between the predicted pattern/sequencing of question functions with the phases of mediation. Results indicate a strong relationship between the predicted sequence of question forms and the opening (T1), middle (T2), and closing (T3) phases of mediation $r(345) = .44$, $p < .05$.

Research Question 5

What differences occur in male versus female mediators' use of question functions across phases of mediation? To answer this question the recoded functions (as in RQ 3) were correlated with mediator gender and phases (T1, T2, and T3). Although the relationships between question function and phase for males $r(200) = .43, p < .05$ and females $r(144) = .46, p < .05$ were quite strong, results indicate no gender differences. To summarize, results indicate a strong relationship between the function of questions and opening, middle, and closing phases of mediation for both male and female mediators.

Research Question 6

What relationship exists between mediators' question functions and forms and disputants' responses to questions? To address this question a 2 x 5 ANOVA was performed with independent variables of question type (open and closed) and question function (information, restate, probe, social control, evaluate) and a dependent variable of disputant's response (agree, neutral, disagree). For question function, a main effect occurred, $F(4, 336) = 3.43, p < .05, Eta = .21$; no significant effect was found for question type, $F(1, 336) = 1.85, p = ns, Eta = .11$. Also, no significant interaction occurred between question type and question function $F(4, 336) = .80, p = ns, Eta = .05$. Table 4.3 shows the breakdown of means and standard deviations for question types by question functions. In short, how a question functioned had more impact on the type of disputant response than the question's form (open versus closed).

TABLE 4.3
Means and Standard Deviations of Question Type by Question Function

| Function | Question Type | | | | | |
| | Open | | | Closed | | |
	N	M	SD	N	M	SD
Information	86	1.20	.56	55	1.29	.64
Restate	11	1.18	.60	43	1.41	.84
Probe	5	1.71	1.50	10	1.93	1.21
Social Control	7	1.14	.38	14	1.79	.98
Evaluate	17	1.48	.75	83	1.45	.81

DISCUSSION

Results of this investigation indicated that mediators used twice as many closed-ended questions as open-ended questions. Because mediators were trained to use the interventionist mediation model, this result is not unexpected. When closed-ended questions are employed, respondents are fairly limited/restricted to their next reply (Folberg & Taylor, 1984; Moore, 1986). It may be that the mediators did not feel confident in their roles as mediators, and, rather than lose control of the mediation, they chose strategies designed to restrict the length and type of disputants' responses. Another potential explanation for twice as many closed questions may be that the roommate conflicts were not as intense (i.e., low affect), for example, as child custody disputes. Thus, mediators in the roommate disputes could ask for specific details instead of "easing into" the specifics of the dispute as mediators in the context of divorce mediation are advised (Folberg & Taylor, 1984). Also, results showed that no differences occurred between male and female mediators' use of question forms. In short, male and female mediators used the same proportion of open and closed question forms.

When looking at the distribution of question form by question function, the majority of open-ended questions functioned as seeking information from disputants whereas closed questions served as restatements or sought evaluations. These results make sense because mediators used open questions when exploring details about the dispute (e.g., "What is the problem?" "How did the dispute begin?"). By contrast, closed questions are used when summarizing participants' positions, clarifying a specific point, or asking for an evaluation (e.g., "Can you accept John's solution?").

The relationship between male versus female mediators' use of question functions and disputants' responses did reveal some gender differences. Disputants were less compliant/cooperative when female mediators asked informational and evaluative questions. Perhaps in attempting to control/manage the interaction, female mediators may have been perceived as pushing too hard toward an agreement, and disputants may have resented the coercive tactics by female mediators. Male mediators received more disagreement when their questions functioned as social controls (asked a series of three questions). Because the social control function occurred so infrequently, this finding is not really generalizable based on the small sample size.

Another important feature of the results that was supported centers on the notion that mediations unfold/progress according to phases (e.g., RQ 4). Mediators' question-asking behaviors began with informational questions (phase 1), then focused on restating, probing, and socially controlling questions (phase 2), and concluded with evaluative questions (phase 3). These results are not inconsistent with Jones (1988) who reports that "specific communication tactics discriminate between phases of interaction in agree and no-agreement divorce mediations" (p. 491). Jones points out that mediations reaching an agreement involve three phases: an agenda-building and information exchange phase, a presentation and evaluation of possible solutions phase, and a resolution phase. By contrast, no-agreement mediations emphasize the exchange of information and deemphasize problem-solving and resolution behaviors (Jones, 1988).

Similarly, most practitioners point out that mediators should first gather information about disputants and the conflict (Folberg & Taylor, 1984; Keltner, 1987; Moore, 1986; Royal & Schutt, 1976; Yeschke, 1987). If mediators are successful in acquiring information, then the number of informational questions should decrease over time. During the middle phase, mediators should be clarifying/restating disputants' positions, probing for additional information and controlling the interaction (Folberg & Taylor, 1984; Moore, 1986). This trend in mediators' questions occurred during phase 2. By contrast, mediators should focus disputants on evaluating/assessing various proposals/solutions in the final phase of mediation (Folberg & Taylor, 1984; Moore, 1986). If mediators are successful in their evaluative queries, then the number of evaluative questions should increase over time. To summarize, what is encouraging about these results is that they contribute to an increasing empirical base that supports practitioners' advice about which strategies/tactics work best in the beginning, middle, and final phases of mediation.

The fifth research question of this investigation centered on male versus female mediators' use of question functions across the phases of mediation. Contrary to the findings in RQ 3, results indicate no gender differences in mediators' use of question functions in the opening, middle, and closing phases of mediation. What this suggests is that over the course of a session, gender differences are minimized.

Finally, results showed that how a question functioned (information, restate, probe, social control, evaluate) had more impact on the type of disputant response (agree, neutral, disagree) than the question form (open versus closed). This finding seems logical because in an interaction, participants are focused on the question's purpose/intent rather than on the question's form. In other words, in the mediation context, disputants are concerned with providing information, responding to the appropriateness of proposals, reframing positions, and so on. Thus, the structure of the mediator's question seems inconsequential in relation to its function.

The research reported must be viewed in light of two important limitations. First, the use of simulated roommate conflicts may have limited the generalizability of the study in that disputants may not have been as committed to their positions as real world disputants. However, the conflict was pretested so that participants were not asked to generate conflicts beyond their experiential domain. Research in progress is comparing the discourse generated through simulated roommate conflicts versus conflicts generated by actual roommates. Clearly, relational histories are an important factor when tracking behavioral routines during conflict episodes. Second, mediator training was limited to four hours in this investigation. This does not generalize to the real world as most states require a minimum of 20 hours of training for community-based mediation (Keltner, 1987).

Finally, the research presented here poses some important questions for future research. An important question for practicing mediators centers on the issue of consistency. Is a mediator's pattern of question-asking similar from session to session? Do disputants respond differently to male and female mediators' question-asking strategies when age and culture are considered? Again, current research in mediation using actual mediation sessions has not addressed these questions. It is hoped that future research will address these two important questions.

III   Negotiation and Bargaining

INTRODUCTION

James B. Dworkin

Bargaining and negotiation are important social phenomena that enjoy widespread coverage in the social science literature. Studies of bargaining and negotiation as key features of the exchange relationship between human actors can be identified with as narrow a focus as family unit interactions and as broad a focus as dealings among countries in the international arena. Every person must negotiate (bargain) over a variety of different issues in many different situations. Indeed, the ability to understand and carry out negotiations may well be one of the more crucial skills of our time. Viewed in this context, the two chapters in this section provide useful information to all who seek to be intelligent users of the process of negotiations.

In their chapter, Dahl and Kienast investigate the effect of competitive versus cooperative bargaining environments on value creation in negotiations. Previous theoretical work in this area has led to differing predictions as to the impacts of integrative versus distributive strategies.

Some authors have claimed that only integrative (cooperative) strategies are geared at value creation or, alternatively stated, the maximization of the joint gain to the parties involved in the negotiations. An opposing viewpoint is that distributive or competitive strategies may also lead to the creation of value in negotiations as the parties seek solutions that may have been overlooked in the absence of a struggle.

Dahl and Kienast conducted a laboratory study to sort out this interplay between competitive situations and value creation. A total of 114 student subjects were randomly assigned to the competitive or cooperative condition. Cooperative/competitive conditions were created through the alteration of the payoff schedules available to the parties.

Two outcome measures were employed, the total joint payoff score for each dyad and the proximity of the dyad's solution to the Pareto Optimal curve. Analysis of variance results on both measures revealed significant effects for the payoff schedule on bargaining effectiveness. Groups with competitive payoff schedules achieved higher joint scores and negotiated solutions significantly closer to the Pareto Optimal curve than did the dyads facing a cooperative payoff schedule. Thus, these authors conclude that a moderate degree of competitiveness may be a necessary element in the creation of value in negotiation. This conclusion tends to be at odds with prevailing thought in the field.

In the second chapter in this section, Allen, Donohue, and Stewart summarize the results of previous laboratory experiments that have compared hardline and softline bargaining strategies in zero-sum situations. A hardline strategy is defined as one involving minimal concessions and extreme offers. According to aspiration theory, one's toughness in bargaining eventually reduces the opponent's aspiration level, which, in turn, causes maximum gain for the negotiator pursuing the hardline approach.

Softline bargaining strategy involves the making of concessions in the hopes of inducing concessions from the opponent. According to reciprocity theory, concessions will be seen as a sign of the desire to cooperate. It is hoped that the other negotiator will in turn offer concessions in the spirit of cooperation. As in the Dahl and Kienast chapter, these authors ask the question: which strategy, hardline or softline, is most effective in improving the final outcome of the situation for the negotiator? As noted above, a controversy exists in the literature as to which strategy is most effective.

The authors discuss four key features of the hardline strategy: initial extreme offers, concession frequency, size of concessions, and competitive orientation. Similarly, four crucial aspects of the softline strategy are giving substantive, frequent and meaningful concessions;

perceived reasons for concessions; development of mutual trust; and perceived costs.

The authors were able to identify 34 relevant experiments where hardline and softline bargaining strategies were compared. The results of their meta-analysis show that the average effect size was positive, which indicates that following a hardline strategy results in more favorable outcomes to the bargainer. Because these experiments were all zero-sum situations, a more favorable outcome for the negotiator following the hardline strategy implies, by definition, a less favorable outcome for the other negotiator in the dyad. This result tends to support the predictions of aspiration theory and not those of reciprocity theory. A major explanatory factor in viewing the failure of reciprocity theory is that the experimental studies analyzed did not permit the disputants to communicate directly with one another. It could very easily be argued that trust and problem-solving behavior is not likely to be engendered where negotiators exchange bids across closed rooms and never meet face-to-face with their actual opponent.

To summarize, both chapters in Part III are concerned with distributive versus integrative strategies in negotiations. Which types of strategies work best? Under what types of circumstances?

In the Dahl and Kienast chapter, payoff matrices are manipulated to provide both competitive and cooperative outcome possibilities. Their main finding is that competitive strategies lead to higher joint payoffs and to solutions closer to the Pareto Optimal curve. The Allen, Donohue, and Stewart meta-analysis chapter also is concerned with the effect of different strategies on bargained outcomes. These authors similarly conclude that distributive (hardline) strategies are more beneficial to the bargainer in terms of the final outcome.

Based on these two similar findings, should negotiators simply forget about integrative bargaining and henceforth adopt hardline approaches? The obvious answer is *no!* Although the following studies are certainly of interest, one must use caution in interpreting their results for a number of familiar reasons. These are both laboratory studies using naive negotiators in highly contrived situations. Further, the scenarios in most cases prevent any direct contact with the opposing negotiator. Hence, a crucial component of real world negotiating situations, face-to-face communication, is absent. Finally, the negotiators are limited to one issue. This is not atypical; however, in many negotiations multiple issues are on the table. In my opinion, future researchers ought to try to create experimental conditions wherein a fairer test of integrative tactics would be possible. I think that researchers should look to real world negotiating situations to test these sorts of competing hypotheses.

I think for now our safest conclusion from the following studies must be that hardline strategies appear to work best for the bargainer and (in variable-sum situations) for the bargaining dyad under these highly contrived laboratory situations. It is also very safe to conclude that much further research on the effects of integrative versus distributive bargaining tactics is needed before we can have definitive answers to the types of questions addressed by both of these studies. The authors of the following chapters are to be commended for taking a first step. Others interested in conflict resolution are encouraged to follow in their footsteps.

5 The Effect of Payoff Matrix Induced Competition on the Creation of Value in Negotiation

Joan G. Dahl and Philip K. Kienast

The 1980s has witnessed increased scholarly attention to the role of negotiations in managerial activity and organizational life. Mintzberg (1986) suggests that the role of negotiator comprises a key managerial behavior. Lax and Sebenius (1986) describe negotiations as comprising a core managerial activity. Others comment on the critical role played by negotiations in various organizational processes, such as resource allocation and budgeting, performance appraisal, and labor relations (Kochan & Bazerman, 1986; Bazerman & Lewicki, 1983). Given the suggested centrality of negotiations to the management of organizations, the question occurs whether a negotiating strategy or approach is superior to others in terms of producing desired organizational outcomes.

THEORETICAL UNDERPINNINGS

The negotiating literature is not unanimous in recommending one approach over another. The prevailing view is that a negotiating strategy variously termed "integrative" (Walton & McKersie, 1965; Lewicki & Litterer, 1985), "principled" (Fisher & Ury, 1981) and "win-win" enhances the creation of value or joint gain. Alternately stated, this viewpoint asserts that a "distributive," "power," and "win-lose" strategy frustrates creation of joint gain (Peterson, Tracy, & Cabelly, 1981).

Lax and Sebenius (1986) rightly point out that a negotiator both claims value, i.e., seeks his or her share of the gains available, as well as creates value, i.e., seeks to increase the gains available to both parties. In their view negotiators' attempts to claim value retard the creation of value. This view is consistent with that of Walton and McKersie's (1965) conceptualization of distributive tactics frustrating integrative bargaining. Fisher and Ury (1981) advocate that negotiators focus on facts and agree upon principle to overcome win-lose tendencies that impede the creation of wise and efficient agreements. Whether such an approach overcomes the tension between claiming and creating value is untested.

The minority viewpoint does not view competition as an impediment to the creation of value in negotiations. This viewpoint envisions competitive bargaining as facilitating the creation of value that would not occur through cooperative bargaining alone. Pruitt (1981) suggests that distributive bargaining often motivates parties to seek solutions that might be overlooked in the absence of a struggle to claim value. He maintains that vigorous advocacy of self-interest discloses the importance and/or motives of parties and leads to a search for integrative agreements that create more value to be divided.

Bacharach and Lawler (1981) state that integrative bargaining cannot be associated exclusively with problem-solving tactics (e.g., open sharing of information). They argue negotiators can reach optimal agreements without employing classic problem-solving techniques. Kimmel, Pruitt, Magerau, Konar-Goldband, and Carnevale (1980) have suggested that more information is learned about the other party's position in a negotiation through argumentation than through open sharing of information. Kienast and Drexler (1983) maintain that labor-management negotiators err when they separate negotiations over integrative issues like quality of work life from negotiations over distributive issues like wages. They argue this separation tends to diminish competitive behavior and, hence, incentives for finding optimal agreements on integrative issues also on the table while at the same time exacerbating the conflict inherent in competitive negotiations. Putnam and Wilson (1989) assert that the tactics used in competitive, distributive bargaining (i.e., tactics used in claiming value) can serve to communicate priorities, signal which items are important, and help to dislodge bargainers from holding a rigid stance. In sum, scholars of negotiation/bargaining disagree about whether negotiators' attempts to claim value necessarily inhibit or enhance the creation of value through negotiations. The question thus remains as to whether more value is created through a competitive negotiation or through a negotiaton that is basically cooperative.

METHOD

To test the effect of cooperation and competition on the creation of value in negotiations, two bargaining situations were created. In the cooperative condition, cooperation was induced by means of a payoff schedule in which several cooperative, win-win payoffs were available to the parties. In the competitive condition, competition was induced by altering the payoff schedules available to the parties so that no cooperative solution was possible.

The payoff matrices evolved over a series of pilot studies involving more than 200 subjects. These studies assisted us in refining the payoff matrices that made the present investigation possible. The following constraints were used in designing the payoff matrices described above. Each issue had five alternative solutions. Pilot testing showed an odd number of solutions discouraged simple tradeoffs. Five alternatives were found to provide an adequately complex bargaining situation (three alternatives made the situation too simple, more than five too complex).

The point distance between the values assigned to the alternatives was set so that all alternatives were feasible solutions to both parties (if the point values had too wide a spread, pilot testing showed the alternative was discarded by the subjects as not feasible).

The bargaining payoff matrices for both conditions are listed in Table 5.1. The various alternative settlements for each issue are indicated by letters. For each alternative settlement the point values assigned to party number one and party number two are listed. The dyad's bargaining score on each issue is equal to the sum of the point values given to each party for that issue. Each party had access only to its own part of the payoff matrix, i.e., either the point values for party number one or the point values for party number two.

Subjects

A total of 114 students participated in the study as part of a course requirement. Subjects were first randomly assigned to the competitive or

TABLE 5.1
Bargaining Payoff Schedules

Cooperative Condition Payoff Schedule	Competitive Condition Payoff Schedule

Dyad Score = Person 1's Score + Person 2's Score for each Settlement Point (SP)

Bargaining Issue 1

SP	#1/#2
A)	80 = 25/55
B)	90 = 55/35
C)	85 = 40/45
D)	75 = 10/65
E)	100 = 70/30

Bargaining Issue 2

SP	#1/#2
A)	85 = 45/40
B)	100 = 30/70
C)	75 = 65/10
D)	80 = 55/25
E)	90 = 35/55

Bargaining Issue 3

SP	#1/#2
A)	75 = 11/64
B)	80 = 24/56
C)	90 = 45/45
D)	100 = 60/40
E)	95 = 70/25

Bargaining Issue 1

SP	#1/#2
A)	80 = 25/55
B)	90 = 55/35
C)	85 = 40/45
D)	75 = 10/65
E)	100 = 70/30

Bargaining Issue 2

SP	#1/#2
A)	85 = 45/40
B)	100 = 30/70
C)	75 = 65/10
D)	80 = 55/25
E)	90 = 35/55

Bargaining Issue 3

SP	#1/#2
A)	-05 = 06/-11
B)	-10 = 12/-22
C)	-15 = 18/-33
D)	-20 = 24/-44
E)	-25 = 30/-55

Bargaining Issue 3
(Continued)

F)	-30 = 36/-66
G)	-35 = 42/-77
H)	-40 = 48/-88
I)	-45 = 54/-99
J)	-50 = 60/-110
K)	-55 = 66/-121
L)	-60 = 72/-132
M)	-65 = 78/-143
N)	-70 = 84/-154
O)	-75 = 90/-165
P)	-80 = 96/-176
Q)	-85 = 102/-187
R)	-90 = 108/-198
S)	-95 = 114/-209
T)	100 = 120/-220
U)	-105 = 126/-231
V)	-110 = 132/-242
W)	-115 = 128/-253
X)	-120 = 144/-254
Y)	-125 = 150/-275

the cooperative condition and then randomly assigned to a bargaining dyad either as "person 1" or "person 2" within the dyad.

Manipulation

Subjects were given a payoff schedule containing three issues to be negotiated. In the cooperative condition, cooperation was induced through the use of win-win payoffs for each issue in the payoff schedule. The three issues to be negotiated involved fringe benefits, working conditions, and compensation. These issues offered several opportunities for both members of the dyad to gain points in the negotiation, a win-win solution. In the competitive condition, competition was induced by altering the payoffs for the third issue on the payoff schedule so that gains to one party resulted in losses to the other, a win-lose solution. Because the payoffs for the first two issues on the payoff schedule remained constant across conditions, it was possible to derive for each dyad two measures of the value derived from the negotiation. One measure, total joint score, was derived by adding together the points earned by both members of a dyad for the first two issues and dividing by the total possible points available on the first two issues. The other measure, called the distance from the Pareto Optima, was ascertained by plotting each dyad's solution of the negotiation simulation and measuring that solution's distance from the Pareto Optimal curve for the negotiation. The Pareto Optimal curve describes the bargaining solutions in a negotiation from which no additional joint gain is possible. It is a visual representation of the optimal solutions to a negotiation. As one moves away from this curve, gains to one party result in losses to another party (Raiffa, 1982).

Procedure

After random assignment to a bargaining dyad, subjects were given a short case to read describing the payoff schedule to be negotiated. Subjects were given only the payoffs available to them for each item and were not allowed to see the payoffs available to the other member of the dyad. Subjects were given 40 minutes to complete the nego-tiation simulation. When agreement was reached, they indicated the terms of the agreement on a paper that was given to the experimenter. Then a short questionnaire was completed. The questionnaire gathered demographic data and data regarding information sharing during the negotiation.

To avoid a possible confound of biasing the subjects toward how they should negotiate, no instructions regarding bargaining theory or technique were given. In addition, subjects were given neither a competitive nor a cooperative motivational orientation, they were given the individualistic orientation to "do the best you can."

Analysis

The data were analyzed using two different measures. Total joint score was derived for each dyad. This score compared the number of points earned by the dyad with the total number of points available to the dyad. The closer this score was to 100%, the closer the dyad came to gaining all the possible points in the negotiation. The second measure of bargaining effectiveness dealt with the proximity of a dyad's solution to the Pareto Optimal curve. Proximity to the Pareto Optimal curve was determined by deriving a "distance from Pareto Optima" measure. This was accomplished by plotting the various possible solutions to the bargaining case given the subjects to derive the Pareto Optimal curve. Then the solutions reached by each dyad were plotted. The horizontal and vertical distance from the Pareto Optimal curve was determined for each solution. The horizontal and vertical distances were added together to derive an overall "distance from Pareto Optima" measure. The data from these two measures were then subjected to analysis of variance. Correlations were computed for the questionnaire data.

RESULTS

The analysis of variance on the first measure, total joint score, revealed a significant effect $F(.95,1,56) = 10.00$, $p < .05$, for payoff schedule structure on bargaining effectiveness. The group with the competitive payoff schedule earned more points and thus achieved a higher total joint score than did the group who dealt exclusively with a cooperative payoff schedule or matrix. The means were .91 and .86, respectively.

With regard to the second measure, distance from Pareto Optima, the results also indicate a significant difference between the groups, $F(.95,1,56) = 9.13$, $p < .05$. The dyads in the group with the competitive payoff schedule negotiated solutions that were significantly closer to the Pareto Optimal curve than the dyads in the cooperative group. Since the Pareto Optimal represents the curve from which no further joint gains are possible, this finding indicates that the dyads in the competitive group were more effective than the cooperative group in deriving all the joint gain possible from the bargaining situation.

The questionnaire data revealed some interesting results. "Information sharing" by person 1 in a bargaining dyad had a correlation of .54 significant at $p < .05$, with "information sharing" by person 2 in the dyad. Thus, the more a person in the dyad shared information, the more likely the other person was to reciprocate. The accuracy of information exchanged was not significantly higher in the cooperative group (Mean = 3.52) than in the competitive group (Mean = 3.50). Interestingly a low but significant correlation, (.28) $p < .05$, between the accuracy of person 1's sharing of information and the accuracy of person 2's sharing of information within the dyads across groups indicates that, as with information sharing, a norm of reciprocity developed: the more one member of the dyad was perceived as sharing accurate information, the more likely the other member of the dyad would reciprocate.

The data from postsession questionnaires revealed no significant differences within or between the groups in demographic variables. Factors such as age, sex, or educational level had no significant impact on the results of this study.

DISCUSSION

In contrast to the dominant theoretical view, the data refute the assertion that the more cooperative the bargaining environment, the more the creation of value is enhanced. This investigation found that subjects in less cooperative environments achieved a higher level of value creation. The study focused on the value created through bargaining, not the process of bargaining itself. Although bargaining outcomes in this study tend to refute the dominant theoretical paradigm regarding the role of cooperation and competition in bargaining, postsession questionnaires revealed some nonsignificant, but nonetheless interesting, trends that support dominant ideas in the literature regarding the process of bargaining.

As predicted by Walton and McKersie (1965), the cooperative group engaged in more information sharing than did the competitive group (with means of 3.4 and 2.8, respectively). Although both groups were told the information they were given was confidential, individuals in the cooperative group chose to share this information with each other more often than individuals in the competitive group. The accuracy of information exchanged in the cooperative group, however, was not significantly higher than in the competitive group. Thus, even though the cooperative group was more willing in general to share information, they did not necessarily share more accurate information. In contrast to what Walton and McKersie might have predicted, a norm of reciprocity regarding information sharing developed within the dyads across both the cooperative and the competitive conditions.

Contrary to findings by Peterson, Tracy, and Cabelly (1981) and assertions by Walton and McKersie (1965), no significant correlation was found between open, honest sharing of information and value maximization or success in bargaining. Apparently, it is possible to maximize joint value available in a negotiation without honest, open disclosure of one's needs.

The significant finding of this study is that the presence of a single win-lose issue, and the mild competitive behavior it induced, enhanced the creation of joint gain. We recognize the limitations of a single laboratory study done with students, yet this result is inconsistent with the majority viewpoint regarding the impact of competition on value creation. Accordingly, we attempt to explain our results within a theoretical framework that can serve as a model to other researchers interested in this phenomenon.

Organizational conflict scholars have used a curvilinear model to posit the relationship between conflict and effectiveness. All things being equal, this model predicts that either the absence of conflict or extreme conflict in organizations is associated with ineffective firms while a modicum of organizational conflict is related to effective firms (Thomas, 1976). The results of this study lead us to posit that a similar relationship may exist between competition between negotiators and the amount of value created as a result of their bargaining.

This study demonstrated that the introduction of a modest amount of competition in negotiations resulted in higher value creation than occurred in a cooperative condition with lower levels of competition. Thus, two elements of the model cited above are satisfied. The relationship of competition to value creation held for low and moderate levels of competition. The model will not be fully tested, however, without the addition of intense levels of competition to the experiment. Therefore the next critical experiment needed to test the model would be to see if a more intensely competitive condition would result in less value creation than the moderate competitive condition used in this study.

We realize the phenomenon under study here is more complex than our laboratory study was able to capture. We know competition results from other sources than issue structure, e.g., personality, previous interactions, and the like. Competition resulting from these sources may impact value creation differently. Only research will tell us whether moderate levels of competition, regardless of source, will conform to the model presented. There is reason to believe they might not. Conflict theory differentiates between constructive and destructive conflict (Deutsch, 1969). Future research may demonstrate a need to similarly differentiate between sources or kinds of competition and their impact on value creation in negotiations.

Finally, we believe the reason the majority of bargaining scholars have concluded that competition has a uniformly dampening effect on value creation arises because of their focus on negotiating situations dominated by win-lose issues and/or a history of intense competitive behavior by one or both parties. For instance, Walton and McKersie (1965) focused their research on labor-management relations in which the parties often had histories of intense competitive behavior. Had they focused on general business negotiations, they may have concluded that moderate competitive or "distributive bargaining" was associated with value creation, i.e., "integrative agreements."

In summation, our findings lend support to the notion that a degree of competition may be a necessary element in the creation of value in negotiations. The effect of varying levels of competition on value creation remains for future investigations. We believe that a moderate level of competition provides the impetus for the search for creative solutions in which the gains available in a negotiation can be maximized to the benefit of all parties involved.

6   Comparing Hardline and Softline Bargaining Strategies in Zero-Sum Situations Using Meta-Analysis

Mike Allen, William Donohue, and Becky Stewart

Most analyses of negotiation behavior make a distinction between distributive and integrative goals (see Putnam & Poole, 1987, for a review). Based on Walton and McKersie's (1965) classic text on bargaining, Putnam and Poole (1987) indicate that "distributive negotiations center on fixed-sum issues (such as wages, hours and distribution of limited resources) characterized by mutually exclusive positions and by inherent conflict of interest between the two sides. Integrative bargaining, in turn, focuses on variable-sum problems (such as rights and obligations) shaped by overlapping interests and flexible initial positions" (p. 566). However, Putnam and Poole note that in most naturalistic negotiations it is difficult to separate the two forms of bargaining. Negotiation often moves from a high conflict to a distributive stage narrowing the differences and finally to a position of supporting the other's position in the form of more integrative bargaining.

According to Putnam and Poole (1987), negotiators often succeed in marking this transition from distributive to integrative strategies in naturalistic negotiations through a variety of interaction processes. For example, individuals might begin exchanging honest information about their expected outcomes or their preferred options for resolving the dispute. Also, bargainers might refrain from attacking the other's position and concentrate on providing more arguments about how both can benefit from some particular option. Another process marking the transition might include increased concession making. One side could show a desire to cooperate by providing a concession as a good faith effort and commitment to bargaining.

Of these transition markers, perhaps concession making is the most often studied, particularly in experimental settings. Most research generally seeks to differentiate between two concession strategies that reflect a negotiator's distributive/integrative orientation. The distributive orientation mandates a hardline bargaining strategy that makes use of minimal concessions and extreme offers, while seeking to maximize the favorability of the outcome. Consistently pursuing this strategy blocks the transition to a more cooperative interaction style. In contrast, an integrative orientation emphasizes a softline bargaining approach that makes strategic use of concessions to promote trust and cooperation among disputants. This second approach stimulates more cooperative interaction by demonstrating sensitivity to the other's problems and needs leading to joint maximum outcomes.

Scholars reviewing the research comparing these two types of bargaining strategies find inconsistent results (Bartos, 1965; Benton, Kelley, & Liebling, 1972; Chertkoff & Conley, 1967). For example, Chertkoff and Esser's (1976) review of this experimental literature claims that the distributive, hardline approach generally yields more favorable outcomes for an individual. Other scholars (e.g., McGillicuddy, Pruitt, & Syna, 1984) contradict this claim by arguing that negotiations conducted in an atmosphere of mutual concession making and cooperation yield more favorable outcomes for an individual.

This chapter quantitatively summarizes and compares the experimental bargaining literature using meta-analysis to determine which of the two types of bargaining strategies (hardline or softline) maximizes the outcome for the bargainer in a zero-sum negotiation structure. Zero-sum structures are those in which a gain for one side means a loss by the other side. The intention of this chapter is to limit the focus to the extreme concession making strategies. Many bargaining studies compare the hardline and softline strategies to various other concession making options that fall somewhere in between these two extremes. For example, the McGillicuddy, Pruitt, and Syna (1984) study compared the effectiveness of a matching strategy (exactly duplicating the opponent's concessions) to both a soft (conceding over twice as often as the opponent) and a hard strategy (conceding infrequently and at only half the amount of the other). In such studies only data from the hard and soft strategies were analyzed. Including the intermediate concessioning strategy data in this study would have hopelessly increased the complexity of this study given that none of the researchers used a standard intermediate concessioning strategy across the various studies. Thus, we made the decision to first explore extreme concessioning conditions to determine how they perform before examining other kinds of concession strategies.

To compare the extreme hardline and softline bargaining strategies, this chapter begins by defining the features of both the hardline and softline bargaining strategies. Following this review, to help clarify the results of this study, is a description of the meta-analysis technique. The methods section, following this discussion, centers on the selection criteria of the studies. Finally, the results and discussion sections compare the two strategies and the implications of the results for both theory and practice.

SUPPORT FOR HARDLINE BARGAINING STRATEGIES

The definition of hardline bargaining strategy involves four elements: initially extreme offers, minimal numbers of concessions, minimal size of concessions, and placing competitive goals over collaborative goals. These four elements can exist in any combination. A bargainer can make an initial extreme offer and no concessions, few concessions, or many concessions of minimal magnitude. Many scholars (cf. Chertkoff & Conley, 1967; Donohue, 1981b; Pruitt, 1981) conclude that a hardline strategy using some combination of extreme offers with infrequent concessions generates the most favorable agreement. The bargainer is trying to minimize the total amount of loss entailed by the process of bargaining. Each of these four elements will be analyzed to show why it increases the favorability of the final settlement for the bargainer.

Initial Extreme Offers

The first hardline tactic makes any concession appear benevolent on the part of the bargainer. The initially extreme offer communicates the bargainer's wish to make an enormous profit from the negotiation. The advantage of an initially extreme offer is that a negotiation strategy of mutual and matching concessions (splitting the difference) means the bargainer with the most extreme initial offer will obtain the most favorable outcome (Pruitt, 1981). Introducing an initially extreme offer gives the opposition a comparison point from which to judge the final negotiated settlement. The opposition might contend after the negotiation that, "The negotiation was successful look at how much the bargainer conceded," when in fact these concessions were planned to be given at certain intervals to support an initially extreme offer.

Concession Frequency

The hardline bargaining position also argues against making concessions to put pressure on the opposition to break the deadlock. Siegel and Fouraker (1960) explain this pressure-inducing process through level of aspiration theory. They argue that the crucial determinate of bargaining outcome is the expectation or aspiration the bargainer brings to a negotiation. An aspiration is the expected or realistically desired outcome from the negotiation. They claim that a bargainer's toughness reduces the aspiration level of the opponent who eventually concedes to obtain an agreement. According to this theory, any sign of weakness by the bargainer results in raising the aspiration level of the opposition leading to increased demands. Conversely, offering no concessions demonstrates high aspirations on the part of the hardline bargainer and should lower the expectations of the opponent, literally wearing him or her down. The famous statement during the Cuban Missile Crisis about the United States and the Soviet Union standing eyeball-to-eyeball until the Soviets "blinked" summarizes this kind of philosophy. A negotiator should stick to the position and force the other side to back down (LaFeber, 1976).

This does not imply that a hardline bargainer should make no concessions. Offering no concessions often leads to a deadlock and decreasing concessions from the opposition (Benton, Kelley, & Liebling, 1972), which can become extremely counterproductive for the bargainer (Hamner, 1974). Rather, this hardline strategy advocates offering a minimal number of concessions and not reciprocating every one of the opponent's concessions with another concession. The hardline bargainer walks a fine line between appearing tough, although also fair, and being accused of not bargaining in good faith. Falling off the line can result in deadlock as the opponent refuses to offer any concessions from initial positions.

Theoretically, a hardline bargainer increases the appearance of sacrifice when making concessions, particularly if they are timed properly. Specifically, if the hardline bargainer concedes slightly just before the opponent reaches the point of terminating the discussion, then the bargainer can create the illusion of sacrificing for the good of the continued negotiation process. This timing process magnifies the concession's significance because what would normally be treated as a minimal concession appears much larger if the general perception exists that the hardline bargainer never makes concessions. Increasing the significance of the concession is particularly effective for the bargainer when the opponent forms the attribution that the bargainer is dedicated to the hardline position for moral or ideological reasons. Faced with this perception, the opponent knows that the bargainer will not suddenly begin offering more concessions if the opponent somehow delays the bargaining process. Rather, the opponent is faced with incurring the costs of a deadlock or offering more concessions.

Size of Concessions

The third element of hardline bargaining is the size of the concession(s) offered by the bargainer. The bargainer can still pursue a hardline approach by offering multiple concessions. However, these concessions must be very trivial. This tactic gives the appearance of flexibility and openness while conceding very little of substance. Labor-management hardline bargaining often employs this frequent, yet trivial, concession tactic by padding their substantive demands with a large number of trivial demands that they are willing to concede to show good faith in the bargaining process. Of course, one danger of pursuing this strategy for hardline bargainers is that they may be unable to stop making concessions once they start. The distinction between trivial and substantive concessions may be difficult to maintain over time.

Competitive Orientation

The last element of hardline bargaining involves treating the negotiation process as a competitive rather than a cooperative venture. For example, bargainers may need to choose between making a concession to obtain an agreement or holding out for that final reward that will yield slightly more than the opponent. In absolute terms, holding out for that final reward does not necessarily maximize the bargainer's outcome. However, holding out has the potential of maximizing outcome in relative terms compared with the opponent.

Experiments in the Prisoner's Dilemma (Minas, Scodel, Marlowe, & Rawson, 1960; Scodel, Minas, Ratoosh, & Lipetz, 1959) show that even when bargainers have an opportunity to maximize their own absolute outcomes, they eschew that choice if the result is an equal payoff for an opponent. Instead, bargainers choose to seek more than their opponents, but less than what the cooperative move involving a concession would provide. This indicates the possibility that hardline bargainers often make competitive choices that in one sense are not rational. The strategy fails to seek the maximum outcome for that bargainer; the bargainer seeks superiority over an opponent.

SUPPORT FOR SOFTLINE BARGAINING STRATEGIES

The softline bargaining position is defined as a bargaining strategy based on the use of concessions to induce more concessions from the opposition. The main goal of this strategy is to create a cooperative context that clears the way for more integrative bargaining, which functionally might include increased information sharing, jointly discussed goals, and an expanded range of settlement options. The cooperative goal is achieved by the softline strategy because the increased concessions are intended to demonstrate responsiveness to the opponent's needs (Kormorita & Esser, 1975).

The success of the softline strategy is based in four elements: the giving of frequent, substantive, and meaningful concessions; the opponent's perception of the reason for the concessions; the extent to which the concessions develop mutual trust; and the perception of the cost associated with the bargaining process. Each of these elements is discussed in detail to gain a better understanding of how this softline strategy works.

Giving Substantive, Frequent, and Meaningful Concessions

Why would a bargainer begin conceding more frequently than the opponent? Theoretically, the basis for this strategy is found in Osgood's

(1962) Gradual Reduction in Tension (GRIT) theory. This theory contends that giving concessions more frequently than the opponent gradually reduces tension by using concessions to show a commitment to the bargaining process. Osgood emphasizes the need to stop concessions at some point when the other party fails to reciprocate the commitment to bargaining. Deutsch (1949, 1958) first observed that the choice by one side to cooperate creates an obligation for the opponent to make more cooperative moves. Gouldner (1960) placed this theoretical notion into a sociological perspective by declaring that the concession making created a "norm of reciprocity." He claims this norm is invoked when persons share the same culture and expectations about how interactions ought to proceed. Benton, Kelley, and Liebling (1972) substantiate this position by pointing to research showing that concessions encourage more concessions. The bargainers begin the interaction with expectations both about their desired outcomes and how the bargaining process sought to proceed. Reciprocating concessions is one expectation about the process of negotiating and bargaining.

Perceived Reasons for Concessions

The extent to which the reciprocity norm is invoked in the bargaining context appears to depend upon the perceived reasons for the concessions. If the concession is perceived as a sign of cooperation then the norm of reciprocity is more likely to surface. However, if the opponent attributes the concession to the bargainer's failing strength in his or her position, the norm is not invoked, and the bargainer's concessions are not reciprocated. Deutsch (1958) points out that the unconditionally benevolent are simply taken advantage of. When the benevolent are not able to persuade the opponent the concessions are a sign of cooperation instead of weakness, the benevolent strategy fails. For example, Hitler attributed Chamberlain's decision at Munich to negotiate away Czechoslovakia as weakness rather than a desire to seek peaceful means of resolving conflict (Shirer, 1960).

From a social exchange perspective, the goal of the soft concession strategy is to invoke a norm of social justice where equal rewards should be given (Liebert, Smith, Hill, & Keiffer, 1968). The concession pattern is intended to be viewed as an effort to "split the difference." The split does not necessarily imply an equal split, only that both sides will be making concessions. This concession moves the bargaining forward toward a better solution, particularly in contrast to those bargaining contexts in which no concessions are made.

The Development of Mutual Trust

If the norms of reciprocity and social justice are invoked because of the bargainer's persuasive skills, the bargainer should be able to develop a long-term relationship built upon mutual trust and cooperation. This is important in any bargaining process involving outcomes with long-term expectations. For example, labor-management negotiations include termination dates for the contract. After the bargaining is over for one contract, the negotiators know that renegotiation will happen at a later date for the next contract.

This long-term expectation may be difficult, if not impossible, to establish in the typical experiment or bargaining situation that has no expectation of future interaction. Those experiments trying to establish cooperative, trusting relationships have attempted to do so by using the Prisoner's Dilemma game over multiple trials. However, even these attempts are probably not capable of creating the level of trust necessary to explore the effectiveness of a softline bargaining strategy. The typical Prisoner's Dilemma game has two people in separate rooms communicating only offers to each other. As a result, an inability to meet this criterion in a short-term experimental setting may bias the results against finding that softline strategies maximize outcomes.

Perceived Costs

Bargaining is often costly. Bargaining takes time and expends resources on the part of both bargainers. This cost means that the length of bargaining will automatically deduct from the potential profits of the bargainers. One net effect of these costs is that they may create pressure to make concessions as bargaining time lengthens (Deutsch & Krauss, 1960, 1962). Hardline bargainers often believe that giving in after holding out for so long admits defeat. In practical terms, making a concession to avoid deadlock after extended and costly bargaining recovers even less of the cost of bargaining. In contrast, the softline bargainer avoids this pitfall by quickly establishing a norm of reciprocity that, in turn, creates a context providing movement toward agreement.

The goal is to keep the costs of the concessions lower by making some of them earlier.

These four points suggest that the real goal in building a softline bargaining position is to change the opponent's views about the bargaining process. This bargainer must make clear, implicitly or explicitly, that the concessions are not a sign of weakness, altruism, or benevolence. Rather, concessions are based on an expectation that such reductions will be matched by the other side. This reciprocation can then serve as the foundation for building a trusting, long-term relationship with the other. Once trust develops, the process of bargaining can be viewed as a problem-solving activity, as opposed to a more distributive, zero-sum activity in which each side demonstrates only minimal concern for the other side's outcomes. In a very real sense the term "softline" is a misnomer. The softline bargainer is soft only regarding the ability to use concessions, not soft toward the final outcome. The softline bargaining strategist believes this strategy of concession making produces the most beneficial outcome because it fundamentally changes the nature of the bargaining relationship and the bargaining process.

META-ANALYSIS AS A METHOD FOR COMPARING STRATEGIES

The traditional way of synthesizing research focusing on a single topic involves giving each study one vote and lining up those studies supporting one position or the other. The "winner" then becomes the preferred position. However, several difficulties arise in using this "vote counting" method for comparing the results of experimental studies (Rosenthal, 1984). First, significance tests used in these studies are often influenced by Type II errors (Hunter, Schmidt, & Jackson, 1982; Allen, Hunter, & Donohue, 1989; Stiff, 1986; Dillard, Hunter, & Burgoon, 1984). For example, assume that every study observed the same effect size. Studies with large sample sizes would report significant results whereas studies with small sample sizes would report nonsignificant results. This produces a set of study results that appear inconsistent with each other when in fact they are perfectly consistent; the same effect was observed by every study. It is the vote counting method of significance test results that leads to a conclusion that the observed effects are inconsistent. A conclusion claiming inconsistent results could be incorrect because of Type II errors (false negatives).

The second problem with the vote counting procedure is that it ignores problems associated with the size of the effect. Studies with an average sample size of fewer than 100 subjects will have low power, and the observed effect size will vary from the population effect size. Sometimes, this random error variance will inflate the observed effect size, and sometimes it will deflate the size of the observed effect. This means that normal sampling error will produce what appears to be inconsistent results (Hedges & Olkin, 1985) rendering the vote counting method results misleading.

Meta-analysis assesses these problems in a systematic manner. Specifically, all the effect sizes are converted to a common metric. A common metric allows the effect sizes to be averaged (Glass, McGaw, & Smith, 1981). Then the variance around the effect size is estimated. If there is more variance in the observed scores than would be expected by random sampling error, there probably exists a moderator variable (Wolf, 1986). If possible, this moderator variable can be identified and included in future analyses. If the variability in the observed scores can be explained by normal sampling error then no moderator may exist. If the variability in observed effect sizes is the result of sampling error, the average effect size is the best estimate of the population effect size.

METHODS

Literature Review

A search was made of *Psychological Abstracts,* the *Social Sciences Citation Index, Dissertation Abstracts, Journal of Conflict Resolution,* and *Communication Abstracts* for articles relevant to this investigation. After the reports were obtained the reference section of each was examined and the relevant materials obtained. This process generated 29 manuscripts with 34 relevant experiments.

An investigation was included if it met the following conditions: the report had to be an experimental investigation providing enough statistical information for the calculation of an effect size (all studies had sufficient information); the report had to compare the effects of softline versus hardline bargaining on the basis of some final offer or amount of concession made by the bargainer; and the bargaining scenario or game had to be competitive such that every gain/loss was expected to be directly related to a direct gain/loss by the opponent.

Coding Categories and Procedures

Studies were each coded for three particular features: whether the study compared hardline and softline bargaining strategies, whether bargaining scenarios were used as the negotiation task, and whether some incentive was used to motivate the bargainer to reach a favorable agreement. Following is a brief discussion of each coding scheme and reliability information based on two coders using this scheme.

Type of Bargaining Strategy

This category judged whether the study compared hardline and softline strategies. Two coders experienced 94% agreement in making this judgment and then worked together to resolve disagreements over the remaining studies. Generally disagreements involved those experiments using the Prisoner's Dilemma game. The studies were coded as comparing hardline and softline strategies if the studies measured some type of final offer or net concession. This meant that studies examining multiple issues (Schurr & Ozanne, 1985; Clopton, 1984) or the sequence of the concession process (Wall, 1977; 1981) were excluded. Many of the Prisoner's Dilemma studies were excluded because the studies sought to measure the amount of cooperation rather than the final amount of gain by the bargainer.

Also, if a study used more than one kind of concessioning strategy, but also included softline and hardline concessioning strategies, then only the hardline and softline were included in the study. For example, the McGillicuddy, Pruitt, and Syna (1984) study used a hardline, softline, and a matching strategy that asked the confederate bargainer to exactly mirror the opponent's concession sizes. In this instance, only the hardline and softline data were used, and the data from the matching strategy were excluded from the analysis. Also, in those studies examining a range of concessioning strategies, the data were treated as linear. For example, if an experiment used a high, medium, or low concession strategy the type of bargaining strategy was interpreted as linear.

Subject of the Bargaining

Each study was coded for the actual content of the negotiation. For example, two commonly used bargaining scenarios included the pricing of a car and the Prisoner's Dilemma game. The coders agreed 100% of the time over the subject of the bargaining. The subject divided into two basic areas: Prisoner's Dilemma games and bargaining over some type of commercial purchase or service.

Type of Motivation for Bargaining

This category assessed whether an experiment offered the subject a reward based on both a successful agreement and the settlement level of contract or game in the scenario. It should be noted that the monetary rewards were typically small (i.e., under five dollars). The reward had to be based on performance, for example, studies offering a reward for participation but not performance were not considered as rewarding. The coders agreed 100% of the time about whether a reward was offered.

Statistical Analysis

The results of all studies were converted to the correlation coefficient. This measure of effect size was used for all the analyses. The correlations were weighted by sample size and then averaged. Each average correlation is assessed to determine if the variance in the observed sample correlations was larger than that expected by random sampling error. The Schmidt-Hunter method of variance-centered meta-analysis describes this statistical procedure (Bangert-Downs, 1987; Hunter, Schmidt, & Jackson, 1982).

This method was chosen because of its high power for detecting moderator variables (Spector & Levine, 1987). If significantly more variance exists in the sample of observed correlations than can be attributed to random sampling error, the particular effect sizes are heterogeneous. This means that the average correlation does not represent the average of a single sample of correlations, in which case a moderator variable probably exists. Two tests are recommended to assess homogeneity. First, 75% or more of the actual variance should be attributable to sampling error. Second, the sum of the squared error should be tested using a Chi-square test. A nonsignificant Chi-square indicates that the amount of variability is not significant.

RESULTS

Comparison of Strategies

Overall the average effect size was positive ($r = .20, N = 2559, K = 34$), indicating that a hardline strategy obtained a more favorable outcome. Table 6.1 contains a list of all the effect sizes associated with each study and how each study was coded. A positive correlation indicates support for the hardline bargaining position. The comparison of expected sampling error to actual sampling error shows that 75% of the actual variance in the correlations can be attributed to sampling error. According to Hunter, Schmidt, and Jackson (1982), this means that the observed effect sizes can be considered homogeneous. A formal significance test confirms that the amount of variation is probably the result of chance rather than the existence of some type of moderator variable (Chi-square = 45.8, $df = 33, p > .05$).

Type of Subject Bargained

Prisoner's Dilemma

Five studies used the Prisoner's Dilemma game. The average correlation for these studies was $r = .16$ ($N = 176, K = 5$). The expected amount of variation accounted for 100% of the observed variation in the correlations. This was an insignificant amount of variation, a finding confirmed by the formal significance test (Chi-square = 2.6, $df = 4, p > .05$).

Commercial Product and Service Contracts[1]

A total of 27 studies was included in this analysis. The average correlation for these studies was $r = .21$ ($N = 2208, K = 26$). The amount of variation accounted for 85% of the actual variation indicating homogeneity. This finding was confirmed (Chi-square = 27.6, $df = 24, p > .05$).

TABLE 6.1

Effect Sizes and Coding of Individual Studies

Study Author*	Study Date	Reward for Agreement	Subject of Bargaining**	r	N
Bateman	1980	No	Wages	.30	72
Benton	1972	Yes	Wages	.20	278
Bixenstine (1)	1963	No	PD	.14	48
Bixenstine (2)	1963	No	PD	.17	80
Chertkoff	1967	No	Car	.12	240
Cialdini	1979	No	Car	.47	21
Druckman	1972	Yes	Food	.30	106
Druckman	1976	Yes	Food	.12	52
Esser (1)	1975	Yes	Appliance	.20	52
Esser (2)	1975	Yes	Appliance	.10	75
Hamner	1974	Yes	Car	-.09	64
Hamner	1975	Yes	Products	.30	78
Harnett	1973	Yes	Commodity	.23	160
Hinton	1974	Yes	Information	-.06	24
Komorita	1965	Yes	PD	.27	80
Komorita (1)	1968	Yes	Commodity	.68	38
Komorita (2)	1968	No	Commodity	.22	36
Komorita	1969	Yes	Commodity	.11	80
Komorita (1)	1975	Yes	Appliance	.16	88
Komorita (2)	1975	Yes	Appliance	.16	119
Lawler	1980	Yes	Iron Ore	.23	120
Liebert	1968	No	Car	.26	40
McClintock	1963	No	PD	.09	32
McClintock	1965	No	PD	-.04	36
McGillicuddy	1984	Yes	Car	-.05	20
Pruitt	1961	Yes	Car	.14	80
Pruitt	1985	No	Car	.48	71
Seholm	1985	No	Car	.31	74
Siegel	1960	Yes	Car	.85	11
Smith	1982	Yes	Points	.05	48
Yukl (1)	1974a	Yes	Car	.10	60
Yukl (2)	1974a	Yes	Car	.29	36
Yukl (1)	1974b	Yes	Car	.33	60
Yukl (2)	1974b	Yes	Car	.22	80

*Author listed is first author only, complete citation given in References.
**PD stands for Prisoner's Dilemma.

Type of Motivation for Bargaining

No Reward for Outcome

Eleven studies offered no reward for a successful outcome. The average correlation was $r = .21$ ($N = 750$, $K = 11$). The expected variance was less than the actual variance observed in the correlations, and 87% of the actually observed variation can be explained by sampling error. The formal significance test also confirms that the variation can be attributed to sampling error (Chi-square = 12.8, $df = 10$, $p > .05$).

Studies Rewarding the Bargainer

A total of 21 studies offered the negotiator a reward for successful bargaining. The average correlation for these studies was $r = .20$ ($N = 1734$, $K = 21$). The expected amount of variation accounted for 100% of the observed variation in the correlations. This was considered an insignificant amount of variation (Chi-square = 19.1, $df = 20$, $p < .05$).

DISCUSSION

The results of this meta-analysis clearly support the hardline bargaining strategy as the most effective for maximizing individual payoff in those zero-sum contexts in which communication between disputants is not permitted. The review also found no differences based on the type of reward offered to the bargainer, perhaps because rewards were very small. Also, a few differences were observed between the commercial product and service contract scenarios and the Prisoner's Dilemma game scenarios.

Theoretically, these results support aspiration theory and do not support the outcomes predicted by reciprocity theory. Recall that aspiration theory argues that individuals will reduce their aspirations for big payoffs when faced with a tough bargainer and increase their aspirations when faced with a bargainer who concedes frequently. The net effect of taking the hardline position is that the bargainer succeeds in wearing down the opposition. In contrast, reciprocity theory holds that conceding frequently will encourage the other to reciprocate concessions thereby increasing the payoff of the bargainer who starts high and concedes first.

Perhaps the main reason subjects failed to create a reciprocity norm in bargaining had more to do with the communicative structure of the experimental studies than the validity of the theoretical explanations. Softline bargaining designed to induce a reciprocity norm needs open communication to persuade the other that the bargainer is conceding, not from lowered aspirations but from a desire for more cooperative interaction. However, in the majority of studies, disputants were forced to bargain from closed rooms, exchanging offers against a mythical opponent. Such bargaining ignores the interpersonal influence processes at work in real negotiation sessions. Part of negotiation is to solve the problems creating the need for negotiation (Putnam & Jones, 1982b; Putnam, Wilson, Waltman, & Turner, 1986; Daniels, 1967). Under these conditions reciprocity theory might become a better predictor of concession behavior. As bargainers get to know each other, trust can develop (Deutsch, 1958), which is most important when bargaining is complex or becomes more long-term. But, in zero-sum circumstances with very simple bargaining tasks, it appears that the default option for bargainers in zero-sum games is to assume that the concessions represent lowered aspirations.

The practical implication of this finding is critical for bargaining in naturalistic situations. Bargainers wishing to move from the typically distributive orientation at the beginning of the interaction to a more integrative perspective probably ought to spend a great deal of time prefacing their concessions with messages about cooperation. Failure to provide such messages before concessioning will result in the default assumption of lowered aspirations. In this case, the context is likely to sustain its distributive orientation, and the bargainer offering the concessions can expect severely decreased payoffs.

Given the extent to which the bargaining games included in this meta-analysis favor aspiration theory, there seems to be an obvious need to undertake another meta-analysis of those bargaining experiments examining the success or failure of different types of reason giving. When the confederate offers a variety of reasons for providing the concessions, is the other bargainer more or less willing to reciprocate these needs? In addition, would such reason giving mark a transition from a more distributive to a more integrative bargaining orientation? Clearly, more research should be directed toward this issue to provide stronger links between experimental and more naturalistic bargaining situations.

Accompanying this lack of emphasis on communication, the studies reviewed here examine bargaining as a structural phenomenon rather than a processual phenomenon. Most of the literature examines strategy, personality variables, and reward systems as structural inputs to the process that produces a given outcome. This emphasis ignores the changes that transpire during the bargaining process that serve to redefine these and other parameters of the situation (Reiches & Harral, 1974). Carnevale and Lawler (1987) suggest that these structural parameters (like time pressure) during an actual bargaining may increase concessions. If time pressures are equal on both sides, then a norm of reciprocal concessions may be established. This suggests a form of meta-communication whereby the negotiators can reflect and remark on the process of negotiation (Daniels, 1967). The result is bargainers that can say to each other, "This is going nowhere," or "Let's try something different." The examination of process is an examination of timing of concessions (when to make) independent of the content of the concession (how much) (Douglas, 1975; Druckman, Zechmeister, & Solomon, 1972). Communication may facilitate the norm of reciprocity by allowing individuals to coordinate their perceptions of their progress in the interaction. A meta-analysis of those experiments using communication in the Prisoner's Dilemma scenario would be desirable to examine the impact of communication on process development.

Finally, these studies only offered bargainers one issue with which to explore. This restriction precluded bargainers from developing multiple concessioning strategies across multiple issues. In many bargaining situations (e.g., labor-management or arms negotiations), bargainers can pursue a variety of possible concession routes that do not require the opponent to match that concession in the same manner. For example, a U.S. concession in an arms deal with the Soviets may be matched by a Soviet concession on emigration of Jews to Israel. Several studies had to be excluded from this analysis because they either dealt with multiple issues or multiple parties. More experimentation might be able to show that reciprocity theory provides a better explanatory framework in contexts offering multiple issues.

The constraints on the meta-analysis results obtained in this research should be placed into a proper perspective. The only study using actual bargainers had a correlation substantially larger than the average correlation obtained in this review (Siegel & Fouraker, 1960), but it had a sample size of only 11. It may be that with actual bargainers in a zero-sum, one-issue, simple-process negotiation, the effect size is larger, not smaller. What this meta-analysis indicates is that a bargainer would be better served in such circumstances (e.g., buying a car) by adopting a hardline bargaining strategy.

NOTE

1. In this analysis two studies were excluded (Siegel & Fouraker, 1960; Hamner, 1974). Siegel and Fouraker's study is the only one in this analysis to allow subjects to actually bargain with each other and not the experimenter. Hamner's study examined how deadlocks could be broken. As a result, the first few trial sessions intentionally created a deadlock. The result is two studies that have major methodological differences from the other studies. More effort in the future should be placed on the examination of both actual bargaining and the breaking of deadlocks. Hamner's study in particular suggests the existence of a deadlock that might be broken with a process increasing trust and making concessions (softline bargaining à la reciprocity theory).

IV
Mediation and Arbitration

INTRODUCTION

Gabriel F. Buntzman

The techniques of mediation and arbitration are probably more highly associated with labor-management conflicts than with the management of conflicts in other contexts (Buntzman, 1989). Nevertheless, mediation and arbitration are found to be important conflict management tools around the world for many kinds of disputes outside the labor relations arena. Mediation and arbitration often prove to be more timely, efficient, and effective than alternatives such as court adjudication (Brett & Goldberg, 1983; Wall & Schiller, 1983).

Scientific studies of arbitration and mediation should continue because both techniques may be expected to play increasingly important roles in conflict management. Given that dispute intervention is a "growth industry" (Rubin, 1983; Maggiolo, 1985), there should be no lack of demand for refinements and innovations to third-party interventions in the management of disputes of all kinds. The two chapters in this section on mediation and arbitration are both worthy additions to the rapidly growing body of research on third-party interventions.

Upon reflection, it should be no surprise to learn from reading the first chapter in this section, James A. Wall, Jr.'s "Mediation in the People's Republic of China," that the practice of mediation is strongly established in that country. Because the People's Republic of China is the most populous nation on earth, one can readily imagine the social and physical pressures with which its citizens must cope. Mediation is but one of many means employed through history to manage those pressures.

Throughout the history of China, great store was placed on harmonious living and respect for the existing social order. This is understandable, for the society could ill afford to expend its scarce resources on conflict instead of on meeting its physical needs for survival. Mediation offers the potential for a relative efficiency in conflict management as well as the opportunity to save face (Brown, 1977), which in turn contributes to the willingness of disputants to accept mediated agreements they might otherwise find unpalatable.

The reader may be startled to learn of some of the differences in style between Chinese mediators and their U.S. counterparts. For example, the mediator may not feel constrained to appear neutral, and parties tangential to the dispute may be brought in to assist the mediator in applying pressure to only one side to make concessions. Another example of differences in the approach of U.S. and Chinese mediators in personal disputes has to do with their reliance on caucusing. Although caucusing (meeting separately with the parties) is an effective conflict management technique in U.S. mediation (Pruitt, Fry, Castrianno, Zubek, Welton, McGillicuddy, & Ippolito, 1989), Wall notes that meeting separately with the parties was reported only rarely by his informants. No matter though. Who would not be satisfied with the 85% success rate claimed by the Chinese mediators?

Three final comments on Professor Wall's chapter seem in order. First, the mediators in his sample were solely from the city of Nanjing. What is typical of Nanjing with regard to mediation practices may not be typical of other parts of this large and varied country.

Second, there may be a dark side to the willingness of the people and government of the People's Republic of China to devote so much time and energy to mediation of disputes. That is, the society simply may have a low tolerance for open, protracted conflict. Professor Wall notes, for example, how assiduously mediators strive to have the parties resolve a problem. From Wall's description of the process, it would seem that Chinese mediators would prefer a mediated resolution procured under pressure to an unresolved conflict allowed to simmer for an unspecified time. Perhaps we should admire the system for this apparent virtue — Professor Wall quite rightly admonishes us to tolerate the differences between the Chinese mediation process and other (Western) ideas about what is appropriate behavior in the mediation process. Yet we cannot help thinking of the June 1989 incident in Tiananmen Square in which, according to reports, many hundreds of nonviolent demonstrators were killed by military troops on orders from the government of the People's Republic of China. We wonder if the systematic institutionalization of mediation in the People's Republic of China and the vigor with which mediated settlements are pursued are no more than symptoms of that society's unwillingness to tolerate open conflict?

Finally, we cannot leave this chapter without noting what a thoroughly engaging piece of writing it is. Professor Wall demonstrates that it is possible to draft a research report that at once is lucid, succinct, and professional as well as conversational in tone with occasional puckish humor. We think this is a combination more writers and editors should strive to attain.

"Consistency in Employee Rights: A Unique Experiment in Conflict Management" is an entirely different piece. In it, Professors Steve Bourne and Jerald Robinson report on the effects of the Arbitration Review Board (ARB) and the rule of precedent on the rate of grievances pursued all the way to arbitration. The chapter may well appeal to a broader audience than those interested only in industrial relations because both the principle of the Arbitration Review Board and the analytical techniques employed appear to have potential applications beyond the industrial relations arena.

The Arbitration Review Board and rule of precedent were designed to reduce the uncertainty regarding likely outcomes of arbitration, thus removing the incentive to arbitrate nonmeritorious grievances. Bourne and Robinson demonstrate an overall decrease in the rate of cases arbitrated per labor hour from 1977 through 1985 and attribute the decrease to the ARB.

As in most field studies and experiments, a number of uncontrolled factors might have accounted for the results reported by Professors Bourne and Robinson. Fortunately, there is other evidence to support their interpretations. Brett and Goldberg (1983) indicated that in a similar time frame mediator-adviser opinions on the likely outcomes of arbitration resulted in lower rates of arbitration in the coal industry. Bourne (1988) also provides additional evidence that the decrease in arbitration rates reported herein was attributable to the influence of the Arbitration Review Board.

The relevance of this article is readily apparent. As this introduction was being drafted, there was great instability in the bituminous coal industry. The Pittston Company and United Mine Workers were locked in a five-month-old strike that could "shape the industry's future" ("Pitted against Pittston," 1989). In an effort to reduce the turmoil in the industry, federal legislation was introduced in an attempt to enforce at least some conformity on certain industry practices. With or without the passage of such legislation, the Bituminous Coal Operators Association and the United Mine Workers may move to reestablish the Arbitration Review Board to restore stability to their industry once the dust has settled over their dispute. Thus we should not be surprised to see a future study titled, "Inconsistency in Collective Bargaining Instruments in the Bituminous Coal Industry: The Rise in Grievances and Arbitration Rates and the Resurrection of the Arbitration Review Board."

Finally, Bourne and Robinson are to be commended for taking their statistical analysis beyond the usual reporting of Chi-square values and significance levels. In discussing cell standardized residuals and their relative contributions to the Chi-square statistic, the authors employ a valuable technique with which a number of readers may not have been familiar.

7   Mediation in the People's Republic of China

James A. Wall, Jr.

Mediation has distinguished roots. In ancient Babylonia, public criers arranged marriages between a father's daughter and the highest paying suitor. Farther east, professional Chinese mediators — meirren — arranged betrothals between children, sometimes even before birth. The meirren along with neighbors also assisted neighbors with quarrels. Often these formal and informal mediators would tender their services because each disputant would lose face by first approaching the counterpart. By relying on the mediation service, both parties could be part to an agreement without suffering a loss of dignity (Latourette, 1942).

More recently, Voltaire mediated between Choiseul and Frederick to end the Seven Years War. And Prince Metternich in 1813 attempted to strike an accord between Napoleon and the allies opposing him. When his mediations failed, the prince joined the allies in their resumed war against France (Williams, 1901).

At high personal cost, Rudolf Hess attempted to mediate World War II. Kissinger was more successful in his mediations of the Yom Kippur War. In the 1970s, Britain's Lord Carrington mediated an important, but little-known, agreement between Rhodesian whites and blacks (Newhouse, 1983). About the same time Jimmy Carter facilitated the Camp David Accords, and this past year, U.N. mediators have gleaned peace in Afghanistan, the Persian Gulf, and Southwestern Africa.

Over the years, mediation has been continually employed because it has proved useful. And currently, we increasingly rely upon it to resolve disputes in the arenas of international (e.g., Touval, 1982; Young, 1972), industrial (e.g., Kochan & Jick, 1978; Kolb, 1983), marital (e.g., Haynes, 1981), and judicial (Wall & Rude, 1987) relations.

As we have utilized mediation, we in the West have come to regard it as a Western phenomenon, and, because we have studied mediation in Western settings, we know a considerable amount about Western mediation. However, we in the West know embarrassingly little about Eastern mediation. This is unfortunate because in one of these — China — mediation has been practiced and refined for hundreds, perhaps thousands, of years. To address this deficiency and set the groundwork for continual studies of this ancient art — or science? — we conducted this exploratory study of 25 practicing mediators in Nanjing, People's Republic of China.

Nanjing, a moderate-sized city by Chinese standards is located in the Jiangsu province — one of the nation's richest. Lying on the Yangtze River, approximately 200 miles upriver from Shanghai, the city holds a population of approximately 4 million; 5.5 million if the close suburbs are included.

Within the city, households in neighboring streets are grouped into "street committees" or precincts that are the urban version of the village communes. The number of streets, households, and residents per street committee varies quite widely, yet an educated guess puts the average number of streets at 3 and the number of residents at 500.

The committee is commanded by a "head" who has at least one female assistant responsible for family planning. In addition, the head oversees a phalanx of red-banded street guards — usually retired workers — who direct traffic, watch for shoplifters, yell at running children, park bicycles, and chat with everyone.

Two to five mediators also serve the residents of each committee. Typically they are middle-aged or older females, appointed by the committee head after a lengthy consultation with most of the committee residents. The mediators' responsibility is to resolve conflicts in their streets. To this end they are dedicated. The streets are their turf. And they brook no distractions from their goal.

THE STUDY

Nanjing was divided into five sectors, and from each sector, five street committees were chosen at random. In each of the 25 street committees, the head was contacted and asked for permission to interview a mediator who was willing to discuss her (or his) mediations. Having gained permission from the head and agreement from the mediator, a Chinese male conducted the interview.

Initially questions were asked about the age of the mediators, their number of years as a mediator, years of schooling, number of disputes handled each month, and the settlement rate in their disputes. Then one-half of the mediators were asked to recall the last intrafamily dispute they had mediated successfully. After describing this dispute and their actions to resolve it, the mediators were asked to recall and discuss the last intrafamily dispute they had been unsuccessful in mediating. The other half of the mediators were first asked to recall the last intrafamily dispute that they had not successfully mediated. Then they recalled and discussed their last successfully mediated case.

For each case the mediators were asked (in Chinese) to note the parties involved in the dispute and to describe the nature of the dispute. Then they were asked to note the specific measures they took to resolve the dispute and to recall the agreement hammered out. All responses were recorded by the interviewer in Chinese and were subsequently transcribed into English.

The Disputes

As noted above the mediators were told to recall intrafamily disputes; this category proved to hold a wide variety of disputes for the Chinese extended families. Table 7.1 provides a concise overview of the disputes and the disputants in the successful and unsuccessful mediations. Many disputes were between husbands and wives; yet, there was a sampling from brothers, sisters-in-law, aunts, grandmothers, and other relatives.

The disputes are quite varied. To the reader, some (such as the broken flower pots) may seem trivial. Others (as the death of a wife) are serious. Many are found within our own families, while some (for instance, the wife's burning of a mosquito net) are more Chinese-specific.

TABLE 7.1
Disputes Handled by 25 Chinese Mediators

Mediator		*Successful Mediation*	*Unsuccessful Mediation*
1	Parties in Dispute	Husband-Wife	Husband-Wife
	Nature of Dispute	Another woman	Husband too sexually demanding
2	Parties in Dispute	Husband-Wife	Husband-Wife
	Nature of Dispute	Mistrust, wife beating	No love
3	Parties in Dispute	Son-Daughter	Husband-Wife
	Nature of Dispute	Support of mother	Husband is dirty; wife leaves
4	Parties in Dispute	Two brothers	Husband-Wife
	Nature of Dispute	Inheritance	Separation by government
5	Parties in Dispute	Wife-Mother in law	Wife's parents-Husband's parents
	Nature of Dispute	Care of Mother in law	Death/murder of wife
6	Parties in Dispute	Sister-Sister in law	Grandson-Grandmother
	Nature of Dispute	Children; attack on sister	Support of grandmother
7	Parties in Dispute	Husband-Wife	Husband-Wife
	Nature of Dispute	Another woman	Another woman; wife beating
8	Parties in Dispute	Mother-Daughter in law	Husband-Wife
	Nature of Dispute	Money; attack on mother	Work in house
9	Parties in Dispute	Mother-Daughter in law	Husband-Wife
	Nature of Dispute	Abuse of mother	Wife treated as slave
10	Parties in Dispute	Husband-Wife	Mother-Daughter in law
	Nature of Dispute	Another man; wife beating	Living arrangement
11	Parties in Dispute	Husband-Wife	Father-Daughter
	Nature of Dispute	Husband's betting	Daughter's marriage
12	Parties in Dispute	Husband-Wife	Mother-Daughter
	Nature of Dispute	Child's education	Daughter's marriage

13	Parties in Dispute	Sister-Brother	Husband-Wife
	Nature of Dispute	Living arrangements	Another woman
14	Parties in Dispute	Father-Son	Father-Daughter in law
	Nature of Dispute	Father's betting	Care of father
15	Parties in Dispute	Father-Son	Mother-Daughter in law
	Nature of Dispute	Household expenses	Money from sale of house
16	Parties in Dispute	Husband-Wife	Mother-Daughter in law
	Nature of Dispute	Another woman	Quarrels
17	Parties in Dispute	Husband-Wife	Husband-Wife
	Nature of Dispute	Husband's gambling	Another man
18	Parties in Dispute	Husband-Wife	Husband-Wife
	Nature of Dispute	Husband beat wife; wife burned mosquito net	Another man
19	Parties in Dispute	Sister-Brother's wife	Husband-Wife
	Nature of Dispute	Quarrels, cursing	Wife's gambling
20	Parties in Dispute	Father-Daughter in law	Husband-Wife
	Nature of Dispute	Quarrel; bowl thrown at father	Sex life
21	Parties in Dispute	Three brothers	Husband-Wife
	Nature of Dispute	Inheritance	Lazy wife, beaten with stick
22	Parties in Dispute	Mother-Children	Father-Son
	Nature of Dispute	Mother's remarriage	Son's poor school performance; beatings
23	Parties in Dispute	Aunt-Sister in law	Husband-Wife
	Nature of Dispute	Money; different life styles	Wife childless and poorly treated
24	Parties in Dispute	Husband-Wife	Father-Daughter in law
	Nature of Dispute	Another woman	Location of citizenship
25	Parties in Dispute	Two sisters	Husband-Wife
	Nature of Dispute	Broken flower pot	Husband not allowing wife to eat

The Mediations: Overview

Fortunately, the mediations were not quite as varied as the disputes. Most of the mediators, because of cultural norms or their training by the army, approached the mediations in a similar fashion.

Because their culture stresses the importance of the group and its harmony, Chinese mediators feel that conflict resolution is the responsibility of the street committee. Because this responsibility has been delegated to them, the mediators view each conflict as a very personal responsibility. For the dispute not to be settled or to move into the court system entails a loss of face for them.

Street mediators also feel little, perhaps no, obligation to remain neutral in their dispute resolutions. Quite often they conclude who is right and who has erred. Subsequently they join forces with the chosen side and pound away at the offender.

When handling a dispute, the mediator follows a well-established protocol: learning of the dispute, the mediator — invited or not — enters the arena and gathers information from the disputants and other relevant parties. Once the information is gathered, the mediator initiates the resolution on an affective/emotional/feelings plane.

The next step entails considerable enhancing of the "other" party's image. That is, in discussions with one party, the mediator plays up the positive attributes of the other, regardless of how irrelevant these attributes are to the dispute. For example, the other is noted to be loving, patient, a good mother, old (a very positive trait), or well respected in community.

As the mediator enhances the other's image, she strokes the feelings of each party. "This is a minor problem," "Life is good," "You are loved by the community," and "You have a very good job," are typical comments.

Remaining on the affective plane, the mediator unleashes a campaign of persuasion, an affective persuasion, not a logical one. Herein the mediator applies tactics that are strange and unconvincing to the Western mind. The parties are told to consider the feelings of the other, to cherish harmony in their families, and not to undermine the respect of the neighbors or the reputation of the family. Most often the major premise is that the parties "should" care less for themselves and their feelings and more for those of others.

As can be noted in Table 7.1, logical discussions about individual rights and pronouncements as to who deserves what are brought into the mediations; yet, at least initially, they play a minor role. The major exception appears to be when a law is broken. In this case, the mediator quickly points out the illegal act (e.g., fighting with knives, beating a wife with a stick, committing adultery) and strongly takes the side of the victim.

At any point within the information gathering, image enhancement, stroking, persuading, and logical arguments, the mediator will bring in third parties. For the most part they — parents, factory leaders, party members, police — are used to persuade or "educate" one or both parties. However, they can be asked to express opinions, provide apartments, contribute money, evaluate one party, or express their personal shame.

As Table 7.2 reveals, the mediators on occasion educate or criticize the parties. Here again the mediator adopts a very biased stance, telling one (or both) parties that he or she is wrong. Wrong! Period! Here there is harassment, along with vehement, sometimes threatening, and most often public, criticism.

As the dispute winds toward agreement, the mediator again strokes the parties and sets the stage for implementation of the agreement. The important step is a "vocal" handshake. Most often one party apologizes. At times the apology is an admission of being wrong, but more often it comes across as "I'm sorry to have contributed to disharmony." The other party reciprocates, at the mediator's bequest, with a statement of forgiveness, tolerance of the other, or a weak apology. The capstones are smiles from all, tea for everyone, and occasionally a gift or two.

Mediation: Specific Techniques

The primary purpose of the study was to identify and categorize the techniques used by the mediators. Table 7.2 shows the techniques found, the groupings used, and the number of times each technique was employed. Because the limited number of observations precluded the use of factor analysis to group the techniques, we used the categories in an earlier study (Wall & Rude, 1985).

As their Western counterparts, Chinese mediators use a variety of procedural techniques. They also rely on a strong mix of paternalistic and logical techniques; less often do they turn to aggressive ones.

As the previous discussion and Table 7.2 reveal, Chinese mediators rely heavily on third parties. This approach differs strikingly from Western mediations. A thorough explanation of this difference must be

TABLE 7.2
Mediation Techniques Used by 25 Mediators

Techniques	Number of Times Used in Successful Mediation	Number of Times Used in Unsuccessful Mediation
Procedural		
Gather information; talking with sides	9	9
Talk to parties separately	1	1
Arrange side payments	1	0
Bring resources into the dispute	1	1
Abandon mediation	0	11
Paternalistic		
"Educate" one party as to how he/she "should" act	15	13
Ask one party to tolerate/forgive other	4	3
Stroking one party	4	5
Advise one party "how" to cooperate	13	7
Enhancement of other	4	4
Protect one party	1	1
Pleas for empathy toward other	9	4
Logical		
Quote point of law	5	5
Logical arguments for compromise (harrassment)	5	5
Note costs to one party of nonresolution	16	3
Argue one party's side to the other	15	15
Suggest settlement point	5	3
Point out benefits of resolution (to the parties)	3	0
Aggressive		
Have one party apologize, acknowledge faults	7	1
Criticize one party	4	5
Third-Party Oriented		
Have third party pressure/persuade/educate one party	15	14
Have third party introduce information	4	3
Ask third party to assist one side	2	0
Point out obligation to a third party	4	3

addressed in later reports. But here we can posit one, tentative, explanation: the Chinese are less inclined (than Westerners) to view people as individuals. Rather they perceive people as members of a group. Therefore the mediator, when encountering a dispute, views the dispute as a group problem (or process) and calls upon the group to mend itself. The group members — third parties — are quick to accept this responsibility and thereby reinforce this approach to dispute resolution.

The most interesting data in Table 7.2 is also explained by this line of thought. Note (second procedural technique) that the mediators only twice mention talking to the parties separately. In Western mediations, separate discussions with the parties are the standard operating procedure. This is not the case in China. Private discussions are not used because almost all social interactions are open to the group and, usually, the public. To exclude the group is to offend it. The group feels it has the right to listen in on conversations, especially if one of the parties is a group member.

Looking again at Table 7.2, it should be pointed out that this study tested no formal hypotheses as to which techniques would be found or as to the number of times each is employed. The findings do, however, shed some light on one important question: "What is the relationship between the number of techniques used by the mediator and the success of the mediation?"

In a recent study (Wall & Rude, 1988) we noted a correlation between the number of techniques used by mediators and the likelihood of a successful mediation. Would this be the case for Chinese mediators? I was unsure of the relationship. On one hand, I felt the more the Chinese mediators hammered away at the disputants, the more apt they would be to resolve the conflict.

On the other hand, I noted that Chinese mediators are dogged and seemingly tireless in pursuing resolution. If the dispute remains open, they continually circle back, using more techniques, expanding the agenda, repeating arguments, playing upon emotions and bringing in more third parties. This devoted persistence, in turn, yields more techniques in the unresolved mediations.

The data from Table 7.2, although tentative, support the first argument — more techniques lead to successful mediations. Specifically, the data shows that 147 techniques were used in the 25 successful mediations and 116 in the unsuccessful ones.

While this difference is not significant, it does seem to indicate that Chinese mediators do cut back on their mediations when they are proving unsuccessful. At some point they probably decide that further mediation efforts are futile and decide to abandon the mediation instead of pursuing it ineffectively.

DISCUSSION

The goals in this study were to examine the Chinese mediation process and to identify the techniques employed within it. Several differences between Chinese and Western mediations were also ferreted out:

Mediation — unlike in the West — is a common practice in China.
Chinese mediators are quite familiar with the disputants.
Seldom are the mediators neutral in their mediations. Rather they educate, criticize, and effectively woo disputants toward their own positions.
In China, mediation is not voluntary; there, as opposed to in the West, any known dispute is mediated.
Whereas Western mediators modify their approaches to fit the dispute, Chinese mediators have a rather standardized approach that they apply to disputes.
A unique feature of this approach is a strong reliance on third-party assistance.

No doubt much more is to be learned about Chinese mediation, and I hope subsequent studies will unearth additional techniques, improve our understanding of the process, and clarify the differences between the Chinese and Western styles of mediation. Such research is important because mediation is the primary method of conflict resolution in China, the world's most populous nation. Not only is it used extensively there; it seems to work. The mediators' responses in this study indicated about 85% of the disputes in China are resolved through mediation. The Chinese courts are not backlogged with litigation. And most of the Chinese interviewed are pleased with the process.

Maybe we can learn from this mediation. The Chinese approach of advancing concomitantly along the affective and logical planes perhaps would prove useful in Western mediations. That is, it seems that focusing the disputants' attention upon the feelings of the other, the emotional payoffs of harmony, and respect and empathy for the other in coordination with assessments of material benefits could prove beneficial in any mediation.

Yet our differences may preclude a fruitful assimilation of Chinese approaches. We write, talk, walk, dress, run, eat, drink, sleep, bathe, drive, ride, smile, point, sit, think, read, laugh, cry, play, entertain, parent, observe, and interact differently from the Chinese. Perhaps we should be content to mediate differently.

8 Consistency in Employee Rights: A Unique Experiment in Conflict Management

G. Steve Bourne and Jerald F. Robinson

> It is obvious that in arbitration, as in other fields, respect
> must be paid to accumulated wisdom and experience.
> — Arbitrator Carl A. Warns

Employee-employer relationships are sometimes viewed as a "web of rules," which may take considerable time to evolve. In a union-free setting, most of the employee rights are either provided under statutes or granted by the employer. Because most employers have traditionally viewed these rights as "residual," all those they do not willingly grant the employees, remain employer rights. Over time, these rights become more fuzzy and often become shared rights, especially among professional, technical, and general white-collar employees. The employer assumes greater responsibilities for the employees, especially when labor market conditions become tight.

Any firm-union relationship or industry-union relationship characterized by inconsistency in arbitration decisions, with little regard given to the precedential value of previous decisions, runs the risk of having an excessive amount of arbitration. The parties continually seek to gain contractual interpretations favorable to their own perspective, despite previous arbitration decisions on the issue in dispute. Thus the stability normally provided to the labor-management relationship by arbitration is greatly reduced in an environment of inconsistent arbitration decisions.

A novel approach to viewing the problem of inconsistency in arbitration decisions was addressed in 1974 in the collective bargaining negotiations in the bituminous coal industry [Bituminous Coal Operators Association (BCOA) and the United Mine Workers of America (UMWA)]. The negotiated product was the Arbitration Review Board (ARB). This board was intended to provide a consistency in contractual interpretation that had been lacking in the industry. The bituminous coal industry had often found itself negotiating about the same contractual clause and work situation but making diametrically opposite arbitration decisions. This occurred, in part, as a result of the high volume of arbitration cases in the industry, which provided the opportunity for a large number of diverse views to be expressed on a topic. Evidence of this high volume is that approximately 30% of the grievances filed under the 1974 National Agreement went to arbitration (Valtin, 1978). The high volume of arbitration decisions for an industry of this size is indicative of both the distrust between labor and management and the litigious nature of the parties. Also, the fact that arbitration decisions were not tradition-ally circulated in the industry in any systematic manner prevented arbitrators from easily accessing previous decisions that might be used as precedents in rendering their own decision (Selby, 1979).

This widespread lack of finality in the arbitration process placed both management and union representatives in a delicate position when confronted with a decision to pursue a grievance to arbitration. The representatives often felt forced to arbitration because there were numerous conflicting decisions on an issue, thus making any lower-level settlement seem suspect. This increased activity then provided additional conflicting decisions, thus creating a continuous cycle that fostered a lack of consistency in arbitration decisions (Benedict, 1981).

The BCOA and UMWA sought to break this cycle of inconsistency and frustration with the formation of the Arbitration Review Board. The ARB, established as an appellate board, possessed the power to review arbitrators' decisions upon the request of either party or upon its own initiative. This implementation of an internal review board was a radical alteration of the grievance procedure traditionally utilized by the coal industry. The basic steps of the grievance procedure had been relatively unchanged from the 1934 Appalachian Agreement to the 1972 National Agreement.

The ARB rendered 207 decisions during its seven year existence under two agreements. These decisions by the ARB were mandated by the collective bargaining agreement to be industry precedent-setting decisions from the date of the decision. The parties have voluntarily continued to incorporate these decisions into their subsequent agreements despite the termination of the board in 1981; BCOA-UMWA panel arbitrators are still contractually obligated to apply the precedents created by ARB decisions.

Despite the perceived importance of the ARB to the arbitration process in the coal industry, there has been little research conducted as to the impact of the ARB's decisions on coal industry arbitration. An exhaustive review of the literature related to the ARB indicates that limited qualitative research has been the rule, with no empirical investigation of the ARB having been undertaken. The speculative analysis that has been conducted previously has not provided the sound empirical evidence to justify various writers' conclusions about the board's effectiveness. The empirical analysis of arbitration decisions conducted in this research provides a more accurate analysis of the board's true impact on arbitrator decision making.

METHOD

Sample

Three hundred arbitration decisions from the coal industry were randomly selected for analysis. Sixty arbitration decisions from each of the following years, 1977, 1979, 1981, 1983, and 1985, were selected. Selection of these particular years was predicated upon the desire to assess arbitrator compliance with ARB precedents at various times throughout the ARB experience. Because the board did not become operational until February 1976, an assessment of arbitrator compliance in the early years of the board cannot begin until 1977. By selecting cases in alternate years from 1977 to 1985, an evaluation of arbitrator compliance over time becomes possible. Also, selection of these years provides an even distribution of time for which the board was in operation, as compared to the time following termination of the board. Since the board was terminated in 1981, the years selected represent two full years of board operation, the year of termination, and two years after termination of the board.

To select the sample of cases for each year, the Coal Arbitration Library System numbering system was utilized. With this system all arbitration decisions for a given year are grouped together and then are arranged by article of the contract. Based on the date of the decision, decisions are placed in chronological order within each article. The decision to select 60 cases for each of the years was based on the utilization of the Chi-square analysis of the frequency distribution for the cases. Because four adherence classifications were being used in analyzing arbitration decisions, the necessary average of 15 observations per cell required 60 cases per year (Graham, 1978).

Cases were selected from the files of Coal Labor, Inc., of Bluefield, West Virginia, an independent labor consulting firm representing various coal companies in grievance and arbitration proceedings; therefore, it augments the BCOA files with the arbitration decisions from non-BCOA signatory companies. By having this larger population from which to sample, inferences from the results of the analysis have greater applicability to the industry as a whole.

The content of selected decisions was analyzed on the basis of compliance with ARB precedent-setting decisions (Weber, 1985). Before this, considerable time was spent becoming familiar with the ARB precedents. This familiarization process was intended to reduce the possibility of classification bias occurring had the classification process commenced with no knowledge of the precedents.

Classification of Cases

Each arbitration decision was analyzed regarding its extent of adherence to precedential ARB decisions. Four classifications were developed to represent varying degrees of adherence to Arbitration Review Board precedents. A set of decision rules was utilized to assist in the content analysis of the arbitration decisions. The decision rules for each classification are presented below:

Classification 1: Strict Adherence to ARB Precedent

An Arbitration Review Board decision was *cited* as the basis for the arbitration decision.

The arbitrator rendered a decision in full compliance with the cited ARB precedent.

Classification 2: Adherence in Principle to ARB Precedent

There was *no citation* of an ARB decision, although there were one or
   more ARB decisions relevant to the issue being arbitrated.
Although there was no citation of an ARB precedent, the arbitrator clearly
   adhered to the principles established by the relevant ARB decision.

Classification 3: Violation in Principle of ARB Precedent

There was *no citation* of an ARB decision, although there were one or
   more ARB decisions relevant to the issue being arbitrated.
In addition to not citing relevant ARB decisions, the arbitrator *violated the
   principles* established by those decisions.

Classification 4: Open Nonadherence to ARB Precedent

The arbitrator *cited* relevant ARB decisions.
The arbitrator rendered a decision that was *contrary* to the ARB
   precedent.

This classification scheme attempted to span the range of possible
degrees of compliance. Assignment of cases into either of these
classifications required first a careful analysis of those ARB decisions
relevant to the case under analysis and then a determination of the
arbitrator's application of the principles from the relevant ARB decisions
to the instant case.

In an effort to assess the reliability of the classification process, a
subsample of the 300 decisions under analysis was selected for review by
a panel of four coal industry labor-relations experts. The subsample,
selected by using a stratified random sample, consisted of 30 decisions.
The strata were based on the overall distribution of cases by
classification, with the subsample reflecting the same percentage of each
classification as did the overall sample. Each panel member reviewed 15
of the decisions, thus yielding a total of 60 decisions from the reviewers
by which to assess the reliability of the investigators' classification
results.

The reviewers were given a copy of the decision rules utilized by the researchers in their analysis, but they had no knowledge of the classification to which each case had been assigned. The decision rules were discussed with each reviewer to make certain there were no misinterpretations of the rules for each classification. The evaluation of the reviewer for each arbitration decision was then compared to the evaluation of the researchers, thus providing an assessment of the reliability of the researchers' classification procedures.

One further set of data was examined to determine the ARB impact on the level of arbitration activity. It might be assumed that if the board were functioning in accordance with the parties' intent, the arbitration rate should decline over time. To evaluate this assumption, arbitration data were collected for each of the five years under analysis. Information on the total employee hours per year was used as a control measure to remove the influence of production levels on the arbitration rate. The arbitration data were then expressed in terms of the "Number of Arbitration Cases per 100 Million Employee Hours."

Analysis

The arbitration decisions for each of the five years under consideration were reviewed and placed in one of the four categories. The frequency distribution for the four categories was subjected to a Chi-square analysis to determine if a significant association existed between the variables (year and adherence classification). In addition, the standardized residual was computed for each cell to determine the contribution of each cell to the overall Chi-square value. The analysis of the standardized residuals allowed a more definite determination of the causes of the variance between the observed and expected values (Haberman, 1973).

RESULTS

There was a high degree of agreement between the classifications of the investigators and of the reviewers. The coal industry labor-relations experts agreed with the classification of the researchers in 93.3% of the cases. The overall consistency between the investigators and the experts in the classification of the arbitration decisions provided the basis for substantial confidence in the classification process. Because there were only four cases from the 30-case subsample in which one expert disagreed with the investigator, and no cases in which both experts disagreed with the classification of the investigator, the interrater reliability of the classification procedures was established. High interrater reliability is a standard for determining reliability for content analysis (Weber, 1985).

The frequency distribution resulting from the classification of the 300 arbitration decisions is summarized in Table 8.1. Of the 300 arbitration decisions analyzed and classified based on their adherence to Arbitration Review Board precedents, 147 (49%) were placed in Classification 1, 128 (42.7%) in Classification 2, 19 (6.3%) in Classification 3, and 6 (2%) in Classification 4. The frequency distribution of the data across four classifications, however, resulted in expected values of less than five for 50% of the cells of Table 8.1.

This presented a problem in analysis of the data because the generally accepted criterion is that the expected values of the cells under analysis should be at least five to ensure the accuracy of the Chi-square statistic. In order to address this problem, Classifications 3 and 4 were collapsed into one joint classification, named Classification 3–4. This technique is justifiable in this instance because both Classifications 3 and 4 address nonadherence by arbitrators to ARB decisions (Agresti, 1984). Thus all of those decisions contained in the combined Classification 3–4 are cases in which the arbitrator failed to adhere to the ARB precedents. The results of the Chi-square analysis are presented in Table 8.2.

TABLE 8.1

Observed Frequencies for Adherence Classifications

Year	1	Classification 2	3	4	Total
1977	20	32	5	3	60
1979	20	34	5	1	60
1981	34	20	5	1	60
1983	34	21	4	1	60
1985	39	21	0	0	60
Total	147	128	19	6	300

TABLE 8.2

Chi-square Test for Arbitration Adherence Analysis

Year	1	Classification 2	3-4	Total
1977	20 (29.4)	32 (25.6)	8 (5)	60
1979	20 (29.4)	34 (25.6)	6 (5)	60
1981	34 (29.4)	20 (25.6)	6 (5)	60
1983	34 (29.4)	21 (25.6)	5 (5)	60
1985	39 (29.4)	21 (25.6)	0 (5)	60
Total	147	128	25	300

Chi-Square = 25.02, $p < .01$
Expected values given in parentheses

Computation of the Chi-square statistic yielded a value of 25.02, which is significant at the .01 level. Given this indication of association between the variables, the standardized residuals for each cell in the contingency table were computed to determine those cells providing greatest contribution to the significant Chi-square. The standardized residuals are presented in Table 8.3.

Analysis of the standardized residuals in this situation yields an unusual result. Standardized residuals are normally considered significant at the .05 level when the absolute value of the residual exceeds 1.96 (Everitt, 1977). Utilizing this approach, only one of the cells in the contingency table appears to be significant in contribution to the Chi-square.

TABLE 8.3

Standardized Residuals for Chi-square Analysis of Frequency Distribution

Year	1	Classifications 2	3-4
1977	−1.7337	1.2649	1.3416
1979	−1.7337	1.6602	.4472
1981	.8484	−1.1068	.4472
1983	.8484	−.9092	.0000
1985	1.7706	−.9092	−2.2360

Chi-Square = 25.02

Further analysis of the residuals, however, indicates a contribution from several additional cells that approach but do not exceed this level. Thus the significance of the Chi-square in this situation is the combined result of cell variances across several cells, not the result of one or two cells.

Another benefit of calculating the residuals in this case is the evidence presented illustrating the trend in variances for each classification. The residuals from 1977 to 1985 for Classification 1 initially indicate a strong negative variance between the expected and observed values (1977 & 1979), then exhibit a moderate positive variance (1981 & 1983), and finally produce a strong positive variance. This illustrates an increasing trend toward strict adherence to ARB decisions by arbitrators.

However, an analysis of the residuals for combined Classification 3–4, those decisions showing nonadherence to ARB precedents, indicates the opposite trend. Initially a relatively strong positive variance between the expected and observed values (1977), the residuals first move toward a slight positive variance (1979 & 1981), then to zero variance (1983), culminating with a significant negative variance (1985). The trend of this data confirms the pattern found for Classification 1 because it indicates a movement away from nonadherence by arbitrators in the industry.

The data for Classification 2 presents a more enigmatic picture for interpretation. The residual for 1977 indicates a positive variance between the expected and observed values, with the residual for 1979 evidencing a further move in this direction. This indicates that arbitrators adhered to the principles of ARB decisions during this period, without utilizing the citation of such decisions. However, this trend was sharply reversed in 1981, with the negative variances stabilizing for 1983 and 1985. The negative variances for these years must be evaluated in light of the residuals for the two other classifications because the movement away from adherence in principle could be evaluated as a positive or negative development, depending on the direction of such movement. Given the analysis of the data for Classification 1 and Classification 3–4, this movement in Classification 2 indicates the overall trend was toward strict adherence rather than nonadherence to ARB decisions.

In the arbitration frequency data (Table 8.4), a remarkable decline (31.55%) is evidenced from 1979 to 1981, and, although not nearly as dramatic as the previous decline, 1981 exhibits the lowest level of arbitration activity for any of the years under analysis. The decline in arbitration activity sought by the implementation of the Arbitration Review Board appears to have been accomplished by 1981, ironically the year of the board's termination. The 22.3% increase in arbitration activity for 1983 as compared to 1981 illustrates a sharp reversal of the trend for previous years. This may be due to a "testing of the waters" by the parties to determine the extent arbitrators would voluntarily comply to ARB precedents in the absence of the threat of an ARB reversal. The data for 1985 illustrate a return to the arbitration levels of 1981, a decline of 18.1% from the 1983 level. This was a logical reaction to the dedication of arbitrators to the ARB precedents.

TABLE 8.4
Arbitration Activity for Bituminous Coal (1977–85)

Year	Number of Arbitration Decisions	Total Employee Hours (100 M)	Decision per 100 M Employee Hrs.	% Change
1977	1823	3.854	473.0	—
1979	1475	4.549	324.2	–31.5
1981	1317	4.163	316.3	–2.4
1983	1326	3.429	386.7	22.3
1985	1114	3.517	316.7	–18.1

Source: Coal Labor, Inc., Health and Safety Analysis Center of the Mine Safety and Health Administration, Denver, Colorado

DISCUSSION

The most significant finding of this study is that the ARB fulfilled its objective of providing consistency in the arbitration process of the coal industry by providing clear precedents for arbitrators to follow. Arbitrator adherence with ARB precedents has increased over time, even after 1981 when the ARB was terminated. This adherence appears to continue even today.

The gains in obtaining consistent arbitration decisions in the industry have not been lost as a result of the termination of the Arbitration Review Board. This may be construed as preference by arbitrators to follow the intentions within the industry. However, a decisive factor must be existence of a "relatively common" contract from 1974 to 1988. Throughout this period, the three relevant contracts before 1988 changed very little, especially in the provisions which tended to be the most frequent objects of arbitration hearings.

However, the 1988 National Agreement includes the addition of potentially controversial issues. This creates an environment in which arbitrators could provide once again inconsistent interpretations of the contractual language, thus increasing the potential for a renewal of the ARB.

Parties in other industries may wish to consider the implementation of an internal review process based on this research. The positive contribution made to the industry should not be overlooked. The arbitration community should find these results of particular value as an analysis of arbitral behavior when confronted with contractually binding precedents. The proper use of precedent decisions is a topic of continuing concern to arbitrators, and the extension of the precedent-setting principle to contractually binding decisions of the board creates an arbitral environment worthy of their scrutiny.

V   Conflict in the Public Sector

INTRODUCTION

Thomas J. Pavlak

It is a truism to say that conflict is inherent in public policy and administration. Politics is about conflict. A raison d'être of the political system is to raise and manage conflict over issues of public concern, i.e., through the "authoritative allocation of values" for society (Easton, 1971, p. 123). Indeed, the framers of our Constitution assured that conflict would be an enduring part of the political system by designing a government of separation of powers with a system of checks and balances. Intended to serve as a structural means to prevent any one faction from gaining too great a share of political power, it also has ensured that there will be opportunities for competing interests to influence the formulation and implementation of public policy.

Conflict in the public sector occurs in many forms and settings, ranging from dramatic electoral contests for high public office, great constitutional struggles over fundamental principles, and bitter clashes over controversial policy issues to the more mundane problems that occur in the daily life of the polity. In the conduct of the public's affairs, conflicts are inevitable between public agency officials and the clients they serve, between units within agencies and across governmental jurisdictions, and between public sector management and labor unions.

Despite the ubiquity of conflict in the public arena, until recently there has not been a systematic effort to study conflict management in the public sector. With the exception of the field of international relations, conflict management is not generally recognized as a subfield of political science, public policy, or public administration, the disciplines most closely concerned with public affairs. It may be that the very pervasiveness of conflict has made it appear unnecessary or even impossible to isolate it for separate and specialized inquiry. After all, it can be argued, the study of politics, policy, and administration is the study of conflict. Whatever the reason, and however odd it may appear to the outsider, conflict management has not received systematic attention as a focus of study in these fields.

This is not to suggest that problems of managing conflict are considered to be unimportant. The vast body of literature in political science, public policy, and public administration addressing conflict-related issues attests to its importance. It is true, however, that there has not been a systematic effort to define the domain of public sector conflict management as a field of inquiry, to identify and debate issues of theoretical and practical import, or to establish an agenda for research. Rather, these efforts tend to be subsumed in the ongoing work in each of the disciplines and their subfields.

The two chapters in this section represent encouraging signs of the growth of interest in the study of conflict management in the public sector. Although they reflect different approaches to theory development, they share several important attributes. Each is a creative, thought-provoking effort to apply lessons learned from the rapidly growing field of conflict management to theory development in public policy and administration. Each reflects a very pragmatic concern with the application of conflict management theory to practice. And each illustrates the rich benefits for theory development that can be derived from the study of conflict management methods, as our understanding of how disputes are effectively dealt with in various settings leads us to reexamine basic tenets of our disciplines.

The chapter by Stephenson and Pops represents an effort to identify those factors that influence the effectiveness of conflict management techniques in public policy development and implementation. They present an analytic framework that depicts the factors that determine the conflict management method appropriate for a given policy situation.

To Stephenson and Pops, four broad factors govern the choice of a conflict management method. These are "structural" variables, such as the number of interested policy stakeholders, the complexity of the issue, the intensity of preference of key stakeholders, and their financial and organizational resources; the stage of the policy process (i.e., policy formulation, development, implementation, or evaluation); the dominant decision mode (coalition, judication, or negotiation); and "tactical" variables, such as the disputants' level of trust, their willingness to share information, and their expected outcomes.

Stephenson and Pops argue that closer attention to these factors in the policy process by conflict resolution scholars and practitioners can lead to more efficient and effective use of conflict management technology.

In Chapter 10, Blackburn employs a "grounded theory" approach to the study of environmental disputes. Based on his review of environmental mediation literature, Blackburn identified 63 components of environmental mediation. He then framed these components into a set of propositions regarding the activities and conditions that favor successful mediation outcomes.

The 63 propositions were then evaluated by 30 environmental mediation practitioners. The mediators assessed each proposition's importance for successful mediation. Based on his analysis of the practitioners' ratings, Blackburn identified three dimensions of environmental mediation practice that are important for successful mediation outcomes. The three dimensions are a flexible approach to the process, accountability, and effective interpersonal relationships between the mediator and participants. These dimensions are examined in some detail, with Blackburn exploring their implications for environmental mediation theory and practice.

The two chapters presented in this section illustrate the breadth of concern and diversity of approaches of scholars who share a common concern for more effective conflict management in the public sector. They are unique contributions to a budding literature. As this literature grows and matures, it also will contribute to theory development in its parent disciplines of political science, public policy, and public administration.

9

Managing Conflict in the Policy Process

Max O. Stephenson, Jr. and Gerald M. Pops

The task of managing conflict in a public organization differs from that same challenge in a private sector organization. Conflict management has two dimensions in the public sector that correspond to two distinct, identifiable levels of operation: organizational and political.

The first, or organizational dimension, is similar in both the public and private milieus. Managers attempt to channel and resolve disputes between employees, between employees and supervisors, and between contending organizational units over power, status, and resources. Approximately 50% of public sector employees are organized nationwide under laws, which, while greatly divergent, have all been modeled after the National Labor Relations Act of 1935 that set the pattern for management-labor relations for private industry.

Nonetheless, there are important differences. First, Freedom of Information Laws, Sunshine Acts, and other legislation require public organization managers to be more open with information. Antidiscrimination policies, although they apply in both sectors, are especially strongly supported by political interest groups and public service ideals and democratic norms. Further, the courts have interpreted both federal and state constitutions to assure protections to public employee rights (particularly free speech and procedural due process) not possessed by their private sector counterparts. Rosenbloom (1983) has supplied a comprehensive list.

The political dimension, however, separates the public sector manager dramatically from the private sector manager. The public sector manager, at all levels of the organization but particularly at its higher levels, is a participant in the political process. To be sure, many early public administration scholars sought to analyze administration and politics (or policy making) as separate activities (Goodnow, 1900; Wilson, 1987), but these efforts have been widely discredited (Waldo, 1948). The relationship between politics and administration, rather than a dichotomy, may most appropriately be described as a continuum. At the upper reaches of management, the relationship between politics/policy making and management is strong and even indistinguishable, but at lower levels, the relationship weakens until, at the operational, technical level of the organization, it is very weak but still present.

This chapter will seek to describe how conflict is managed in the public policy process. We develop a model that may serve as a guide to scholars and practitioners to become more discriminating in their application of evolving conflict management tools and techniques by paying more systematic attention to variables that appear to structure and to condition the utility of those efforts in the intensely political sphere of government activity.

CONFLICT AND THE POLICY PROCESS

The central feature of the model outlined here is the policy process. Having no real counterpart in the private sector, it is essential to our analysis that that process be carefully described and explained.

Political conflict is managed through the policy process. Policy making is the essence of what government does; it is the process by which who gets what, when, and how is decided (Lasswell, 1958). Public policy, the product of politics, inevitably addresses Lasswell's famous concerns. Therefore, to study policy making is to study the most significant aspects of what a government actually does and how it does it. The policy process is the means by which the government authoritatively allocates values and resources on behalf of the citizenry it serves (Easton, 1965, p. 21). In a heterogeneous, representative republic like our own, the process will serve as the harbinger, the vehicle, and principal symbol of the aspirations and demands of the populace. Small wonder, then, that policy development and implementation so frequently serve as the battleground for debate and resolution of a wide range of challenges confronting society. Should the nation embrace tax system reform? Launch a new type of warship? Develop programs to assist the homeless? These and like questions suggest the enormous significance of the policy process as both mirror for conflict within our society and as principal vehicle for its effective resolution.

Precisely because government acts via policy, regime actions of even modest magnitude imply a range of consequences across a number of dimensions. Perhaps most obvious is the fact that any course the government adopts involves (typically implicitly) a value framework. For example, when the nation's legislature and chief executive jointly settle upon a course of increased defense (or social spending) that choice implies not only a concern that one or another broad aim be targeted but also that some other goal receive proportionately less emphasis. The government's priorities reflect, in a fundamental way, the most deeply held values of its elected leadership and, thereby indirectly, its citizenry. Although our example here is a national one, this argument applies with equal force to the state and local levels of government.

As a result, nearly any action by a representative government touches the interests and values of subpopulations within society. In practice, regime action both shapes and reflects widely held sentiments and values. Individual groups may press their claims upon government even as the regime develops its own perception of the legitimacy of those demands and moves to accept, modify, deny, or ignore them (Truman, 1951). Public policy results from the interaction of parties who often possess widely divergent perspectives. The interorganizational implementation literature has amply demonstrated that this intense and often stylized political process of negotiation and consideration yields social phenomena worthy of study, regardless of the outcomes (O'Toole, 1986; Kettl, 1988). Certainly, it will exhibit great potential for conflict and confrontation. Table 9.1 illustrates some of the latent sources for conflict in policy decision making.

The differences in values, interests, resources, and methodology detailed in Table 9.1 suggest the wide variety of influences that can separate both officials within the policy process and those outside the process who wish to shape its outcomes. Significantly, many of these variables or factors will exist regardless of the specific issue or policy under consideration. Table 9.1 suggests that long-standing policy consensus will likely be difficult to achieve in the dynamic of the U.S. pluralistic context. Instead, consensus and cooperation are likely to be attained for delimited periods on specifically defined issues among particular process participants. The model described here should help to define the context in which policies are likely to be considered and the mechanisms by which conflicts concerning them are apt to be addressed.

Even a glance at Table 9.1 also suggests that policy actions may carry with them a wide range of consequences. Certain parties may profit while others will undoubtedly lose, for example, when government sponsors pollution clean-up and control efforts. Indeed, more broadly, it might be argued that the mere existence of tax-supported institutions in an economy dominated by the private sector implies an opportunity cost to players in the nonpublic sector as resources (capital) are diverted to purposes over whose selection they exercise little or no control. The perceived implications of public policy decisions will surely bring sustained debate and conflict.

We assume that policy is the result of all governmental action concerning a specific problem and is most readily understood in terms of process (Eulau and Prewitt, 1973, p. 465; Jones, 1984, p. 26). To study the dynamic by which decision makers came to adopt a course of action (or inaction) is to reveal the sum of why government acted as it did. Moreover, it is into this developing policy chain that conflict management efforts are interjected. It is, therefore, crucial to understand who the players are and how they relate to one another in the process.

The basic elements of the policy process may be stated in terms of their relationship to what government does to act on problems. There are basically four stages of action in public policy making: policy formulation, program development, program implementation, and program evaluation. The transition between stages may prove neither smooth nor sequential. In fact, the process is quite fluid and dynamic. Nevertheless, phases of the process are identifiable even if not always linearly related (Greenberg, Miller, Mohr, & Valdek, 1977, p. 1532). Each stage of the policy process evidences characteristics closely linked to the set of functions that set of activities serves (Jones, 1984, pp. 27–30). These stages must be carefully observed by those who are involved in managing conflict in the policy process because each demands different behavior of those engaged in it.

The policy formulation phase of the policy process is concerned with those activities that bring a problem to government for action. Some individual, group, or groups, either within or outside government, must perceive that a problem exists, conclude that it requires public action,

TABLE 9.1
Some Salient Value, Interest, Resource, and Methodological Differences Fueling Conflict in the Policy Process

VALUES

Belief in the efficacy of government decision-making	vs.	Belief in the superiority of leaving decision-making in the private and corporate sectors
Belief in the superiority of centralized control of government programs	vs.	Belief in the superiority of local control of government programs
Importance of client, citizen	vs.	Importance of agency or "public interest"
Faith in voluntary, self-compliance to gain public support	vs.	Belief in active government policing to ensure program compliance

INTERESTS

General Role Orientation:
Line agency administrator vs. Overseeing Agency Administrator (e.g. EEOC, OPM) vs. Special Interest Spokesperson vs. Professional Association Spokesperson vs. Government Generalist (e.g. legislator, representative of chief executive)

Specific Role Orientation:
Chief Executive Officer (of agency, organization; elected official) vs. Designated Agency Official (lacking authority to bind CEO) vs. Hired Advocate vs. Unpaid Volunteer

RESOURCES

Holds large share of the budget   vs. Holds small share of the budget

Has a growing share of the budget   vs. Has a declining share of the budget

Claims large number of votes and/or political influence   vs. Claims small number of votes and/or political influence

Strong organization (assets, size, geographic distribution)   vs. Weak organization (assets, size, geographic distribution)

Possession of knowledge and information   vs. Lack of knowledge and information

METHODS OF ANALYSIS

Training and education in different professional disciplines and in different environments of human activity lead to difference in defining:

- How problems are identified and how programs are formulated, implemented, and evaluated
- What data are determined to be relevant in analysis
- How much data are needed to trigger decision-making
- How much uncertainty can be tolerated
- What method to use to link cause to effect when attempting to predict consequences of alternative courses of action

develop the wherewithal to press that perspective and successfully obtain a place on the decision-making agendas of otherwise busy and preoccupied officials. This process is neither neat nor necessarily sustained. Issues may languish unnoticed only to receive unexpectedly feverish attention in changed political circumstances (Cobb & Elder, 1983).

What most concerns us here is the function itself and not each of the activities underpinning it. There are nearly limitless patterns of legitimation, representation, and agenda setting. Study of these is no doubt important, but we need only note that this stage of the policy process is broadly concerned with getting government to acknowledge and devote attention to an issue. Such attention need not be closely defined. Indeed, participant definitions of precisely what is at issue may vary over time. Vagueness of problem specification also may often be considered a political virtue by policy process participants.

The program development phase of policy making concerns action within government on an articulated issue. In this stage, proposals designed to address identified problems are framed and supportive constituencies amassed. Typically, this phase results in identifiable programmatic action and, as such, claimants' agendas are wholly or partially legitimated by regime action of some type. Perhaps the surest measure of definitive governmental acceptance of a specific problem is the devotion of resources toward its resolution. Budgets fuel programs by which services are delivered. They are the lifeblood of the public enterprise and an important indicator that a policy concern has attained legitimacy.

The program implementation phase of the policy process finds government officials seeking actually to accomplish the goals set during earlier stages. Specific agencies are now charged with responsibility for delivering a service of some kind. Unfortunately, that product is often not well defined. Many previously unresolved conflicts are often carried into this stage requiring whole new rounds of bargaining and negotiation between officials charged with a program's implementation and those most deeply interested in its fate. Implementation will necessarily prove a complex and potentially conflict-filled process of choice and change.

Finally, the policy evaluation stage finds government assessing the relative merits of its programs and processes. This function may occur more or less formally and may be conducted either within or outside the confines of a particular public program or agency or in (or for) Congress (or state or local legislative bodies). Because evaluation commonly requires an increased degree of goal specification, it is often a conflict-ridden activity. Government, or those interested in its efforts, embrace evaluation for a wide variety of reasons, which may be unrelated to the merits of specific activities. Program evaluation, as Jones' work has suggested, can as often serve to obscure as to illuminate and to justify as to examine (Jones, 1984, pp. 196–232).

The managers of public organizations are active players throughout each phase of the policy process. Their involvement is likely to be relatively limited in the first, policy formulation stage, in proportion to the greater involvement of political interest groups and elected officials. As the need for technical knowledge and expertise increases apace during the program development and program implementation stages, however, managers become more central in the interactions between parties and can be expected to play an enlarged role in managing the conflict that is likely to arise and persist among them. When the evaluation stage is reached, managerial involvement will likely decline somewhat. The original players in the policy's formulation may reenter the decision arena because evaluation is inextricably linked to the policy termination, modification, or renewal. Nevertheless, managers can be expected to become active in the decision process in order to defend the manner in which their programs were operated. That stance, however, finds them in a notably different mode of behavior vis-à-vis conflicting parties than when they are actively involved in detailed program management efforts.

AN OVERVIEW OF THE MODEL

The model depicts a set of structural variables, process variables, decision modes, tactical variables, and conflict management methods, and it points up the relationships among them. Figure 9.1 sketches our conception of the relationships between these elements. They are dynamic and likely to evolve over time within loose interorganizational structures (Heclo, 1978). The question of prime interest depicted in Figure 9.1 is, "How does a distinct cluster of variables operate within the policy process to cause players to select a particular decision mode and method to approach or resolve conflict?" We are especially interested in suggesting the analytic utility of disaggregating the policy process into its component stages and attempting to discern which decision modes and conflict resolution methods are most likely to be employed by participants as various functions and activities occur within the process.

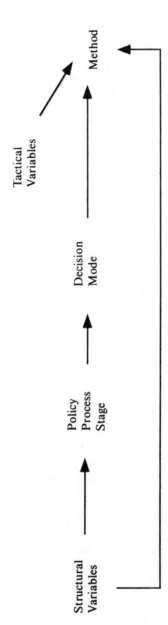

FIGURE 9.1 — Model for Managing Conflict in the Policy Process

Structural variables condition the social, political, and economic environment in which policy process participants will play their roles. They share the feature, which distinguishes them from tactical variables, that they are not controlled by the parties attempting to manage political conflict. Together with the policy process stage, they comprise the "givens" for the policy maker.

Although additional structural variables undoubtedly constrain or affect policy makers, those treated here include the number of parties interested in the policy (including policy problem or program) and the intensity of their interest, the relative complexity of the policy at issue, the resources (both organizational and financial) possessed by participating parties, the existence or absence of legal mandates concerning the type of decision process to be used, and the general salience of the policy problem.

The interaction of these structural variables, set in the conditions of a particular phase of the policy process, determines the decision mode participants are apt to use in addressing their conflict. Different stages of the policy process are likely to demand different types of activities that will be closely linked to general types of decision making.

Four types of decision modes are generally recognized and so employed here: coalition, rational planning, judication, and negotiation. Each decision mode is typically associated with a discrete set of conflict management methods (see Table 9.2).

Finally, a set of tactical variables will produce the particular conflict management method or methods that ultimately will be employed. Tactical variables are factors over which the parties possess control or which each may influence significantly. They include level of trust among the disputants, the willingness of participants to utilize third-party neutrals with skills in promoting agreement, participant-generated assessments of whether the issues in contention are integrative or competitive in nature, and the relative willingness of each player to share information with other players. This list should not be considered exhaustive. Other important tactical variables may not be identified here.

DECISION MODES

Dahl (1955) and Zartman (1978) have both argued that there are three distinct modes of social decision making although each employs different

TABLE 9.2
Decision Modes and Associated Decision Methods

Mode	Methods
Coalition	Political convention
	Voting
	Legislative process
	Informal rulemaking
Judication	Judicial trial
	Administrative adjudication
	Binding arbitration
	Advisory arbitration
	Formal rulemaking
Rational planning	Strategic planning
	Delphi technique
	Informal problem-solving
Negotiation	Position-based bargaining
	Interest-based bargaining
	Unassisted bargaining
	Assisted bargaining (mediation and facilitation)
	Mediated arbitration

labels to describe them. Dahl labeled the modes coalition, hierarchy, and bargaining. Zartman, drawing heavily upon Dahl's formulation, uses the terms coalition, judication, and negotiation. We have adopted Zartman's nomenclature and to it have added an often described fourth decision mode: rational planning (Dror, 1986).

Coalition is the social process of making collective choices by numerical aggregation (Zartman, 1978, p. 69). The decision results from a series of dealings in which participants aggregate their numerical strength in order to achieve the legally required standard (a majority, an extraordinary majority, or a defined plurality). All parties exercise influence only in relation to the process of choice itself. Thus, one party's ability to influence another player "counts" only insofar as the second party lends its support to the first participant. Any party can make the decision alone, provided it becomes powerful enough, in a numerical sense, to do so. Coalition decisions are normally of prospective effect; that is, they relate to events in the future.

Judication is a process in which each party offers facts and arguments to a judge or executive in an effort to persuade that arbiter to render an authoritative decision on its behalf. The judgment aggregates conflicting values and interests within a single decision, normally by choosing one side over the other (Zartman, 1978, pp. 69–70). Thus, the process results in winners and losers.

It often happens that coalition decisions are challenged through judication. Those who lose (for instance, those participants who do not prevail in having their interests included in a legislative enactment) often seek to block the enforcement of the law through appeals, which are made either to the administrative agencies responsible for implementing the law or to the courts (Sacarto, 1985, pp. 34–35). Normally, appeals must first be directed to responsible implementing agencies, and agency appeal processes exhausted, before the courts will accept jurisdiction.

Even when coalition decisions are not challenged, administrative agencies must make judgments about how existing policies and rules will be applied to the circumstances of particular cases. These occasions require agency managers to make decisions through some type of process of choice — they may choose to employ judication or rational planning. If they use judication, they may reconsider the factual assertions and arguments advanced by policy process participants.

The advantages and disadvantages of employing judication as a decision mode in policy making are well documented (Horowitz, 1977). Orderly consideration and the ability to judge the applicability and effect of a policy in light of a particular set of facts are obvious assets. Also, when the veracity of a claim is at issue, the judicial process brings to the task a valuable set of techniques for examining the relevance of evidence and testing the validity of contending parties' assertions. These advantages begin to diminish, however, as the number of parties increases and as the issues become less factually oriented and more closely linked to conflicting perceptions about the likely social consequences of alternative courses of action.

Rational planning is a decision process in which logic ideally plays a dominant role. Managers generate a set of possible paths for achieving policy objectives. A search process occurs in which data are sought and fitted to each of the alternatives for the purpose of exploring the feasibility and likely consequences of that alternative. Finally, an option is selected which ideally optimizes (that is, most efficiently reaches) the policy objective (Simon, 1959, pp. 262–64). Rational planning norms have long been associated both with administrative expertise and with a perceived administrative role in faithfully executing the democratically determined aims of the state. As is well known, the intent of this mode is never fully realized; that is, decision makers cannot consider every possible alternative, nor can they always optimize the choices they make. We treat this mode separately, however, because it suggests a decision process in which managers consciously attempt to employ as systematic a search process as possible before making a policy decision. More often than not, this mode is characterized by heavy reliance on technical/ analytical expertise as decision makers prepare to make choices. Indeed, one frequent criticism of decision processes that seek to approximate rationality is that they run a severe risk of becoming unrepresentative even as they rely on technical expertise to pursue "truth" (West, 1988, pp. 774–75).

Negotiation is a voluntary process involving two or more individuals or groups who attempt to gain objectives through mutual consent (Bingham, 1984). The procedure (for instance, the parties may be compelled by law to bargain in good faith using the auspices of a government agent acting as a third-party facilitator), but not the outcome, may be imposed. The participants must believe there is more to gain than to lose by their interaction and that somewhere among the array of possible alternative solutions there exists at least one that is optimal and more than one promising more satisfaction than dissatisfaction (Rubin & Brown, 1977, p. 8).

Negotiation may appear at first blush to be much like coalition. Both may involve tradeoffs of interests in order to bring the participants to a common position. In the policy formulation stage, fundamental positions are frequently altered or obscured in order to attain a decision. As with collective bargaining between management and unions, conflict may be deferred to a later time. Nonetheless, negotiation differs in that the parties bind themselves to each other legally by virtue of the agreement they reach, usually for a specific period of time, whereas the relationship between coalition partners is nonbinding and likely to be temporary and shifting.

POLICY STAGES AND DOMINANT
DECISION MODES

Each stage of the policy process has functions and activities that tend to dictate the use of a particular decision mode. The policy formulation stage performs the functions of perceiving and defining the problem or problems, aggregating interests, organizing and determining representation for participant groups, and setting the agenda for decision making. Usually, the principal players are political interest groups and elected officials, with administrative managers playing a lower profile role. Although collaborative activities are involved (suggesting negotiation as a mode), this is preeminently a set of functions served by the coalition decision mode. Political party conventions, election campaigns, and the legislative process are all well suited to raise policy issues, argue about what the problems and their relative importance are in the effort to court supporting constituencies, and array participants and their sympathizers on various sides of the identified issues (Jones, 1984).

It seems likely, however, that if the structural variables are such that a large number of groups, with intensely held interests, hold clear and conflicting definitions of a problem so that none of the participants and their natural allies can attain a majority, there is more apt to be pressure for negotiating binding agreements among disparate interests in order to move toward a majority. However, at some point in the process, as consensus upon defining the problem builds, negotiaton will prove a less attractive alternative.

Because a program represents one path to reaching policy objectives, the program development stage appears to be naturally associated with the rational planning mode. Expertise is normally sought by policy makers in determining the general means to efficiently and effectively attack the policy objectives. Coalition can also be an appropriate decision mode at this stage. Many of the fundamental differences dividing the parties may have been finessed or deferred at the policy formulation stage, leaving crucial value decisions to be supplied through debate. Still, there are usually technical issues of design, staffing, budgeting and procedural controls that require the help and leadership of the knowledgeable insider.

The implementation stage continues and strengthens the need for inputs from managers and technocrats and, thus, for a continued orientation to rational planning. It is at this stage, however, that unforeseen challenges arrive from those critical of a program who wish to impede it, as well as from those whom a program benefits and who seek to prevent delays and negative interpretations by agency managers. Judication now emerges as an apparently appropriate decision mode to test the actions and interpretations of those persons executing the program. Judication is frequently employed because it is tailored to making decisions concerning a specific set of facts relating to individual complaints of either noncompliance or administrative arbitrariness. The problem, of course, is that the delays and expense associated with judicialized procedure in both courts and agencies may well jeopardize a program's effectiveness.

Because of the threat to program effectiveness caused by dysfunctional aspects of the judication or coalition mode, negotiation may be viewed as an attractive alternative. Agency managers may be well advised to bring supporters and detractors together and to have them engage in a bargaining process that will allow program implementation to proceed with a reasonable prospect for success (Harter, 1983). Indeed, the dynamics of the process may result in negotiation — whether intentionally launched or not. Such negotiation tolerates a high degree of issue complexity and a moderate number of parties. Of course, as the number of parties involved grows, the coalition mode becomes more attractive.

Program evaluation tends to focus on technical issues but also revisits arguments first addressed at the policy formulation stage. The latter have to do with varying perceptions of the policy problem and of the linkage between cause and effect in the strategy embraced by the initiative. Program managers predictably defend their programs and, in so doing, structure data in a way that blurs the original issue of whether the effort, no matter how well or poorly run, worked toward achieving the policy objective. Political interest groups and elected officials reemerge as players because they are vitally concerned about the link between the issue of how well the program has achieved the sought-after policy goal and the matter of how the next battle over the policy domain will be fought.

In this environment, administrators, political interest groups, elected officials, and evaluation specialists are likely to engage in a process of negotiation concerning a range of program-related matters (Weiss, 1972). Some of the participants may choose to press their claims in the legislative arena through the coalition process.

The relationship between policy stage and dominant decision mode may be summarized, although it should be recognized that a particular mix of structural variable values may negate the mode. Policy formulation typically employs coalition; program development fosters rational planning; program implementation frequently employs judication and/or negotiation; and program evaluation is likely to spur negotiation.

DECISION MODE TO DECISION METHOD

Both the structural variables discussed above, over which participants have no control, and a set of tactical variables, which they can influence, work to determine which decision method is likely to be used. These intervening variables shape the selection of method from among the set of decision types associated with each decision mode.

As already noted, a variety of structural and tactical variables influence which decision method is selected. For example, when the tactical variables include a high degree of trust between participants, high willingness to share information, an unwillingness to use third parties as neutrals, and a belief among the parties that the issues are integrative rather than competitive and when the decision mode is negotiation, then participants are likely to engage in unassisted, interest-based bargaining. Conversely, when the tactical variable values are the opposite of those just outlined (low degree of trust, low willingness to share information, willingness to work through third parties, and a belief among the parties that the issues are essentially competitive) and when the decision mode is negotiation, then position-based bargaining will result and will likely involve arbitration or mediation.

Another example may be helpful. When tactical variable values include a low degree of trust, low willingness to share information, a willingness to use third parties with skills, and a shared belief that the issues are competitive and when the decision mode is rational planning, the method likely to be chosen is the Delphi technique, in which face-to-face contact is not allowed and the process is managed by experts who summarize predictions and report back to the parties. This method is further encouraged by the structural variable value of a large number of parties and intensely held values.

We will not attempt to delineate here, in a chapter having as its purpose the presentation of a general model, the myriad hypothetical relationships that may potentially exist between decision mode, various mixes of tactical and structural variables, and decision method. The reader familiar with managing conflict or studying the management of conflict can suggest research hypotheses at least as appealing as those we might offer. Our interest at this point is simply to develop a framework that permits such relationships to be conceived and analyzed.

CONCLUSION

We have presented a general framework that describes how conflict is managed in the public policy process. The approach we have employed recognizes the environment in which political decisions are made, identifies a variety of important factors that condition the type of decision mode used, and suggests some of the relationships that may exist between the decision mode and decision method that is ultimately selected. Above all, the model takes into account the critical influence of the policy process and the way in which conflict is treated at each of its various stages.

We believe that this framework can be usefully employed as a heuristic tool by conflict management researchers and practitioners both to understand better and to predict decision modes and methods that are likely to be used by public policy decision makers to address conflict.

10   Theoretical Dimensions of Environmental Mediation

J. Walton Blackburn

Environmental mediation is merging as an alternative to litigation in the settlement of environmental disputes. A literature on the theory and practice of environmental mediation is beginning to develop as practitioners reflect upon the techniques and approaches that have worked best and as theoreticians attempt to synthesize the key elements of successful environmental mediation.

This research is an effort to develop the theory of environmental mediation from a "grounded theory" approach. Bailey (1982) describes grounded theory as an approach in which theory is discovered or generated from data rather than being abstract and tentative. It is developed by entering the fieldwork phase without a hypothesis, describing what happens, and explaining why it happens on the basis of observations.

The author examined the literature on environmental mediation to identify the activities mediation practitioners performed and the conditions they claimed were conducive to successful mediation efforts. The literature search itself was a challenge. Despite a computer search and examination of indexes and bibliographies, little work on environmental mediation was found.

In the search of the mediation literature, the author found 63 elements, considerations, and activities of environmental mediation that were evident in or had been used in different mediation efforts. These 63 components of mediation were shaped into 63 propositions about which activities and conditions favor successful mediation outcomes. They were also organized into ten categories, called the "Ten Stages of Environmental Mediation," as a means of structuring environmental mediation for ease of understanding.

The next step in the development of the theory was to test the 63 propositions developed from the literature. To do this, the author identified several organizations that conducted environmental mediation from a directory of alternative dispute resolution organizations and from the list of attendees at the Second National Conference on Environmental Dispute Resolution held in Washington, D.C., in 1984. Contacts with these organizations produced the addresses of several environmental mediation practitioners. In addition, names of practitioners were identified through the case study literature.

A questionnaire was developed listing the 63 propositions. Respondents were asked to rate each proposition as irrelevant, moderately important, very important, or critical to successful environmental mediation. From the list of 40 practitioners, the author obtained 30 completed questionnaires. The pattern that emerged from this practitioner evaluation revealed three theoretical dimensions of environmental mediation practice.

To assist the reader in understanding the theoretical dimensions of environmental mediation, the nature of this approach is described, the Ten Stages of Environmental Mediation are listed, and the virtues of mediation presented.

THE NATURE OF
ENVIRONMENTAL MEDIATION

Environmental mediation is an approach employing mediation to resolve environmental disputes. The Institute for Environmental Mediation uses the following definition when discussing the mediation process:

> Mediation is a process in which those involved in a dispute jointly explore and reconcile their differences. The mediator has no authority to impose a settlement. His or her strength lies in the ability to assist the parties in settling their own differences. The mediated dispute is settled when the parties themselves reach what they consider to be a workable solution (Cormick, 1980:27).

A number of important considerations are implicit in this definition. Involvement of the parties in the mediation process and their acceptance of the mediator is voluntary. The parties jointly explore and debate the issues, both in joint sessions and in caucuses of one or more of the parties with the mediator. The mediator facilitates the negotiation process by assisting the parties to reach a settlement acceptable to them. An agreement requires the support of all parties. The mediator shares with the parties the responsibility of ensuring that any agreement reached represents a viable solution that is technically, financially, and politically feasible to implement (Cormick, 1982).

STAGES IN THE MEDIATION PROCESS

An examination of the literature on environmental mediation revealed a number of discrete activities undertaken and factors considered in the mediation process. These were structured into a set of stages of mediation. The series of activities and considerations fell into the pattern shown in Figure 10.1, and described below.

1. Identify Mediator. Identify a mediator who has no personal interest in the outcome of the dispute and who does not have great technical expertise on the subject of the dispute.
2. Assess Preconditions. Assess the presence of mediation preconditions, such as whether the issues are concrete, whether there are real consequences for not entering into mediation, whether there is uncertainty about possible outcomes in contexts other than mediation, whether there is a balance of power among contending parties, and whether the dispute has potential to set legal precedents.
3. Recruit Participants. Recruit participants who are representatives of all parties with a substantial interest in the dispute and educate them in the mediation process.
4. Design Process. Design mediation and obtain approval of ground rules.
5. Identify Issues. Clearly identify the issues in the dispute.
6. Establish Information Base. Establish the information base for the issues in dispute.
7. Develop Preliminary Agreement. Examine alternative solutions, communicate with parties that will be responsible for implementing an agreement, and put the preliminary agreement into writing.

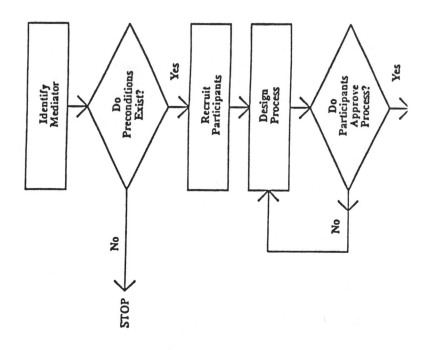

154

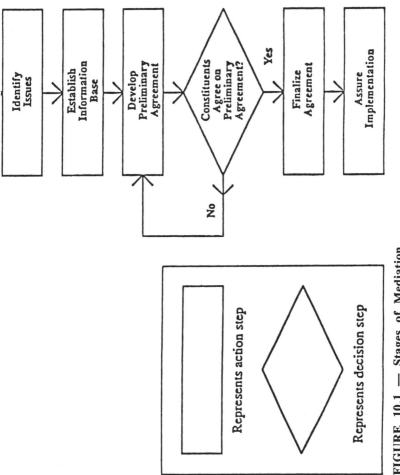

FIGURE 10.1 — Stages of Mediation

The flowchart contains the following action steps: Identify Issues; Establish Information Base; Develop Preliminary Agreement; then the decision step Constituents Agree on Preliminary Agreement? If No, return to Develop Preliminary Agreement. If Yes, proceed to Finalize Agreement; then Assure Implementation.

Legend: Represents action step (rectangle); Represents decision step (diamond).

8. Consult Constituents. Consult constituents on the suitability of the preliminary agreement.
9. Finalize Agreement. Incorporate recommendations for changes in the preliminary agreement into a final agreement and obtain approval of all parties to mediation.
10. Assure Implementation. Assure implementation by getting the agreement ratified by the constituents of parties to mediation, by obtaining public support for mediation, and by providing for monitoring the agreement and means for revising the agreement.

THE VIRTUES OF ENVIRONMENTAL MEDIATION

Writers on the subject of environmental mediation have made a number of claims about the benefits of the practice of environmental mediation. Three different sources extol the virtues of environmental mediation, as follows:

Mediation can provide conflict resolution for environmental disputes far less expensively, in terms of time and money, than can litigation. Moreover, it can provide all participants a greater sense of satisfaction because of their active role. It allows the participants to maintain a degree of control. It allows the consideration of more creative environmental options than does litigation. Most important, mediation promotes cooperation, which is the missing element in the solution of most environmental problems. It also allows consideration of a more comprehensive range of expertise and technical data affecting environmental decisions than does litigation. Environmental mediation is an attempt to manage resources and make decisions that incorporate as many relevant factors and consequences as possible (Folberg & Taylor, 1984).

The flexibility of mediation is probably one of its principal strengths. The mediators and parties to a dispute have had to design a process and ground rules to fit the specific circumstances of their particular case (Bingham, 1984).

[Mediation] is generally less expensive in time and money. . . . It deals more satisfactorily with the issues. In contrast to judicial review, which typically examines whether the administrative and procedural requirements have been adequately addressed, a mediated settlement deals directly with the "substance" of the dispute. It is this crucial aspect of the mediation process that should, over the long run, encourage greater use of the process (McCarthy & Shorett, 1984).

An evaluation of the success rate of environmental mediation efforts provides a favorable picture. Bingham (1984) indicates that by 1984, a decade after environmental mediation had first been attempted, mediators had been involved in at least 160 environmental disputes. Results of many of those efforts were successful, remarkable for the positive climate of public opinion they fostered and for the sense among the parties that they had won, each of them. In the cases in which the purpose was to achieve an explicit agreement, the success rate was 78% (Bingham, 1984). Among the 103 cases in which an agreement was reached, approximately 70% had been fully implemented, 14% had been partially implemented, and 15% were unlikely ever to be implemented (Bingham, 1984). Environmental mediation is achieving substantial legitimacy.

THEORETICAL DIMENSIONS

The Ten Stages of Environmental Mediation contained 63 propositions about the practice of environmental mediation. These propositions were evaluated by 30 environmental mediation practitioners in terms of their importance in achieving a mediated settlement. The 34 propositions receiving an average importance rating from practitioners of "critical" or "very important" in reaching a mediated settlement were termed the "Essential Model of Environmental Mediation." The 29 propositions receiving an average importance rating of only "moderately important" or "irrelevant" in effective mediation were termed the "Secondary Model of Environmental Mediation."

A careful comparison of the Essential Model and the Secondary Model indicated three striking patterns. The first pattern indicated a contrast between the two models. In the Essential Model, a "flexible, adaptive, general, participative" dimension of mediation was found. In contrast, in the Secondary Model, a "formalistic, structured, specific, authoritative" dimension was evident.

A second pattern observed was accountability. This dimension was found entirely within the Essential Model. The third pattern, the interpersonal dimension, indicated a striking, and counterintuitive, difference between the Essential Model and the Secondary Model.

Dimension One:
Flexible, Adaptive, General,
Participative versus Formalistic,
Structured, Specific, Authoritative

A comparison of the Essential Model of environmental mediation with the Secondary Model revealed a dimension that can be labeled the "flexible, adaptive, general, participative" aspect, as opposed to the "formalistic, structured, specific, authoritative" approach to mediation. The elements in the Ten Stages of Environmental Mediation of greater importance in achieving mediated settlements were the flexible, adaptive components. They are, therefore, included in the Essential Model. The elements of less importance in reaching mediated agreements were the formalistic, structured aspects, and they are included in the Secondary Model. For the sake of simplicity in description, these two dimensions will be referred to simply as the flexible aspect and the formalistic approach.

In the flexible approach, the criteria by which disputes are evaluated for their suitability for mediation are general, rather than highly specific. If conflicts have certain broad characteristics, they are evaluated as suitable for mediation. In the formalistic approach, particular, sharply defined criteria are used to determine whether a conflict is suitable for mediation.

In the flexible approach, the mediator and the participants together develop and shape the process to fit the characteristics of the dispute and their own needs and predispositions. The joint activity of the participants with the mediator in creating the process as it develops helps to give all individuals a sense of ownership in the process and helps to ensure that it is suitable to the issues being addressed and to the background and inclinations of the actors in the process. In the formalistic approach, the mediator assumes primary responsibility for evaluating the suitability of the dispute for mediation. The mediator takes an authoritative role in certain steps in the process.

The structure of the mediation effort is subdivided at certain points under the formalistic design; in the flexible approach, the participants maintain participation as an integral group.

In the formalistic approach, certain kinds of information are gathered and parameters for the process are specified in some detail as the process advances; in the flexible approach, information is gathered only to ensure that participants have an understanding of the situation enabling them to move forward together toward solutions. In the formalistic process, considerable precision and definition of information is required. In the flexible approach, only enough precision and information is needed to keep the mediation effort moving forward.

The following two sections use representative elements of the Ten Stages of Environmental Mediation to illustrate the flexible, and the formalistic, approaches and describe the rationale for the inclusion of each example within the contrasting dimensions.

Flexible, Adaptive, General, Participative Approach

Several of the propositions in the Ten Stages of Environmental Mediation illustrate the flexible perspective. One of the elements states that

The mediator should not have an interest in the outcome of the dispute.

This qualification is critical to the flexible approach simply to ensure that the mediator will allow the process to produce a solution that meets the needs of the participants rather than develop a result that suits the concerns of an agency the mediator represents or of his personal interests (Cormick, 1980).

An important preliminary to mediation is an assessment of the suitability of a dispute for this particular method of dispute resolution. Two general criteria were found to be useful in establishing the appropriateness of a conflict for mediation. They were:

There should be real consequences to the parties if mediation is not attempted, which makes mediation the best alternative.

There should be uncertainty about possible outcomes of the dispute in a context other than mediation, i.e., in the courts, before a regulatory body, etc.

The generality of these propositions makes them appropriate to the flexible approach. Simply "real consequences," and "uncertainty" qualify these disputes for mediation (Cormick, 1982). The mediator has substantial flexibility for assessing their suitability to mediation, rather than basing such a determination upon more precise criteria.

The participants in mediation are generally unfamiliar with such an approach to dispute settlement. Because of the novel nature of mediation, therefore, the mediator must spend time explaining how the process generally works and what is expected of participants (Bingham, 1982). This knowledge enables the participants to shape the approach according to their particular needs and to the dimensions of the conflict being addressed (Huser, 1982; Faning, 1979). They are not dependent upon the mediator to give them detailed directions at every step in the process. This gives the effort flexibility, rather than formality:

The mediator should educate the contending parties on the mediation process.

Two elements in the flexible approach involve the participants intimately in shaping the mediation effort in a way that meets their inclinations and concerns and the particular characteristics of the conflict (Kennedy & Lansford, 1983). They allow flexible participation. These are:

Contending parties should participate in designing the mediation process.

The participants and the mediator should develop ground rules for the process.

The identification of the issues in dispute is a key stage in mediation (Carpenter & Kennedy, 1980). Substantial leeway exists, however, in the amount of effort expended in defining the issues. In the flexible approach, only a general knowledge of the issues is needed so that the participants know the nature of their disagreements. As they work toward defining the issues at the level of specificity needed, they discover where they need additional information. This avoids the collection of enormous amounts of detailed information that may not be germane to the concerns of the contending parties. Although a general agreement on the dimensions of the dispute is needed, too great a focus upon explicit determination of facts may lead to a preoccupation with obtaining information that supports a particular position. An adequate understanding of the facts is appropriate, rather than a detailed and exhaustive comprehension as in the following elements:

The issues in dispute should be clearly identified.

Efforts should be made to be sure that all representatives of parties to mediation have an adequate understanding of the facts relevant to the dispute.

Once the participants in mediation have obtained the amount of information they feel is appropriate to their own understanding of the issues in contention, they can begin to develop possible solutions. The development of a variety of alternatives allows the different perspectives to put forward ideas that incorporate their particular concerns (Carpenter & Kennedy, 1980). By avoiding the temptation to focus upon a particular solution too early in the process, the creative development of options is fostered. The development of variety provides participants the opportunity to pick and choose among diverse solutions and to select portions of different approaches to be combined into a solution representing the interests of all parties. The process continues to reflect the diverse needs and concerns of the opposing perspectives without favoring any particular position, nor one precise, technically correct resolution:

A variety of alternative solutions should be generated by the participants in mediation.

An important dimension of flexibility and adaptability is the use of an informal structure in mediation, rather than always gathering in highly organized meetings (Susskind, 1981). This informality allows the members to try out ideas that they might hesitate to put forth in a formal setting. It also enhances the creativity of the process. Less articulate participants may generate proposals that otherwise might be lost. Unusual and offbeat ideas may be developed that may be combined in a way leading to unique resolutions of the conflict, yet informality allows the elimination of unusual ideas without denigrating the value of such contributions. An atmosphere of exploration and flexibility, rather than one of rigid adherence to strict technical feasibility, is developed:

The contending parties and the mediator should hold informal meetings.

Another stage in mediation is reaching an agreement. It is desirable to achieve a consensus result that meets the needs of all parties (Talbot, 1983). Majority vote may not be satisfactory. This requires a settlement reached through a flexible process that adapts the solution to the needs of each perspective in mediation. A technically correct solution reached through a highly rational and formal process may settle differences in the short run, but by sticking to highly rational criteria, the irrational, perhaps emotional, concerns of some participants may be excluded. This leaves the potential for a lawsuit to block the implementation of the settlement. The positions of all parties should receive respectful consideration (Shorett, 1980). This condition is met by the element:

> An agreement should be reached which is approved by all parties to mediation.

One last element of the flexible, adaptive orientation is the provision for revisions of the agreement once implementation has begun. Conditions and circumstances in the environment may change in unpredictable ways, and the process of implementation may uncover unanticipated obstacles (Lee, 1982). By being aware of the possible eventual need for revising the agreement, even while the mediation process is underway, the need to make changes will not be demoralizing to participants, who may have invested great time and effort in reaching a feasible solution. They will simply understand that the complexity, unpredictability, and interrelated nature of changes in the environment may require future adjustments. This flexibility and adaptability of the settlement enhance the feasibility of a solution that meets the spirit, if not the letter, of the mediation effort and the concerns of the participants. This indicates the importance of the proposition that

> Means should be provided to re-make, or re-decide the agreement, if necessary.

Formalistic, Structured, Specific, Authoritative Approach

The first point in the stages of mediation at which the formalistic orientation enters into the processes is in the criteria for evaluating the suitability of a dispute for mediation. Three of the propositions illustrate the formalistic aspects of the Secondary Model (McCarthy, 1976; Susskind & Weinstein, 1981; Cormick, 1982). They constitute more precise, specific criteria for evaluating the suitability of a dispute for mediation than the criteria employed in the flexible model:

> There should be a perceived balance of power among contending parties.

> It should be clear that the parties to the dispute have reached a stalemate, or an impasse.

Contending parties should have potential to experience economic costs if a
mediated settlement is not reached.

In the formalistic perspective, structuring the mediation process is
helpful in maintaining the momentum of the effort and in keeping
participants intensively involved (McCarthy, 1976; Susskind, 1981).
Two provisions of this approach are as follows:

Clear and enforceable deadlines should be developed to provide an impetus for
a mediated settlement.

Contending parties and the mediator should hold regularly scheduled meetings.

Those who would use a flexible approach might consider such
constraints on the process to be too limiting. At times, the participants
may need time to attend to other concerns in their lives, and a mediation
effort should not be so totally demanding that it becomes prohibitively
expensive in time and effort so as to preclude the participation of
individuals who have only limited time available. In addition, at times the
members of a mediation effort may need time to explore and research
certain issues in depth. Although it may be important to maintain
momentum in the process, usually the desire of the participants to achieve
a resolution, and their ownership of the process, will keep the process
moving. Such artificial conditions may be unnecessary in the flexible
approach, but they may be very appropriate from the formalistic
perspective.

In working toward the definition of the issues in dispute, defining the
conflicts in time and space may be appropriate (Susskind & Weinstein,
1981). From the formalistic perspective, this would justify the following:

Agreement should be reached among contending parties on the geographical
boundaries and time horizons of the issues in dispute.

From the flexible perspective, this level of specification would be
seen as limiting.

From the formalistic perspective, substantial agreement among
contending parties is needed on the facts and data relevant to the dispute
as a beginning point for discussion (Carpenter & Kennedy, 1980; Clark,
1980). This information provides a framework for discussion. From the
flexible orientation, however, it is more appropriate to have only an
adequate understanding so that the contending parties feel comfortable

discussing the issues. Reaching actual agreement on facts, in itself, may consume substantial time and effort and will not necessarily move the process forward. Addressing different concerns about the issues, rather than the details of the factual circumstances, is considered more productive. From the formalistic viewpoint, however, the following component is useful:

Agreement should be reached among participants in mediation on the facts and data relevant to the dispute.

In the formalistic approach, the structural arrangements of the mediation process are used to facilitate mediation (Talbot, 1983). This is useful in addressing technical questions that may be beyond the interest or expertise of some of the participants, as follows:

Small groups should be used to address technical questions in the dispute.

Advisors, or advisory groups, should be used.

From the flexible approach, however, this structure may interfere with the participative aspect of the process. By fragmenting the effort into subgroups, the effort may lose coherence. The small groups, or advisory groups, will have to report to the plenary mediation body. These reports will then need to be incorporated into the process. This subdividing and reconstituting may damage the integrity of the process. From the flexible perspective, it may be more desirable to use as little technical information as possible so that attention is maintained on involvement in the process. When technical details are important, it may be most desirable to educate the participants in a way that allows them to assess the information from their own perspective rather than have them accept the information as "fact" from a subgroup or advisors, who may have their own perspective on and interpretation of the data.

In the formalistic perspective, the mediator assumes three authoritative roles:

The mediator should assist in drafting the wording of the preliminary agreement.

The mediator should put forth trial solutions.

The mediator should assist in drafting the final agreement.

These activities by the mediator may help to move the process toward a solution faster (Shorett, 1980; McCarthy, 1976; Susskind & Weinstein, 1981). The neutral position of the mediator may enable him to develop wording more satisfactory to all positions than the participants are capable of with their contrasting interests. Trial solutions may incorporate all positions in a fair and equitable manner.

These roles for the mediator were not found in the flexible approach. If the flexible model succeeds in obtaining the commitment and involvement of participants in working toward a solution, the members themselves should be able to complete drafting chores. The involvement of the mediator in drafting agreements denigrates the abilities of the participants. Similarly, the development of trial solutions by the mediator infringes upon the right of the participants to fashion their own unique settlement. It may be better to take more time to draft the wording of the agreements and develop solutions, which intimately reflect the concerns and the interests of the participants, than to rush the process at the risk of alienating the parties from the solution.

Dimension Two: Accountability

The accountability dimension of environmental mediation has two aspects. One aspect is the need to develop a mediated settlement that takes into account the orientation, resources, motivations, and concerns of those parties who may not be involved in the mediation effort but who will be responsible for implementing a mediated agreement. The other face of accountability is the need for the settlement to reflect the concerns and interests of the constituents of the representatives in mediation.

The accountability propositions in the Ten Stages of Environmental Mediation were all rated so important by the mediation practitioners that they are all a part of the Essential Model (Blackburn, 1987). This indicates simply that accountability is a necessary foundation for effective environmental mediation and for the successful implementation of mediated settlements.

The accountability components of the Essential Model are straightforward and self-evident. Three elements illustrate accountability:

Parties responsible for implementing a mediated agreement should provide assurances that they will follow through.

The participants in mediation should consult with their constituents on the suitability of the preliminary agreement.

The agreement should be ratified, or approved, by the constituents of representatives to mediation.

Dimension Three: Interpersonal Aspects

The interpersonal aspects of mediation reveal a surprising dichotomy in approaches to mediation between the Essential Model and the Secondary Model. In the Essential Model, the relationships between the mediator and the participants are rated as important in successful mediation. The interpersonal components of the Secondary Model indicate that the relationships between the contending parties are not as critical to successfully mediated outcomes as are the interactions of the mediator and participants.

In the Essential Model, three components were important in effective mediation. These were:

The mediator should obtain the trust of the contending parties.

The mediator should spend time interacting with participants in mediation on a one-on-one basis.

The contending parties and the mediator should hold informal meetings.

This pattern indicates that the development of interpersonal relationships between the parties and the mediator is a foundation for successful mediation (Carpenter & Kennedy, 1980). At times, the mediator may need to be privy to positions that must be kept secret from the opposition parties. The mediator may help the parties to evaluate how sound their position is and which arguments may be weak in the larger context of mediation (Lee, 1982; Faning, 1979). The mediator helps to ground the parties in reality. In order for the parties to be willing to reveal this sensitive information, there must be strong trust that this information will be handled in confidence.

In contrast, the fact that the following two components were important enough to be included only in the Secondary Model suggests that the interactions among opponents in mediation are not a critical factor in reaching settlements. These propositions are:

The opposing parties should not have a history of contentious relationships.

Positive attitudes and interaction should develop among representatives of contending parties to mediation.

Mediation practitioners have argued that a history of contention among conflicting parties can poison the atmosphere so severely that participants are unable to work together toward a settlement (Carpenter & Kennedy, 1980; Talbot, 1983). Antagonisms inhibit the ability of the parties to see any merit in the position of their opponents. Similarly, it has been maintained that a settlement can be achieved more readily in an atmosphere in which the parties develop positive attitudes and interactions. These conditions, however, may be irrelevant to achieving a settlement.

Participants in environmental mediation will recognize that they have substantially different interests and perspectives on a dispute. It may be difficult, or impossible, to develop a pleasant and friendly atmosphere for a mediation effort, particularly if parties have been at each others' throats on many previous occasions. Yet, if the process is developed carefully, respecting the interests of all parties, participants have substantial involvement in the development and design of the mediation process, and accountability relationships are firmly established. The desire to achieve a settlement of the dispute and the personal investment of the participant in the process will override any feelings of animosity or an atmosphere that is less than positive. Sophisticated participants in mediation realize that the goal of the process is much more important than inter-personal relationships. The time and effort needed to develop friendly interpersonal relationships in mediation may not be resources wisely spent in a mediation effort as they have little bearing on a successful outcome. If by chance, they may develop, that is all to the good. They are not a precondition for mediation.

CONCLUSIONS

The comparison of the Essential Model with the Secondary Model reveals three theoretically important dimensions. First is the contrast between flexible, adaptive, general, participative elements and the formal-istic, structured, specific, authoritative components. An accountability dimension was of such importance that all elements of this aspect were found within the Essential Model. An analysis of interpersonal aspects of mediation showed some elements important enough to be included in the Essential Model; others of less importance were placed in the Secondary Model.

The contrast between the flexible, adaptive, general, participative dimensions of the Essential Model and the formalistic, structured, specific, authoritative aspects of the Secondary Model could be characterized in terms of a group process approach, as opposed to a rational, analytical approach to mediation. It is not clear whether these dimensions reflect fundamentally different approaches to mediation by different practitioners. This first factor appeared in a factor analysis of 17 components, indicating that a great many of the propositions in the Ten Stages of Environmental Mediation are highly interrelated.

Even though the flexible elements and the formalistic elements in the Ten Stages of Environmental Mediation did not show a high level of interrelationship, it does seem likely that the group process model and the rational, analytical model represent general tendencies among different practitioners. These tendencies probably relate to the general philosophy, personal predisposition, and professional background of different mediators.

Another possible explanation of the differences in mediator orientation is that different conflicts require different approaches. Disputes involving a large number of contending interests and highly complex, interrelated environmental impacts may require a formalistic approach to sort through highly technical issues and to organize participants in a way that allows the desired level of participation for each individual. Disputes involving few parties and relatively simple environmental impacts may be much more amenable to the use of the flexible approach.

The relevance of the theoretical dimension that contrasts the flexible with the formalistic approach to environmental mediation practice needs empirical research.

The importance given to the accountability dimension by mediation practitioners, which placed it entirely within the Essential Model, indicates that this theoretical dimension of mediation is fundamental to resolving environmental disputes effectively. By developing the mediation effort with full communication with parties responsible for implementation, the process is grounded in reality. The solution will reflect the imperatives of environmental conditions and the realities of bureaucratic and resource constraints. When the representatives of parties to mediation consult with their constituents before reaching the final agreement, the mediation effort is grounded upon political feasibility. The accountability dimension greatly enhances the feasibility of implementing agreements and increases the legitimacy of environmental mediation as an approach to dispute resolution. It is a key to effective environmental mediation.

The surprising split of the interpersonal dimension between the Essential Model and the Secondary Model has important practical implications. Developing trust and positive interactions between the mediator and each of the contending parties is critical to mediation success. Developing friendly interactions between opposing parties is not critical to success, however desirable it might be for other reasons. The investment of time and resources to develop a close relationship of the mediator with the different parties is extremely productive, but efforts spent to engage the contending parties in positive interactions is not necessarily productive.

VI International Conflict

INTRODUCTION

Roderick Kramer

Throughout the 1960s and into the first half of the 1970s, research on psychological aspects of international conflict flourished. Major conceptual contributions were made by de Rivera (1968), Deutsch (1965), Etzioni (1969), Jervis (1976), and Kelman (1966), to name only a few. Early innovative research using the Prisoner's Dilemma game initiated an intensive and productive line of laboratory research on the determinants of cooperation and conflict (Rapoport & Chammah, 1965). In addition, pioneering developments in the simulation of international conflicts were begun (Guetzkow, 1963). The *Journal of Conflict Resolution* and *Journal of Social Issues* devoted substantial space to the examination of issues pertaining to the management of international conflicts in general and prevention of nuclear war in particular. As a result of this activity, significant conceptual and methodological progress was made, and the future of research in this area seemed promising.

Then, for well over a decade there seemed to be a hiatus of sorts as interest in international conflict waned. Social psychologists turned their attention to other topics, such as social cognition and attribution theory. The number of journal articles and scholarly books concerned with international conflict decreased markedly. And, for a while, it seemed as if the entire area was destined to become just another chapter in the history of psychological research.

Fortunately, in the second half of the 1980s, the study of international conflict appeared once again to be enjoying a much-deserved and much-needed vogue. One evidence of this vogue is the renewed interest in previous work, as evidenced by the fact that SPSSI (the Society for the Psychological Study of Social Issues) recently issued a compilation of major contributions from the past several decades (White, 1986). And several major original contributions have appeared (e.g., Jervis, Lebow, & Stein, 1985; Levinger, 1987).

A prominent feature of this new research on psychological aspects of international conflict is its conceptual vigor and diversity. New research on international conflict incorporates the latest findings from all areas of psychological research, including research on cognitive processes, motivation, and decision making. There have been major reexaminations of the psychological foundations of deterrence theory (e.g., Levinger, 1987), as well as a focus on new approaches to the promotion of peace that attempt to transcend reliance on deterrence (Wagner, de Rivera, & Watkins, 1988).

In addition to the theoretical breadth and conceptual richness of recent work in this area, there has also been an impressive range of methodologies adopted in studying these topics, ranging from social psychological experiments (Plous, 1987), content analyses of policy makers' rhetoric (Tetlock, 1988), clinical interviews (Kull, 1988), and even grounded theory (Sutton & Kramer, in press).

The two contributions included in this section were selected in part because they are representative of this conceptual and methodological diversity. The chapter by Kozan uses a survey methodology to examine differences between the conflict management styles of managers from two developing countries — Jordan and Turkey. Kozan's study adopts an individual differences approach to understanding the conflict management style of managers in these countries. He uses the Rahim Organizational Conflict Inventory to examine the extent to which managers in Jordan, Turkey, and the United States use integrating, obliging, dominating, avoiding and/or compromising styles in managing their relationships with others.

One notable aspect of Kozan's chapter is that it provides useful information on two subject populations not previously examined. Such cross-cultural comparisons are essential in determining the generalizability of findings using Rahim's Inventory. They also have important implications, of course, for understanding the interaction of managers from different cultures.

The chapter by Kramer, Meyerson, and Davis examines international conflict at the nation-state level. They use an experimental approach to examine the role of cognitive processes in deterrent decisions. The basic question they address is how decision makers decide "how much" of a deterrent is needed to guarantee their security. Implicit in their analysis of attack behavior is also a concern with the conditions under which deterrence fails. Classical approaches to deterrence theory have often assumed, somewhat uncritically, that decision makers can be conceptualized as rational actors engaged in a systematic or orderly calculation of the costs and benefits associated with their strategic behavior. In contrast with this rational view of such decisions, Kramer, Meyerson, and Davis' results underscore the subjectivity and "bounded rationality" of decision makers.

The two chapters have in common their emphasis on factors that affect conflict management behavior. But the assumptions they make about the nature of the relationships among the parties to a conflict differ markedly. Kozan's research is concerned with conflict within organizational settings. In these settings, individuals can communicate more or less openly and directly about the issues that divide them. Moreover, when disputes cannot be settled by negotiation and compromise, they can rely on hierarchy and other institutional mechanisms to facilitate conflict resolution. The study by Kramer, Meyerson, and Davis focuses on management of conflict in situations where decision makers do not have such opportunities to communicate directly. As they point out, in the anarchic international environment, where each nation is assumed to pursue its own self-interests, "talk is cheap" and actions speak louder than words (Axelrod, 1984).

11 Relationships of Hierarchy and Topics to Conflict Management Styles: A Comparative Study

M. Kamil Kozan

With the globalization of business activities, a greater need seems to exist now than ever before for studies of organizational behavior in different cultures. This is especially true for empirical studies of managerial practice in developing countries. A review of this literature found this need even more pronounced for conflict management (Kiggundu, Jorgensen, & Hafsi, 1983).

Conflict has emerged as a major subfield of organizational behavior in the West, as both scholars and practitioners realized its inevitability in organizational life. The emphasis in the field has gradually shifted from harms or uses of conflict toward its management, including the different styles of handling conflict.

Studies of conflict management styles in non-Western cultures, including the third world, should have important implications for management practice. Increasing numbers of third world countries are choosing rapid industrialization and encouraging domestic firms to adopt new technologies and open up to global markets. Hence, an understanding of how their managers deal with conflicts may help both these countries to deal more effectively with the pains of modernization and Western managers to understand better the styles of their counterparts.

The objective of this study is to investigate the conflict management behavior of managers in two Middle-Eastern countries: Turkey and Jordan. Both of these countries are in a period of transition from a traditional to a modern industrialized society. However, their achievements have been modest. They share a level of per capita income that fluctuates around $1200. Their growing industries, which include chemicals, paper, textiles, and food processing (plus durables and automotive in Turkey) is heavily protected from foreign competition. The state operates public works and utility companies in both countries.

Several cultural commonalities exist between the two countries as well. They are geographically close and have been part of the same empire for several decades. The overwhelming majority of both populations are Sunni Moslems. A couple of differences may nevertheless have to be mentioned, lest we overlook the uniqueness of these seemingly close cultures. First, Turkish and Arabic are totally different languages, the former belonging to the Ural-Altaic and the latter to the Indo-European language family. More will be said later on the implications of this language difference and its relation to verbal behavior in the two countries. Second, the extended family or tribe seems to be a key factor to an understanding of the Jordanian society, but it is not as much a prominent aspect of most of the Turkish society. Despite differences, however, the modernization efforts of the two countries against a basically traditional background undoubtedly creates an interesting setting for the study of conflict in their organizations.

Organizational conflict takes various forms, such as dyadic conflict, involving persons or groups, and coalition behavior, involving more than two parties. This study was confined to dyadic interpersonal conflict behavior of managerial personnel. The study used a model of conflict management styles that has had widespread application in the field (Blake & Mouton, 1964; Thomas, 1976; Rahim, 1983a). The model identifies five styles of conflict management, based on different combinations of high and low levels of a party's concern for self and for the other. The *dominating* style involves the use of power to have one's position get accepted. At the other extreme, *obliging* represents trying to satisfy the other party's wishes at the expense of one's own. In between these two extremes lies *compromising,* or splitting the difference, with both parties giving up something in order to find a middle ground. *Avoiding,* a style reflecting low concern for self and others, takes the form of sidestepping the issue and shying away from its open discussion. *Integrating,* which is high in both dimensions, involves facing the conflict, bringing all pertinent issues and concerns out into the open, and, as a result, reaching a solution that integrates the different points of view.

A manager's preference for one or another style may depend on a variety of factors. A review of the literature led Thomas (1976) to identify several such factors including the personality characteristics of the conflicting parties, behavioral norms encouraged by relatively neutral onlookers, the reward structure, and the rules and procedures governing decision making once conflict arises. The present study likewise examined how the likelihood of using each style was affected when certain aspects of the conflict situation were altered. The variables chosen for this purpose were the authority position of the other party and the topic of conflict.

The authority position of the other party, whether he/she is a superior, subordinate, or peer, seems to influence a manager's style. In a large-scale survey of U.S. managers, Rahim (1986b) found that managers were primarily obliging with superiors, integrating with subordinates, and compromising with peers. Rahim explains these findings in terms of the constraining influence of hierarchical relations on the behavior of members in an organization. The hierarchy dimension can be expected to be at least as salient a factor in organizational conflicts in both Turkey and Arab countries, where power distance between superior and subordinates is high (Hofstede, 1983). Centralized decision making seems to characterize managerial practice in both Turkey (Bradburn, 1963; Badawy, 1980) and Jordan (Adwan, 1983; Badawy, 1980). These characteristics may lead us to expect more assertive and less accommodative styles to be used toward subordinates in the two countries than, for example, in the United States.

Studies in the United States have also shown that conflict management styles are affected by the topic and the source of conflict. Renwick (1975) found a tendency to use problem solving when salaries, promotions or performance appraisals were involved and to rely on compromising in dealing with conflict concerning personal habits and mannerisms. She further reported that disagreements originating from substantive factors were more likely to be openly acknowledged and confronted than affective conflicts, which have their sources in personality or attitude differences. Phillips and Cheston (1979) also found problem solving to be used more in conflicts caused by communication failures and structural factors, such as conflicting objectives, than in conflicts resulting from incompatible personal goals or values.

The impact of culture needs to be examined here again. The organizational atmosphere in Latin America and the Middle East has been described as embodying a personal tone of administration and emotionally involved relationships (Bourgeois & Boltvinik, 1981; Badawy, 1980). Would this result in more assertive styles in dealing with conflicts involving personality issues than those concerning organizational policies or salaries?

The present study aimed at understanding conflict-handling behavior over a variety of topics and with different parties within each culture studied. It did not adopt an interactive perspective, examining conflict between managers from different cultures, for example, between Western managers and their counterparts in Turkey and Jordan. However, comparisons with conflict management practice in the United States are drawn whenever comparable findings are available.

METHOD

Subjects

Data in Turkey were collected from 14 private and 8 public organizations in Istanbul, the industrial and commercial center of the country, and Ankara, the capital and second largest city. Jordanian data were collected from 10 private and 5 public organizations in the capital city of Amman, which contains nearly 40% of the country's population. In both countries, up to a maximum of 12 respondents were chosen in an organization, the choice being randomly made if the total numbers of the managers exceeded 12. As a result, 259 managers were contacted in Turkey and 150 in Jordan, resulting in usable returns from 215 (83%) and 134 (89%), respectively.

About half of the sample in each country came from manufacturing and mining firms. The remaining half was divided between utility companies, service organizations, and construction firms. The emphasis on major commercial, industrial, and administrative centers in both countries resulted in the exclusion of agricultural enterprises from the sample.

The Jordanian sample was 98% male and had an average age of about 40. Half of the managers had at least a college degree and about one-third were high school graduates. Among the college graduates, 34% had degrees in engineering, and 33% had degrees in business and economics. Top management constituted 14% of the sample, middle management 49%, and the first-line supervisors 37%.

The Turkish sample was 93% male and had a similar average age of 40. Those with college degrees (or higher) constituted 85% of the sample, with an additional 12% having a high school education. Engineers made up 39% of the college graduates, and business and economics majors, 40%. The distribution of respondents in the hierarchy was 22% top management, 60% middle management, and 18% first-line supervisors.

Measurement

Data were collected by means of a questionnaire. The five styles of handling interpersonal conflict were measured by statements adopted from the Rahim Organizational Conflict Inventory-II (Rahim, 1983a). Each statement was worded so as to represent, as much as possible within a sentence, different behaviors depicted in the multi-item ROCI-II. These statements, representing avoiding, dominating, obliging, compromising, and integrating, respectively, are as follows:

I stay away from disagreement and avoid open discussion of differences.
I am firm in my position and use my power to get my view accepted.
I try to accommodate his/her wishes.
I propose a solution halfway between my and his/her wishes to break any deadlock.
I try to bring all of my and his/her concerns out in the open and work for a solution together.

The respondents were asked to indicate how well each statement described their behavior in terms of a 5-point Likert scale (strongly agree to strongly disagree) in Jordan and a dichotomous response scale (agree or disagree) in Turkey. The same set of statements was repeated over different conflict topics. Hence, each manager rated his conflict behavior, using the same set of statements, in conflicts concerning performance appraisal and salaries, proper performance of responsibilities and compliance with rules and procedures, work methods to be used and organizational policies, and personal habits, mannerisms, and values.

The use of a single item for each style made possible repetition and measurement over various conflict topics, as well as calculation of a composite style score covering those topics. The internal consistency (Cronbach's Alpha) of these composite style scores was, for avoiding, obliging, compromising, dominating, and integrating, respectively: .65, .73, .71, .65, and .73 for Turkey and .50, .77, .85, .79, and .77 for Jordan. On the average, 70% of the variance in the composite style scores can therefore be attributed to a common factor, i.e., the style in question.

The questionnaires were translated into Turkish and Arabic, and retranslated into English to ensure reliability, by bilingual colleagues of the author in each country. The respondents filled out the questionnaires alone during work hours at their place of work. Anonymity of responses was assured and questions answered before the questionnaires were administered.

Three different sets of questionnaires were administered, each one involving a different party to the conflict, i.e., subordinate, peer, or superior. A respondent randomly received only one of these sets, which identified, at the beginning and when each topic was introduced, who the party to the conflict was.

RESULTS

Because of language and response scale differences in the questionnaires, analyses were carried out separately for Turkey and Jordan. In both countries, managers seem to prefer some styles over others in general. Table 11.1 shows the preference rankings obtained in each country. Rahim's (1983) findings on U.S. managers are also shown for comparison. A difference in ranking indicates a statistical difference at the .05 level of significance, two tailed, using the paired-samples version of the t-test. A tie is shown where rankings do not differ significantly. On the one hand, both Turkish and Jordanian managers report using integrating the most often, like their counterparts in the United States. On the other hand, they prefer obliging the least and in this regard differ significantly from the U.S. managers. The major difference between Turkey and Jordan is obtained in the use of the dominating style. In their relatively lower preferences for dominating, Jordanian managers resemble U.S. managers more than they do Turkish managers.

The effect of party on style was tested by means of profile analyses, separately run for Turkey and Jordan. In both countries, parallelism of profiles was rejected at the .001 level of significance. A series of multiple discriminant analyses was run in each country to ascertain which style distinguished conflict behavior with different conflict topics. The topical classification used for analysis was based on Renwick (1975) and

TABLE 11.1
Rankings of Preferences for Different Conflict Management Styles in Three Countries[1]

	Turkey	Jordan	United States
Integrating	1	1	1
Compromising	2.5	2	2.5
Dominating	2.5	3.5	4
Avoiding	4	3.5	5
Obliging	5	5	2.5

[1]All parties (superiors, subordinates, and peers) combined; highest prefence = 1.

covered performance appraisal and salaries; personal habits, mannerisms, and values; and work related conflicts. This last category was obtained by combining "proper performance of responsibilities and compliance with rules and procedures" and "work methods to be used and organizational policies." The discriminant analysis used a stepwise selection procedure utilizing Mahallanobis distance as selection criterion. The canonical discriminant functions were rotated using the varimax method. Table 11.2 summarizes the results of the discriminant analyses, including the percentage of cases correctly classified by the rotated discriminant functions.

The styles that distinguish conflict behavior toward different parties in Turkey, irrespective of topic, seem to be dominating with subordinates, obliging with superiors, and avoiding with peers. In Jordan, avoiding and compromising discriminate conflict behavior of managers with peers. The dominating and obliging pattern found in Turkey, which distinguished between conflict with subordinates and superiors, does not seem to hold for Jordanian managers.

The managers in Turkey resemble their counterparts in the United States in their preference for avoiding with peers and obliging with superiors. However, in reporting a preference for dominating with subordinates, they deviate significantly from U.S. managers who prefer integrating with subordinates. Jordanian managers do not seem to be dominating with subordinates, either. Unlike the U.S. managers,

TABLE 11.2
Discriminating Styles of Conflict Management with Different Parties in Turkey and Jordan

		% of Cases Correctly Classified	The Other Party in Conflict		
Country	Topic of Conflict		Subordinate	Superior	Peer
Turkey	Salaries & Performance Appraisal	40	Dominating	—	—
	Work-Related Issues	54	Dominating	Obliging	—
	Personal Habits & Mannerisms	44	Dominating	Obliging	—
	Overall	50	Dominating	Obliging	Avoiding
Jordan	Salaries & Performance Appraisal	51	—	Compromising	Avoiding
	Work-Related Issues	50	Avoiding & Obliging	Compromising & Integrating	—
	Personal Habits & Mannerisms	49	Avoiding & Obliging	Compromising & Integrating	Avoiding
	Overall	45	—	—	Avoiding & Compromising

however, neither integrating nor any other style emerges as the discriminating style against subordinates in Jordan. Furthermore, in reporting little use of obliging toward superiors, managers in Jordan appear to be quite unique in their conflict behavior.

The dominating-obliging pattern found in hierarchical relations in Turkey seems to hold for most topical areas, as well. In both work-related conflicts and personal habits, mannerisms, and values, superiors appear to be dominating and subordinates obliging. In performance appraisal and salaries, the effect of hierarchy is not as strong as in other topics, although some dominating down the hierarchy still exists.

Conflict behavior of Jordanian managers continues to be quite varied from those in Turkey when we consider each individual conflict topic. In work-related issues, Jordanian managers are likely to use more avoiding and obliging than other styles toward subordinates, who, in turn, are inclined to use compromising and collaboration with their superiors. The assertiveness of subordinates increases when we move into personal habits, mannerisms, and values, where they resort to a dominating style along with compromising toward superiors. This behavior is matched by superiors' tendencies to be somewhat obliging and integrating toward their subordinates on these more sensitive issues.

In summary, the results of the study show significant differences between the two Middle-Eastern countries, as well as between each and the United States. Obliging on the part of subordinates is matched by integrating from superiors in the United States. But in Turkey obliging is achieved by dominating by superiors. Obliging does not seem to characterize subordinate behavior toward superiors in Jordan. In Turkey, the impact of hierarchy is most prominent in work-related conflicts, but it seems to carry over to personal habits, mannerisms, and values, as well. In total contrast to Turkey, Jordanian managers are less assertive toward subordinates, even to the point of being obliging when personal issues are at stake.

DISCUSSION

Studies of organizational behavior in Turkey support the pattern of conflict management behavior found in the present survey. The Turkish culture is distinguished by high power distance (Hofstede, 1983), respect for authority (Kagitcibasi, 1970), centralized administration, and an authoritarian leadership style (Bradburn, 1963; Lauter, 1968). In a study of 16 firms in Turkey, eight of which were subsidiaries of U.S. firms, Lauter consistently found superiors to display a paternalistic, but rather tough and uncompromising, attitude toward their subordinates. Even when participation was encouraged, Lauter reports that subordinates expected top managers to make propositions and then limited their participation to a very careful way identifying possible problem areas without, however, directly contradicting their executives. This tendency complements perfectly the obliging style toward superiors found in the present study.

The underlying authoritarian culture in Turkey may also explain the relative lack of compromising found in conflict behavior. As Dereli (1968) has pointed out, parties to a conflict in Turkey have difficulty in openly and aggressively defending their interests because this stance is likely to find expression in an aggressive phraseology and offend the other party. This difficulty has its roots in family upbringing. Bradburn (1963) reports that few of the businessmen he interviewed in Turkey had ever argued with their fathers and that those who had did so at the price of an open break. Most of the conflict management in the Turkish family is undertaken by a third party, the mother. Hence, the socialization process does not seem to provide the language and emotions with which compromise could be undertaken in adulthood.

Bradburn has further noted that very little differentiation exists in Turkey between personal authority and the authority of the office. This lack of differentiation may explain why the dominating-obliging pattern was observed in conflicts involving personal habits and mannerisms in addition to work-related issues. According to Bradburn the Turkish manager is always "in role" and must be treated as a superior in all situations. Any breakdown of the behavior patterns that characterize superior-subordinate relations would tend to destroy the respect on which authority is based. Consequently, lack of obliging on the part of subordinates in differences involving personal habits and mannerisms is likely to be interpreted as the equivalent of lack of obliging toward superiors in work-related issues.

The conflict management profile that emerged for Jordanian managers poses more problems for interpretation compared with the profile for Turkey. These managers avoided dominating subordinates, but this tendency should not be mistaken for a participative style of management. Centralized decision making is an acknowledged characteristic of management in Jordan (Adwan, 1983), as well as in other Arab countries

(Badawy, 1980; Wright, 1981). For example, nearly three out of four high-level Jordanian public administrators surveyed by Adwan reported that they made decisions without involving their subordinates.

Despite a high level of centralization, though, the absence of a dominating-obliging pattern in superior-subordinate relations in Jordan is quite apparent to the observer who has had a chance to compare organizational functioning in the two cultures. Unlike their counterparts in Turkey, Jordanian employees can easily question decisions made or methods used, resulting in detailed, and sometimes heated, discussions with a superior. Judging from the responses of superiors, such behavior seems acceptable and within the existing norms of conduct. The superiors' basic defense may be to avoid subordinates, as the findings on work-related conflict showed. In the presence of persistent subordinates, however, the ideal manager should be soft and tolerant and, at the same time, skillful in persuasion. The style of Jordanian managers can best be described in terms of Hersey and Blanchards' (1988) "selling" approach.

This managerial style and the ensuing conflict handling behavior fit well within the cultural context these managers function. The Arab culture differs significantly from the Turkish culture in terms of temperament and tolerance of differences. Socialization may play a role here, as individuals experience a more relaxed childhood in Jordan and clearly are treated with more tolerance by elders.

Another aspect of the two cultures, where differences are quite ostensible, is verbal behavior. Observers of Arab culture have argued that Arab society is an expressive verbal society, characterized by an emotional responsiveness to language (Ajami, 1981). Almaney (1981, p. 12) has suggested that "the intrinsic characteristics of Arabic (musicality, resonance, and elegance) coupled with the Arabs' infatuation with sound and form rather than content" lead to extended discussion and debate over issues, often culminating in argumentation for its own sake. Such behavior typically characterizes the way differences are dealt with, regardless of the relative positions of the parties.

In contrast, the handling of differences in Turkey is brisk and clear-cut if an authority relationship between the parties exists. The difficulty in this culture is in dealing with differences by parties on an equal footing, which may call for bargaining and compromise.

The aversion to dominating by Jordanian managers, and the lack of obliging on the part of their subordinates, may have been reinforced by still another cultural feature of this country. It was noted earlier that the tribe was a much more prominent aspect of Jordanian society in comparison with Turkey. The presence of a powerful status system in the social environment of Jordanian organizations competes and interferes with their formal status systems. Consequently, formal position may not strongly correlate with actual status and power in these organizations. Managers may be well advised to reduce their use of position power and take into consideration the intricacies of inter- and intratribal relationships when dealing with conflict. In conclusion, the dissimilarities found in the present survey on conflict behavior of managers may be the likely outcome of the contrasting temperaments and tolerances of differences embodied in these two cultures and of their varying social structures.

IMPLICATIONS FOR CONFLICT
MANAGEMENT ACROSS CULTURES

The contrasting pattern of conflict handling behavior of Turkish and Jordanian managers may seem unexpected in the light of the outward similarities of the two cultures. International management scholars have placed heavy emphasis on factors like level of economic development, geographical proximity, and religion in understanding culture and their effects on management practice. As a result, advice to practicing managers in the international field sometimes perpetuates our ignorance of differences in a seemingly homogeneous region. Writers who give blanket treatment to a region or countries sharing the same religion, under titles such as "styles of Mid-Eastern managers" or "organizational behavior in Islamic firms," may actually be offering limited help. A more useful but tedious approach is to determine the unique characteristics of each national culture in order to draw implications for international management.

The prevalence of a strong authoritarian management tradition is the key to understanding Turkish managers' handling of differences. This tradition is also quite pervasive, affecting the more Westernized organizations, as well. For example, little difference in leadership style was found between Turkish firms and subsidiaries of U.S. firms operating in Turkey (Lauter, 1968). Foreign managers doing business in this country should appreciate the importance of "being in control" for Turkish managers and should be careful not to undermine their authority over subordinates. The leadership style that employees favor the most in Turkey is that of the benevolent autocrat (Ilter, 1983). Hence, expatriates who are comfortable with working at both the giving and receiving end of such authority relationships may have the best chance of success in foreign subsidiaries in Turkey.

Working with Jordanians, however, may require a totally different attitude and set of skills. Western managers who have found a working style in eliciting an obliging response from subordinates in return for their participative approach should not expect the same here. Unlike Turkey, where subordinates were quite obliging, albeit in response to a dominating style, an obliging attitude from subordinates could not easily be achieved in Jordan. Handling of differences called for extraordinary patience and use of persuasive skills on the part of managers.

This undoubtedly contrasts with popularly held views of Arabs in the West, reinforced largely through media coverage of political conflicts in the region. This is not to imply that conflict was basically played down or smoothed over in Jordanian organizations. Actually, bargaining and compromising were quite widespread. Yet, this was done in a style that conformed to cultural norms. A thorough understanding of these values is essential to doing business in this country. For example, a Western manager who feels pressure for faster results should nevertheless avoid forcing the issue. Deliberate use of power tactics is likely to have adverse effects in this culture. It may also turn the disagreement into a personal issue, making it altogether unmanageable.

Jordanian managers were quite sensitive over personal habits and mannerisms, and their superiors seemed to be cautious concerning their subordinates' sensitivity by being a little obliging on these issues. Hence, an understanding of rituals and behavioral norms may be required here. Foreigners who do not feel confident in this area should avoid trying to solve differences on their own. They may rather let their Arab counterparts to deal with subordinates or peers as they are much better equipped with the art of persuasion and compromising used in handling differences in this culture.

The effectiveness of the contrasting profiles of conflict management in Turkey and Jordan remains as a question. The present survey was limited to describing how managers dealt with differences in these two cultures. The reluctance of Jordanian managers to use their authority to attain organizational goals seems to lower the efficiency of organized effort. The effects of this style were already apparent in the extraordinarily slow way in which Jordanian organizations functioned. By contrast, Turkish managers seem to get quicker results from subordinates.

But the cumulative effect of overreliance on authority may prove counterproductive as well. It seems to work best under crisis situations, where use of power is more easily justified. In the long run, however, it may reduce, to a minimum, initiative and innovativeness on the part of subordinates. Further studies assessing the effectiveness of the different styles of handling conflict for various topics are needed to address these issues.

12   Deterrence and the Management of International Conflict: Cognitive Aspects of Deterrent Decisions

Roderick Kramer, Debra Meyerson, and Gerald Davis

> A healthy and fully functioning society must allocate its resources among a variety of competing interests, all of which are more or less valid, but none of which should take precedence over national security (p. 32).
> — Herman Kahn (1984), former RAND nuclear strategist

> National Will involves far more than the readiness to use military power . . . it includes a readiness to allocate the resources necessary to maintain that power . . . (and) a clear view of where the dangers lie (p. 54).
> — Richard Nixon (1980), former U.S. president

Individuals and organizations rely on many constructive approaches to keep conflict within manageable limits. The two members of a business partnership, for example, may rely on the norm of reciprocity in order to ensure that, on balance, each partner is able to achieve fair outcomes in the relationship. Trust in reciprocity helps them avoid potentially destructive conflict. Along related lines, organizations regulate their competition with other organizations by means of a variety of implicit normative and legal constraints. Although they might engage in derogatory advertising, for example, they do not destroy a competitor's warehouses or physically attack its corporate officers. Moreover, if serious conflict does erupt, they have available to them various formal remedies, such as third-party arbitration or criminal prosecution.

In contrast, nation states face unique difficulties when trying to avoid conflict with other nations. The difficulties encountered by the United States and Soviet Union in trying to avert a nuclear confrontation are in many respects prototypic of such difficulties. First, because the costs of misplaced trust are potentially catastrophic, approaches such as reciprocity, which are predicated on voluntary compliance, are likely to be regarded as ineffective or risky. Second, to the extent that nations typically do not recognize the authority of other nations to interfere with their sovereign affairs, third-party remedies are often ineffective. In this sense, the international environment is fundamentally anarchic. Consequently, each nation must protect its own self-interests and guarantee its own security by whatever means it has available to it.

As this example illustrates, many of the conflict management mechanisms available for dealing with interpersonal and interorganizational conflicts are not applicable to the international level. What mechanisms do nations use, then, to avoid conflict and enhance their security? For the past 40 years, the theory of deterrence has played a singularly important role in conceptualizing how nations avoid conflict with potential adversaries (Frei, 1986; Kahan, 1975; Miller, 1984). In suggesting that the theory "works," proponents of deterrence have cited the historical record. Although half a dozen nations possess nuclear arsenals and more than 50,000 nuclear weapons are deployed around the world, these weapons have not been used during any international conflict since the end of World War II. Moreover, despite several periods of acute confrontation, nuclear war between the United States and Soviet Union has been avoided for four decades. Given the enormous destructive potential of these weapons and the ever present danger of inadvertent or miscalculated war, this record has bred neither confidence nor complacency. Instead, there has been a resurgence of interest among social scientists in the problem of managing international conflict in the nuclear age and in clarifying the role that deterrence plays in doing so (Jervis, Lebow, & Stein, 1985; Oskamp, 1985; Tetlock, 1986; White, 1986).

In its purest form, deterrence theory possesses a compelling, if not beguiling, logic: deterrence entails dissuading potential adversaries of the United States from initiating aggression against it by posing the prospect of risks and costs that outweigh any gain such adversaries might contemplate (Snyder, 1961). The theory thus posits that possession of a credible and sufficient nuclear deterrent will enhance a nation's security whereas the absence of such a deterrent will undermine it. As simple as this sounds, it has proven enormously difficult to achieve an enduring sense of security through deterrence alone (McNamara, 1968; Smoke, 1984).

One reason that a sense of security has remained so elusive may be a consequence of the fact that efforts by one nation to increase its security by building up a massive nuclear deterrent tend to threaten the security of others. This is the essence of what Robert Jervis termed the "security dilemma" (1978). As a consequence of this dilemma, deciding just how much of a nuclear deterrent to deploy in order to avoid conflict has remained problematic for those responsible for formulating nuclear strategy and national security policy. On the one hand, too little may fail to deter. On the other hand too much may provoke adversaries to reciprocate, leading to dangerous and costly arms races whereby each nation ends up less secure than it was in the beginning.

Decisions about "how much is enough" obviously depend, to a large extent, on decision makers' perceptions of the level of threat in the strategic environment and their judgments regarding the need for additional security (Jervis, 1982, 1985). Because of the central role that perceptions play in such decisions, recent critical discussions of deterrence theory have emphasized the need for more research on the relationship between psychological processes and deterrent decisions (Fischer, 1983; Jervis, 1986; Tetlock, 1986).

How do decision makers decide how much security is enough in these situations? How does one country assess the threat posed by the other's nuclear arsenals? Many of the classic studies of these questions have focused on the role rational or objective criteria play in national security decisions and threat assessments (e.g., Enthoven & Smith, 1971). More recently, attention has been drawn to the need for a better understanding of how psychological factors affect these decisions (Fischer, 1983; Fischhoff, 1983; Jervis, Lebow, & Stein, 1985; Lebow, 1987; Stein, 1988; Tetlock, 1986). Stein (1988), for example, has commented that "current theories do not systematically consider the critical interaction among cognitive heuristics and biases and their cumulative impact on the misperception of threat in international relations" (p. 246).

The present research was designed to investigate the relationship between cognitive processes and security decisions. The research was motivated by the security salience hypothesis (Kramer, 1989). According to this general hypothesis, the decision to allocate resources to security is influenced by the perceived need for additional security. In the experiments described in this paper, we examined how three cognitive processes — imagining hypothetical scenarios, psychological accounting, and decision framing — affect the salience of security needs and individuals' decisions to allocate economic resources to security.

"GUNS VERSUS BUTTER" TRADEOFF

From a psychological standpoint, decisions regarding "how much is enough" are complex because they require decision makers to make a tradeoff between increasing their security (guns) or wealth (butter). Because each country's economic resources are finite, allocating substantial resources to security means fewer resources available to achieve other goals, such as reducing a national deficit or improving social welfare.

As a result of this "guns versus butter" tradeoff, decision makers must choose between gaining security (and enduring the economic losses associated with doing so) or increasing their economic wealth (but at the risk of losing security). Both historical case studies and laboratory experiments have found that decision makers often find tradeoffs of this sort difficult to resolve (George, 1980; Jervis, 1986; Slovic, 1975; Steinbruner, 1974; Tetlock & McGuire, 1986). Instead, they tend to avoid them or attempt to minimize their psychological consequences.

The avoidance of decisional tradeoffs can reflect a number of different psychological mechanisms, including the desire to maintain the appearance of consistency of balance among cognitions (Steinbruner, 1974), as well as cognitive limitations of decision makers (Abelson & Levi, 1985; Tetlock & McGuire, 1986). One way in which decision makers resolve tradeoffs is to "focus on *one salient value dimension* on which choice alternatives vary and *screen out* of consideration any countervailing differences on *other value dimensions*" (Abelson & Levi, 1985, p. 288, emphases added). In the present experiments, we were interested in examining how the salience of information during decision making affects the resolution of "guns versus butter" tradeoffs. We propose that the extent to which one attribute of a decision (e.g., security) tends to dominate or "loom large" relative to another (e.g., wealth) during decision making is influenced by at least three distinct psychological processes.

The "guns versus butter" dilemma arises because it is impossible for decision makers to simultaneously maximize both security and wealth. Consequently, gains in one domain necessarily entail losses in the other. According to normative or prescriptive models of choice, individuals should evaluate such gains and losses in terms of their absolute outcomes or consequences (Tversky & Kahneman, 1986). For example, they should evaluate the acceptability of a given "guns versus butter" allocation in terms of the resultant gains and losses in security and wealth it entails.

In contrast with these normative models, recent studies of "psychological accounting" processes in decision making have shown that, rather than evaluate gains and losses in terms of absolute or final outcomes, individuals often evaluate them relative to initially presented values (Kahneman & Tversky, 1982, 1984a; Thaler, 1985). These initial values represent implicit reference points against which alternative states or outcomes are subsequently compared.

For example, the purchase of a $750 car stereo may be perceived as a large (and unacceptable) cost when evaluated by itself. However, when contemplated along with the purchase of an expensive new car, the price of the stereo may seem like a relatively small additional expenditure. As this example illustrates, the evaluation of monetary expenses or losses can be affected by the psychological "accounts" in which they are placed. When the cost of the car stereo is evaluated in terms of a mental account that includes the total costs of the car, it is perceived as more acceptable than when evaluated in the context of an account that assumes a reference state of zero expenses. Because of psychological accounting, decision makers tend "to evaluate gains and losses in *relative* rather than absolute terms, resulting in large variations in the rate at which money is exchanged for other things" (Kahneman & Tversky, 1984a, p. 347).

In Experiment 1, we investigated how implicit reference points associated with "guns versus butter" decisions influence decision makers' willingness to allocate resources to security. These reference points, we argue, define initial states of health and security that affect the salience of the tradeoff between them. Specifically, we hypothesize that when decisions are described in terms of reference points implying security is low relative to wealth, the perceived need for additional security will be high. Consequently, individuals will allocate more resources to security in order to reduce this perceived deficit. Under these circumstances, the tradeoff between security and wealth has low salience. In contrast, when decisions are described so as to suggest that both security and wealth are low, individuals must explicitly choose between increasing one or the other. As a result, salience of the tradeoff between them will be high, and they will allocate fewer resources to security (Hypothesis 1).

IMAGINING HYPOTHETICAL SCENARIOS

Even if individuals decide they need to increase their security, determining precisely how much additional security is needed is problematic because of two sources of uncertainty characteristic of security dilemmas. First, decision makers may be uncertain of an adversary's intentions. Because nuclear weapons can be used either offensively or defensively, it is often difficult to determine the intentions behind an adversary's military expenditures (Jervis, 1976, 1978). Uncertainty may also exist with respect to an adversary's nuclear capabilities (Kahan, 1975). Because nations often use disinformation and strategic deception to try to misrepresent or conceal their actual capabilities, others may be uncertain how many nuclear weapons they secretly possess (Downs, Rocke, & Siverson, 1986; Kahan, 1975; Smoke, 1984).

Uncertainty regarding an adversary's intentions and capabilities poses a severe dilemma for decision makers trying to decide "how much is enough." Independent of any real increase in the number of weapons it stockpiles, a nation can attempt to mislead others into believing that it has many more or fewer weapons than it actually does. In the late 1950s, for example, the Soviet Union attempted to convince U.S. leaders that Soviet nuclear capabilities were substantially greater than they were at the time. This led U.S. decision makers to be concerned about the possibility of a "missile gap" between the United States and Soviet Union (Smoke, 1984).

Historical evidence suggests that decision makers often respond to such uncertainties by adopting "worst-case" assumptions when determining how much security they need (Kahan, 1975; Lebow, 1987). For example, U.S. national security decisions have frequently been based on worst-case scenarios regarding Soviet intentions and capabilities. Although there is a normative logic to such worst-case forecasting (Garthoff, 1978), virtually no empirical research has examined how the act of imagining such scenarios actually affects decision makers' judgments regarding security needs. In Experiment 1, we addressed this issue by experimentally manipulating the content of scenarios individuals imagined before making security decisions. Specifically, we compared decision making under conditions of worst- versus best-case assumptions regarding an adversary's intentions and capabilities.

Why should imagining purely hypothetical events affect decision making? A number of studies have found that actively visualizing and rehearsing possible outcomes caused decision makers to judge those outcomes as more likely to actually occur (Carroll, 1978; Hoch, 1984; Kahneman & Tversky, 1984b; Ross, Lepper, Strack, & Steinmetz, 1977; Sherman, Cialdini, Schwartzman, & Reynolds, 1985). For example, Sherman et al. (1985) reported that individuals' estimates of the probability they would contract a disease were affected by having first imagined symptoms associated with contracting it.

Based on these studies, we hypothesized that imagining hypothetical outcomes would have two effects. First, we predicted that when decision makers imagine worst-case scenarios regarding an adversary's intentions, they will perceive such scenarios as more probable. Second, we predicted that they will respond to such worst-case expectations by increasing their own security (Hypothesis 2).

To investigate these hypotheses, a laboratory analogue of a security dilemma was developed. The purpose of an analogue experiment is to recreate those abstract properties or processes of a real-world social system of interest to a researcher, but in a scaled-down version that enables him or her to examine them under the controlled conditions of the laboratory. The results from two recent studies are described here.

STUDY 1

Method

Design of the Study and Subjects

Experiment 1 employed a 2 x 2 (Salience of Tradeoffs x Type of Scenario Imagined) between-subjects factorial design. Forty-eight students participated in the experiment to complete a course requirement and to earn money.

Procedure

On the arrival at the laboratory, subjects were put in isolated cubicles. The task was described as a decision-making study involving the allocation of scarce resources. Subjects were informed they would be interacting with one other student located in another cubicle. Each of them would have a monetary account and a security account. At the start of each trial, they would both be given 50 resource units ("points") and would have to decide how many to secretly allocate to their monetary accounts and how many to allocate to their security accounts. After making these secret allocations, they would then make a second strategic or "announced" decision, which would be relayed by the experimenter to the other person. Subjects were told that their announced security allocations could be larger or smaller than their secret allocations, subject to the constraint that they be within 20 points of their secret decisions. Thus, subjects could use their announced decision to misrepresent (i.e., under- or over-report) their true security levels to the person with whom they were paired.

Subjects were informed that the points they allocated to their monetary accounts were worth money. At the end of the experiment, they would be paid one cent for every point in their secret monetary accounts. Security resources were not worth money, but they could be used either offensively to try to seize the other person's monetary resources or defensively to protect their own monetary resources from seizure.

Subjects were told that if they accumulated at least 300 security points, they could use a "take option" to try to seize (attack) the other's monetary resources. An attack was successful if the attacker had more resources in his or her secret security account than the defender. If successful, the attacker received all the defender's monetary resources. If unsuccessful, the attacker lost all his or her monetary and security resources. Because each subject's actual security allocations were secret, it was not possible for them to determine how much security the person with whom they were interacting had accumulated. Moreover, because direct communication between subjects was prohibited, they could not determine whether the other person's intentions were offensive or defensive.

Salience of the Tradeoff between Security and Wealth. To manipulate the salience of the tradeoff between wealth and security, we varied the initial reference points associated with subjects' decisions. Subjects were given "accounting ledgers," ostensibly to help them keep tract of their allocation decisions. These ledgers were used to introduce the experimental manipulation. In the Low Salience of Tradeoffs Condition, subjects were told to initially add all their 50 resources to their monetary account at the start of the first trial. They then had to decide how many of these monetary resources to reallocate to security. In the High Tradeoffs

Condition, subjects did not deposit their 50 resources in their monetary accounts initially. Instead, they were told they had to decide how many resources to allocate to their monetary account and how many to allocate to their security account.

To understand the logic of this manipulation, it is important to note that these two decisions are economically equivalent from the standpoint of their final outcomes. For example, in either condition, allocating 10 resources to security resulted in a net increase of 10 units of security and 40 units of wealth. Thus, on the one hand, if decision makers evaluate their choices in terms of their absolute outcomes, these two decisions should be perceived as identical. If, on the other hand, psychological accounting leads decision makers to evaluate their options in terms of initial states of security and wealth, then these conditions may seem quite different. In the Low Tradeoffs Condition, subjects initially have a maximum amount of wealth, but no security. Thus, the perceived need for additional security should be high. In the High Tradeoffs Condition, in contrast, subjects' initial states of wealth and security are equal (both at "0"). Relative to this starting point, they must explicitly choose between increasing their wealth or security. Thus, we argue, the tradeoff between increasing wealth and security should be more salient.

Imagining Manipulation. Subjects were told that earlier research with this task had found that individuals often use a variety of strategies when deciding how to allocate their resources. Some use primarily defensive (protective) strategies whereas others use offensive (competitive) strategies. Accordingly, one purpose of the present study was to better understand how individuals think about the strategic possibilities inherent in these situations. Half of the subjects were then asked to list as many allocation strategies as they could think of that others might use if they had primarily offensive or competitive intentions. This was the Worst-Case Scenario Condition. In the Best-Case Scenario Condition, subjects were asked to list strategies others might use if they had primarily defensive or cooperative intentions. Subjects worked on their lists for ten minutes and then completed a pretrial questionnaire.

Upon completion of the questionnaire, subjects made what they thought was the first of a series of allocation decisions. They recorded their secret allocation in their ledgers and wrote their announced decision on a slip of paper, which the experimenter collected. After a brief pause, the experimenter returned and gave each subject a similar slip of paper, ostensibly written by the person with whom they were paired. Actually, each subject received identical false feedback indicating that the other person had announced a security allocation of 25 points.

Subjects recorded the other person's announced decision in their ledgers. At this point, the experimenter informed subjects there would be no additional trials. Subjects completed a brief questionnaire, were debriefed, thanked, and paid $5 for their participation.

Results

Manipulation Checks

To assess the impact of the experimental manipulations on subjects' perceptions, two pretrial questions were included. First, before making their allocations, subjects estimated how likely they thought it was that the other person would use the attack option at some point during their interaction (7-point scale; 1 = Not at all likely; 7 = Very likely). These data were analyzed by means of a 2 x 2 (Salience of Tradeoffs x Imagining) analysis of variance (ANOVA). There was a main effect for imagining, $F(1,44) = 16.60$, $p < .01$. Individuals estimated the likelihood of being attacked to be substantially greater in the worst-case condition ($M = 6.4$) than in the best-case condition ($M = 5.0$).

Subjects also indicated whether they thought the need for additional security was low or high (1 = low; 7 = high). There was a main effect for the salience of tradeoffs manipulation, $F(1,44) = 6.60$, $p < .02$. Subjects perceived the need for security to be greater in the Low Tradeoff Condition ($M = 6.1$) compared to those in the High Tradeoffs Condition ($M = 5.3$). There was also a marginally significant main effect for imagining, $F(1,44) = 2.97$, $p < .11$. Subjects tended to perceive less need for security after imagining best-case scenarios ($M = 5.4$) compared to those who had contemplated worst-case outcomes ($M = 6.0$).

Security Allocations

The primary dependent variables in this study are individuals' secret (actual) and announced security allocations. Because each subject made both an actual and announced allocation, these data were analyzed by means of a 2 x 2 (Salience of Tradeoffs x Imagining) ANOVA with repeated measures, using subjects' secret and announced security allocations as dependent variables.

There was a main effect for the salience of tradeoffs variable, $F(1,44) = 5.49, p < .05$. Hypothesis 1 was supported: individuals allocated more resources to security in the Low Tradeoffs Condition ($M = 38.08$) compared to those in the High Tradeoffs Condition ($M - 27.33$). There was also a main effect for imagining, $F(1,44) = 6.74, p < .01$. Consistent with Hypothesis 2, individuals who had imagined worst-case scenarios allocated more resources to security ($M = 36.00$) compared to subjects who had imagined best-case scenarios ($M = 29.28$).

There was also a highly significant main effect for the repeated measure, $F(1,44) = 25.05, p < .001$. Subjects chose to announce lower security allocations ($M = 23.58$) than they were secretly making ($M = 32.70$). Thus, the level of strategic deception across conditions was quite high.

Discussion of Study 1

The results of Experiment 1 provide strong support for the hypothesis that implicit reference points affect how decision makers resolve tradeoffs between guns and butter. This pattern is consistent with the assumption that psychological accounting leads individuals to evaluate such tradeoffs in relative rather than absolute terms. In assessing the external validity of this result, it is important to consider the extent to which such reference points vary in the case of real-world national security decisions. What correspondence is there between these experimental manipulations of reference points and the structure of decisions confronting actual policy makers? We suggest that policy makers may implicitly evaluate defense expenditures in terms of at least two distinctive psychological accounts. One natural reference point places defense expenditures in the context of the total wealth available for allocation (e.g., the total federal budget for a given year). Our results suggest that, when evaluated with this reference point in mind, a given defense allocation might be perceived as moderate or reasonable for at least two reasons. First, the expenditure may seem small because it constitutes only a tiny proportion of resources that might have been allocated for defense. As Thaler (1985) noted, losses tend to be less aversive when placed in the context of large accounts. Second, when decisions are described in ways that make the "stakes" appear large, the costs of protecting those stakes are likely to be perceived as more legitimate because they provide insurance (Slovic, Fischhoff, & Lichtenstein, 1982).

An alternative reference point available to policy makers assumes a state of zero expenditures for defense. Relative to this starting point, decision makers must explicitly decide how to divide their allocatable resources between security and wealth. Under these circumstances, we argue, the explicit tradeoffs between increasing security and wealth "loom larger" during decision making. It should be noted that real-world policy makers often intentionally manipulate reference points in just such a fashion. The practice of zero-based budgeting entails evaluating allocation decisions in terms of a reference state that assumes no expenditure for a given budget item. Our experimental results suggest why this practice is effective.

The results of Experiment 1 also suggest that selectively imagining best-case versus worst-case scenarios can influence individuals' perceptions of threat and judgments regarding how much security they need to meet those threats. Why should the act of imagining purely hypothetical outcomes affect decisions in this fashion? Previous studies suggest that imagining or "cognitively rehearsing" outcomes increases their availability in memory. Because decision makers may use ease of recall or availability as a cue when judging the probability of future events (Kahneman & Tversky, 1984b; Sherman et al., 1985), imagining a particular scenario may lead to inflated estimates of the likelihood it will subsequently occur.

Consistent with this interpretation, analysis of posttrial data collected during the experiment revealed that subjects who had imagined worst-case scenarios attributed more competitive motives to the person with whom they were supposedly interacting compared to subjects in the best-case condition. This result is rather striking because identical information regarding the other's announced allocation was provided to subjects in both conditions. Thus, there was no objective basis for this differential appraisal.

In this first study, we focused attention on how variations in initial endowments of wealth and security affect decision making. Decisions can also be "framed," however, in terms of their perceived outcomes or consequences (Kahneman & Tversky, 1982, 1984a). To investigate the impact of decision framing on security decisions, we conducted a second study.

STUDY 2

According to the security salience hypothesis, when the perceived need for security is high, decision makers focus attention primarily on increasing security. The results of Experiment 1 demonstrated that implicit reference points can affect how much weight or attention is given to the costs associated with doing so. One reason why individuals may give less attention to such costs is that outcomes or consequences that are "out of sight" tend to remain "out of mind" during decision making (Slovic, Fischhoff, & Lichtenstein, 1982). Slovic et al. (1982) have characterized this as the "dominance of explicit or surface information," noting that "decision makers appear to use only the information that is explicitly displayed in the formulation of a problem. Information that has to be inferred from the display or created by some mental transformation tends to be ignored" (p. 24).

One implication of Slovic et al.'s analysis is that increasing the salience of those dimensions of a tradeoff that are "out of sight and out of mind" should ameliorate the tendency to underweight them during decision making. In Experiment 2, we investigated this possibility. A major factor found to affect the salience or dominance of surface information is decision framing (Kahneman & Tversky, 1984a; Tversky & Kahneman, 1986). According to Kahneman and Tversky's prospect theory (1982), when decisions are framed in terms of gains, decision makers tend to be risk averse, preferring smaller but certain gains over larger but uncertain ones. In contrast, when decisions are framed in terms of losses they tend to be risk seeking, preferring to risk the prospect of larger but uncertain losses rather than accept certain (sure) losses. On the basis of prospect theory, we hypothesized that individuals would allocate less to security when their decisions were framed in terms of monetary losses (the costs of security) compared to when they were framed in terms of monetary gains (the savings from not spending on security) (Hypothesis 3).

The effects of decision framing may also depend, however, on the initial reference points associated with individuals' decisions. Experiment 1 found that the extent to which decision makers are sensitive to the costs of security was dependent on the initial status of their wealth and security. Therefore, we expected that framing decisions in terms of economic losses associated with security allocations would have the greatest impact when the perceived need for security is low. When the need for security is high, framing effects should be attenuated because security needs "loom large" relative to monetary losses (Hypothesis 4).

Method

Design of the Study and Subjects

Fifty-six students participated in the second experiment in exchange for an opportunity to earn money. The experiment employed a 2 x 2 (Salience of Tradeoffs x Decision Framing) factorial design. To manipulate the salience of tradeoffs between wealth and security, we employed the same reference point manipulation that we used in Experiment 1. Decision frame was varied so as to make salient either economic gains (savings) or losses (costs) associated with security allocations.

Procedure

The task used in Experiment 2 was similar to Experiment 1, except for the following procedural differences. First, in Experiment 2 subjects actually interacted with each other by means of a DEC-20 computer, which controlled pairs of linked terminals. Thus, on each trial, subjects actually did send their announced allocation to another person with whom they were linked. To guarantee that subjects did not communicate any other information or violate the constraint that their actual and announced decisions had to be within 20 points of each other, the experimenter monitored all subjects' decisions at a third terminal. The other main procedural difference was that, rather than terminate the experiment after the first allocation, the trials continued until either one of the subjects in a dyad attacked the other or the time allotted for the experiment had elapsed.

Subjects were told it was possible to earn up to $10 ($.50 per trial x 20 trials) during the experiment. In addition to the accounting ledgers used in Experiment 1, each subject was given a scale that ranged from $0 to $10, calibrated in $.20 increments. Decision frame was manipulated by varying the instructions subjects received regarding how to use these scales. Subjects in the Gains Salient Condition were told the scale should be used to keep track of their monetary gains across trials. These subjects were told to add the number of resources they had allocated to their monetary accounts on each trial to the scale, starting at the $0 point. Subjects in the Losses Salient Condition were told they should use the scale to keep track of the costs of security during the trials. Starting at the $10 endpoint on the scale, they subtracted the number of resources they had allocated to security from the monetary scale. Thus, in the first condition, subjects kept track of how much they were saving by not spending on security; in the second they kept track of how much they were spending for security.

Results of Experiment 2

Our primary concern here is with the impact of the experimental manipulations on subjects' first trial allocations. These initial decisions provide the cleanest test of the hypotheses because they were made before subjects had received any information regarding the announced allocations of the other person and are thus free of any influence from this person's behavior.

Initial Allocation Decisions

We performed a 2 x 2 (Salience of Tradeoffs x Decision Frame) ANOVA with repeated measures, using subjects' initial secret and announced decisions as the repeated factor. There was a significant main effect for decision frame, $F(1,52) = 4.12$, $p < .05$ and a marginally significant effect for salience of tradeoffs, $F(1,52) = 3.74$, $p < .06$. There was also a significant interaction between them, $F(1,52) = 8.10$, $p < .01$. As predicted by Hypothesis 4, subjects in the High Tradeoffs Condition secretly allocated fewer resources to security when monetary losses were salient ($M = 23.31$) than when gains were salient ($M = 39.60$). In other words, feedback regarding the economic losses associated with security had the greatest impact on subjects' decisions when the need for additional security seemed low. When security needs "loomed larger" (the Low Tradeoffs Condition), in contrast, there was no difference between the gains ($M = 34.85$) and losses frame ($M = 35.43$).

As in the first experiment, there was a highly significant main effect for the repeated measure, $F(1,52) = 31.61$, $p < .001$. Across the experimental conditions, subjects chose to consistently announce less security ($M = 23.96$) than they were secretly building up ($M = 33.12$).

Process Data

In addition to these behavioral effects, we also found evidence that the experimental manipulations had affected subjects' perceptions of threat and security even before they had started interacting with each other. Before the first trial, subjects were asked to estimate the likelihood (7-point scale, 1 = Not at all; 7 = Very) that the other person would use the take option against them during the experiment. There was a significant main effect for the salience of tradeoffs manipulation, $F(1,52)$ = 11.14, $p < .002$, as well as a significant interaction with decision frame, $F(1,52) = 7.13$, $p < .01$. The nature of this interaction was that the threat of attack was perceived to be substantially lower ($M = 4.6$) in the High Tradeoffs/Losses Salient Condition compared to the other conditions (Ms of 6.0, 5.8 and 6.6). This pattern, it should be noted, is consistent with their subsequent allocation decisions.

GENERAL DISCUSSION

Although it has been frequently observed that policy makers find it difficult to resolve complex choice tradeoffs, there has been relatively little research suggesting why such tradeoffs are problematic. Instead, it has been rather uncritically assumed that decisions about deterrence are the product of logically coherent, rational calculations of costs and benefits (see, Jervis, Lebow, & Stein, 1986, and Steinbruner, 1982, 1983, for excellent overviews). In contrast with these approaches, the experiments described in this paper indicate how three distinct cognitive processes can affect how decision makers approach and resolve tradeoffs.

There are, of course, many other factors affecting deterrent decisions. For example, numerous studies (e.g., Domke, Eichenberg, & Kelleher, 1983; Johnson & Wells, 1986; Russett, 1982) have demonstrated that such decisions are complex events and subject to many influences, including macroeconomic conditions, organizational routines, budgetary politics, and emerging technological imperatives, to name only a few (Allison, 1982; Enthoven & Smith, 1971; Hitch & McKeen, 1960). In the present experiments, we did not attempt to simulate any of these important casual elements.

At the same time, we would argue that psychological processes are not necessarily eclipsed or dwarfed by these other factors. Indeed, increasing historical data suggest that cognitive factors do play a major role in national security decisions (Jervis, 1985; Kull, 1988; Stein, 1988; Tetlock, 1986). One direction for future research is to seek evidence of the convergent validity of the present hypotheses by examining policy makers' public statements and memoirs, as well as archival documents, describing the evolution of national security decisions. Content analyses of such statements might provide evidence as to how military and political decision makers spontaneously frame their decisions. Do they tend, for example, to frame them narrowly in terms of security needs alone, ignoring or minimizing the social costs of such decisions? The quotations at the front of this chapter suggest that sometimes policy makers frame allocation decisions in precisely this way. Such statements, we would argue, are highly suggestive of implicit reference points and tacit values that shape a policy maker's professional judgments regarding the priority of security needs relative to other national needs.

Although the results of both experiments support the security salience hypothesis, considerable caution must be exercised when generalizing experimental results to nonlaboratory settings. One limitation of these experiments is the relative inexperience and lack of sophistication of the decision makers. It is not clear how closely the behavior of subjects in these simulated security dilemmas resembles that of real-world political elites. This is a recurring problem with laboratory-based decision research (see Ebbesen & Konecni, 1980, for a recent discussion). For example, are the risk-taking propensities and competitiveness of these subjects similar to that of more experienced decision makers? Do they attend to the same features of the situation when deciding "how much is enough"?

Although this is a difficult question to answer, it has frequently been observed that policy makers confronting real-world security dilemmas have been extremely risk averse and loss averse. As noted earlier, given their belief that failure to maintain a "credible and sufficient" nuclear deterrent might result in a catastrophic loss (e.g., "destruction of the American way of life"), they have often asserted that it is better to err on the side of spending too much on defense rather than too little. A similar pattern of behavior was observed among the participants in these experiments. Subjects regarded the prospect of the sudden loss of all their economic resources to an exploitative other as a significant threat. Realizing that failure to spend enough for security left them vulnerable to such a loss, they appeared to be more than willing to invest substantial resources in security in order to protect their economic well-being.

Obviously, the costs of miscalculating deterrent requirements in these simulations were trivial compared to real-world situations. At the same time, subject involvement with the task was quite high. Process data and postexperimental interviews revealed that the individuals who participated in these experiments regarded the potential monetary gains as significant. In fact, the willingness of defensively oriented individuals to suffer economic losses in order to acquire a deterrent that might or might not turn out to be necessary suggests how motivated such individuals were to minimize their losses given their perception of the situation. Even though these subjects indicated they had no intention of using the take option themselves, they felt the need to have substantial security. As one subject put it, "I would have liked to have earned more, but I had no choice. I knew the other person would 'take' me if I didn't have enough security." Or, as another commented, the problem was to "balance profits and protection, knowing there are others out there who can't be fully trusted." Such comments suggest that the experimental analogue used in this research did capture, even if on a modest scale, some of the psychological facets of a domestic security dilemma. In many respects, such declarations strikingly echo assessments of threats to national security offered by contemporary political leaders (Nixon, 1980, 1983).

Another important question that needs to be addressed in evaluating the external validity of this research is, "In what specific ways might decision frame, as operationalized here, resemble how real-world policy makers imagine or formulate their decisions?" Obviously, in the real world decisions are not as artificially framed as those in the laboratory. However, one might characterize policy makers' images of large-looming windows of vulnerability and threatening missile gaps as manifestations of decision frames imposed by policy makers on complex problems. Of course, such images are also subtly prescriptive: windows ought to be closed and gaps narrowed.

In discussing the relevance of framing research to understanding real-world decisions, Kahneman and Tversky (1984a) speculated that presidential advisors and other decision makers might influence important decisions by inadvertently formulating them so as to increase the attractiveness of certain options. The results of the present experiments may be regarded as at least suggestive of this possibility.

Although many experiments have demonstrated the deleterious effects of decision frame on decision making, relatively little attention has been given to the study of how decisions might be more constructively or "positively" framed in order to offset such effects. This raises an interesting theoretical question: would more positive decision frames increase cooperative interaction among decision makers? And, if so, what would such positive frames look like? One possibility is to frame decisions so that the joint (self-other) consequences of decisions are made salient to individuals. Earlier research on decision framing has examined only how decision frame affects individuals' preferences regarding their own payoffs. In situations involving decisional interdependence, such as security dilemmas, allocation decisions obviously affect both own and others' outcomes. Therefore, one way to increase decision makers' sensitivity to the effects of their own behavior on others might be to frame their decisions so that they incorporate information about the impact of strategic choices on each actor's outcomes. Decisions framed so as to increase, for example, the salience of bilateral gains in security rather than relative gains might promote more cooperative outcomes. This is an important direction for framing research to pursue. If decision frames influence policy decisions to the extent research suggests is possible, and if decision makers are unaware of such effects, then further research is needed to discover general heuristics or approaches that might help attenuate the negative impact of decision frames on strategic allocations.

In the first study, it was observed that individuals tended to overallocate economic resources to security when the decision frame suggested there was much wealth, but a deficit of security available to protect that wealth. One way to reduce this tendency might be to reframe these decisions so that more neutral reference points or status quo positions become salient. Selection of a neutral frame could help decision makers become more aware of the explicit tradeoffs associated with the options available to them. A similar rationale is given, in fact, for the use of cost control practices such as zero-based budgeting and sunset legislation, which force decision makers to reappraise periodically the costs or tradeoffs associated with their allocation decisions.

In addition to reframing decisions by using neutral reference points, decision making may also be influenced by increasing the salience of the consequences or outcomes associated with particular choices. Several studies suggest why this might be a useful approach. First, one reason that decision frames adversely affect choice behavior is that they vary what Slovic et al. (1982) have termed the "dominance of explicit information" (p. 24). Information that is "out of sight," they argue, tends to remain "out of mind," especially in cases involving complex, multiattribute decisions. Second, research on psychological entrapment (Brockner & Rubin, 1985) and escalation of commitment in decision making (Staw & Ross, 1987) has found that decision makers often continue to overallocate resources in pursuit of a goal when the cumulative or long-term costs of those investments are not immediately obvious to them. Rubin and Brockner (1975), in particular, found that decision makers were more likely to remain committed to an unprofitable course of action when information about the costs of their commitments was low in salience. Thus, making more explicit the cumulative economic consequences associated with maintaining a costly deterrent may reduce the tendency to overallocate resources for this purpose.

It is difficult to predict what role deterrence theory will play in future efforts by nations to prevent conflict. On the one hand, it is easy to dismiss deterrence as an outmoded approach to international relations. As Booth (1987) has noted, "Unless one defines peace in the most negative sense — as the mere absence of war — the deterrence has not worked. . . . Indeed, nuclear deterrence as practiced between the super-powers . . . is antithetical to peace conceived in a positive sense" (p. 265). And, to be sure, dissatisfaction with deterrence theory is increasing, as evidenced by what Steinbruner (1983) has appropriately termed a "struggle for new conceptions." Such a struggle is both healthy and essential from the standpoint of developing alternative approaches to fostering cooperation among the nuclear powers.

At the same time, there is some evidence that deterrence has worked, and worked reasonably well for more than four decades (Nye, 1987). Furthermore, it remains an enormously influential concept among U.S. policy makers and will in all likelihood continue to exert an influence on strategic theory. Thus, it is important that psychologists and other social scientists contribute to our understanding of the conditions under which deterrence might help maintain stability, if not equanimity, among the nuclear powers. Such research may lead to insights that reduce the likelihood that, until more positive approaches to managing international relations are found, deterrence will fail. Even more important, perhaps, such research might lead to an understanding of how nations can move away from reliance upon negative approaches to peace, such as deterrence, and toward more positive approaches, such as problem-solving and negotiation.

One would like to think, of course, that decisions made by real-world policy makers reflect considerably more sophistication and rationality. Yet, the logic and justification for much of this country's nuclear deterrent strategies have remained surprisingly atheoretical and aempirical. As Fischer (1983) concluded in a thoughtful review of conceptual models of nuclear threat assessment, "Some of the most widely cited threat assessments are based not on any theory, but rather on simple mental images. More is better. Equality of force implies security. And so forth. Such simple images provide an inadequate basis for decisions involving the most destructive force known to man" (p. 88).

Bibliography

Abdel-Halim, A. A. (1982). Social support and managerial affective responses to job stress. *Journal of Occupational Behavior, 3,* 281–295.

Abelson, R. P., & Levi, A. (1985). Decision making and decision theory. In Lindzey & Aronson (Eds.), *Handbook of social psychology, II* (3rd ed., pp. 231–309). New York: Random House.

Adwan, Y. M. (1983). Patterns of administration-citizen relationship: Administrator's view. *METU Studies in Development, 13,* 325–338.

Agresti, A. (1984). *Analysis of ordinal categorical data.* New York: John Wiley.

Ajami, F. (1981). *The Arab predicament: Arab political thought and practice since 1967.* Cambridge, MA: Cambridge University Press.

Allen, M., Hunter, J., & Donohue, W. (1989). Meta-analysis of the self-report data on the effectiveness of communication apprehension treatment techniques. *Communication Education, 38,* 54–76.

Allison, G. T. (1982). What fuels the arms race? In J. F. Reichart & S. R. Sturms (Eds.), *American defense policy* (pp. 463–479). Baltimore: Johns Hopkins Press.

Almaney, A. J. (1981). Cultural traits of the Arabs: Growing interest for international management. *Management International Review, 21,* 10–18.

Axelrod, R. (1984). *The evolution of cooperation.* New York: Basic Books.

Bacharach, S. B., & Lawler, E. J. (1980). *Power and politics in organizations*. San Francisco: Jossey-Bass.

____. (1981). *Bargaining: Power tactics and outcomes*. San Francisco: Jossey-Bass.

Badawy, M. K. (1980). Styles of mideastern managers. *California Management Review, 22*, 51–58.

Bailey, K. D. (1982). *Methods of social research*. New York: Free Press.

Bales, R. F. (1950). *Interaction process analysis: A method for the study of small groups*. Cambridge, MA: Addison-Wesley.

Bangert-Downs, R. (1987). Review of developments in meta-analytic method. *Psychological Bulletin, 99*, 388–399.

Baron, R. A. (1988). Negative effects of destructive criticism: Impact on conflict, self-efficacy, and task performance. *Journal of Applied Psychology, 73*, 199–207.

Bartos, O. (1965). Concession-making in experimental negotiations. In J. Berger, M. Zelditch, & B. Anderson (Eds.), *Sociological theories in progress* (pp. 3–29). New York: Houghton-Mifflin.

Bazerman, M. H., & Lewicki, R. J. (1983). *Negotiating in organizations*. Beverly Hills, CA: Sage.

Beisecker, T. (1970). Verbal persuasive strategies in mixed-motive interactions. *Quarterly Journal of Speech, 56*, 149–160.

Benedict, R. C. (1981). Industry relations in the coal industry: The UMW perspective on industrial relations. *Labor Law Journal, 32*, 569–574.

Benton, A., Kelley, H., & Liebling, B. (1972). Effects of extremity of offers and concession rate on the outcomes of bargaining. *Journal of Personality and Social Psychology, 24*, 73–83.

Berger, C. A. (1973, November). *The acquaintance process revisited: Explorations in initial interactions*. Paper presented at the annual meeting of the Speech Communication Association, New York.

Berger, C. A., & Kellermann, K. A. (1983). To ask or not to ask: Is that a question? In R. B. Bostrom (Ed.), *Communication yearbook 7* (pp. 342–368). Beverly Hills, CA: Sage.

Bergmann, T. J., & Volkema, R. J. (1989). Understanding and managing interpersonal conflict at work: Its issues, interactive processes, and consequences. In M. A. Rahim (Ed.), *Managing Conflict: An inter-disciplinary approach* (pp. 7–19). New York: Praeger.

Betts, R. K. (1982). *Surprise attack: Lessons for defense planning.* Washington, D.C.: The Brookings Institution.

Bienenfeld, F. (1983). *Child custody mediation.* New York: Science and Behavior Books.

Bingham, G. (1982, Summer). Metropolitan Water Roundtable formed to build consensus on meeting Denver's long-term water needs. *Resolve, 1–3.*

___. (1984). *Resolving environmental disputes: A decade of experience.* Washington, D.C.: Conservation Foundation.

Blackburn, J. W. (1987). *Environmental mediation: Expert assessment of an eclectic theory.* Unpublished doctoral dissertation, Virginia Polytechnic Institute and State University.

Blake, R. R., & Mouton, J. S. (1964). *The managerial grid.* Houston: Gulf.

Booth, K. (1987). Nuclear deterrence and "World War III": How will history judge? In R. Kolkowicz (Ed.), *The logic of nuclear terror* (pp. 251–282). Boston, Allen & Unwin.

Borah, L. A. (1963). The effects of threat in bargaining: Critical and experimental analysis. *Journal of Abnormal and Social Psychology, 66,* 37–44.

Bourgeois III, L. J., & Boltvinik, M. (1981). OD in cross-cultural settings: Latin America. *California Management Review, 23,* 75–81.

Bourne, G. S. (1988). The rise and fall of the Arbitration Review Board. *Labor Law Journal, 39,* 470–475.

Bradburn, N. (1963). Interpersonal relations in Turkish organizations. *Journal of Social Issues, 19,* 61–67.

Brett, J. M., & Goldberg, S. B. (1983). Mediator-advisers: A new third-party role. In M. Bazerman & R. J. Lewicki (Eds.), *Negotiating in organizations* (pp. 165–176). Beverly Hills, CA: Sage.

Brockner, J., & Rubin, J. Z. (1985). *Entrapment in escalating conflicts: A social psychological analysis.* New York: Springer-Verlag.

Brown, B. R. (1977). Face-saving and face-restoration in negotiation. In D. Druckman (Ed.), *Negotiations* (pp. 275–299). Newbury Park, CA: Sage.

Bullis, C. A., & Putnam, L. L. (1985). *Bargaining as social construction of reality: The role of stories and rituals.* Unpublished manuscript. Purdue University.

Buntzman, G. F. (1989). Mediation: Introduction. In M. A. Rahim (Ed.), *Managing conflict: An interdisciplinary approach* (pp. 197–199). New York: Praeger.

Burrell, N. (1987). *Testing a model of mediation: The impact of disputants' expectations.* Unpublished doctoral dissertation, Department of Communication, Michigan State University, East Lansing.

Burrell, N., Donohue, W. A., & Allen, M. (1988). Gender-based perceptual biases in mediation. *Communication Research, 15,* 447–469.

Calabrese, R. J. (1975). *The effects of privacy and probability of future interaction on initial interaction patterns.* Unpublished doctoral dissertation, Department of Communication Studies, Northwestern University, Evanston.

Caplan, R. D., Cobb, S., French, J. R. P., Harrison, R., & Pinneau, G. R., Jr. (1975). *Job demands and worker health* (Publication No. NIOSH 75–160). Washington, D.C.: Department of Health, Education, and Welfare.

Carnevale, P., & Lawler, E. (1987). Time pressure and the development of integrative agreements in bilateral negotiations. *Journal of Conflict Resolution, 30,* 636–659.

Carpenter, S., & Kennedy, W. (1980). Environmental conflict management. *Environmental Professional, 2,* 67–74.

Carroll, J. S. (1978). The effect of imagining an event on expectations for the event: An interpretation in terms of the availability heuristic. *Journal of Experimental Psychology: Human Learning and Memory, 14,* 88–96.

Chertkoff, J., & Conley, M. (1967). Opening offer and frequency of concession as bargaining strategies. *Journal of Personality and Social Psychology, 7,* 181–185.

Chertkoff, J., & Esser, J. (1976). A review of experiments in explicit bargaining. *Journal of Experimental Social Psychology, 12,* 464–486.

Clark, P. (1980). Mediation energy, environmental, and economic conflict over fuel policy in New England. In L. Lake (Ed.), *Environmental mediation: The search for consensus.* Boulder, CO: Westview Press.

Clopton, S. (1984). Seller and buying firm factors affecting industrial buyers' negotiation behavior and outcomes. *Journal of Marketing Research, 21,* 39–53.

Cobb, R., & Elder, E. (1983). *Participation in American politics: The dynamics of agenda building.* Baltimore: Johns Hopkins University Press.

Cohen, J., & Cohen, P. (1983). *Applied multiple regression/correlation analysis for the behavioral sciences.* Hillsdale, NJ: Erlbaum.

Cohen, S. (1980). Aftereffects of stress on human performance and social behavior: A review of research and theory. *Psychological Bulletin, 88,* 82–108.

Cohen, S., & Edwards, J. R. (1989). Personality characteristics as moderators of the relationship between stress and disorders. In R. W. Neufield (Ed.), *Advances in the investigation of psychological stress* (pp. 235–285). New York: Wiley.

Colosi, T. (1983). Negotiation in the public and private sectors. *American Behavioral Scientist, 27,* 229–253.

Conrad, C. (1985, November). *Gender, interactional sensitivity and communication in conflict: Assumptions and interpretation.* Paper presented at the Speech Communication Association convention, Denver, CO.

Constable, J. F., & Russell, D. (1986). The effect of social support and the work environment upon burnout among nurses. *Journal of Human Stress, 12,* 20–26.

Cormick, G. W. (1980). The "theory" and practice of environmental mediation. *Environmental Professional, 2,* 24–33.

___. (1982, Winter). Interventions in self-determination in environmental disputes: A mediator's perspective. *Resolve,* 1–6.

Coulson, R. (1983). *Fighting fair: Family mediation will work for you.* New York: The Free Press.

Crott, H., Kayser, E., & Lamm, H. (1980). The effects of information exchange and communication in an asymmetrical negotiation situation. *European Journal of Social Psychology, 10,* 149–163.

Dahl, R. (1955). Hierarchy, democracy, and bargaining in politics and economics. In R. Dahl (Ed.), *Research frontiers in politics and government.* Washington, D.C.: The Brookings Institution.

Daniels, V. (1967). Communication, incentive, and structural variables in interpersonal exchange and negotiation. *Journal of Experimental Psychology, 3,* 47–74.

de Rivera, J. (1968). *The psychological dimension of foreign policy.* Columbus, OH: Merrill.

Dereli, T. (1968). *The development of Turkish trade unionism.* Istanbul: Istanbul University Publications.

Deutsch, M. (1949). A theory of co-operation and competition. *Human Relations, 2,* 129–152.

___. (1958). Trust and suspicion. *Journal of Conflict Resolution, 2,* 265–279.

___. (1965). A psychological approach to international conflict. In G. Sperazzi (Ed.), *Psychology and international relations* (pp. 44–48). Washington, D.C.: Georgetown University Press.

___. (1969). Conflicts: Productive and destructive. *Journal of Social Issues, 25,* 7–41.

___. (1973). *The resolution of conflict.* New Haven, CT: Yale University Press.

___. (1980). Fifty years of conflict. In L. Festinger (Ed.), *Retrospections on special psychology* (pp. 46–77). New York: Oxford University Press.

Deutsch, M., & Krauss, R. (1960). The effect of threat upon interpersonal bargaining. *Journal of Abnormal and Social Psychology, 61,* 181–189.

___. (1962). Studies of interpersonal bargaining. *Journal of Conflict Resolution, 6,* 52–76.

Dillard, J., Hunter, J., & Burgoon, M. (1984). Sequential-request persuasive strategies: Meta-analysis of foot-in-the-door and door-in-the-face. *Human Communication Research, 10,* 461–488.

Domke, W. K., Eichenberg, R. C., & Kelleher, C. M. (1983). The illusion of choice: Defense and welfare in advanced industrial democracies, 1948–1978. *American Political Science Review, 77,* 19–35.

Donohue, W. A. (1978). An empirical framework for examining negotiation processes and outcomes. *Communication Monographs, 45,* 247–257.

___. (1981a). Analyzing negotiation tactics: Development of a negotiation interact system. *Human Communication Research, 7,* 273–287.

___. (1981b). Development of a model of rule use in negotiaton interaction. *Communication Monographs, 48,* 106–120.

Donohue, W. A., Allen, M., & Burrell, N. (1985). Communication strategies in mediation. *Mediation Quarterly, 10,* 75–89.

___. (1988). Mediator communicative competence. *Communication Monographs, 55,* 104–119.

Donohue, W. A., & Diez, M. E. (1983, November). *Information management in negotiation.* Paper presented at the annual convention of the International Communication Association, Dallas.

Donohue, W. A., Diez, M. E., & Hamilton, M. (1984). Coding naturalistic negotiation interaction. *Human Communication Research, 10,* 403–425.

Donohue, W. A., Diez, M. E., & Stahle, R. (1983). New directions in negotiation research. In R. W. Bostrom (Ed.), *Communication yearbook 7* (pp. 249–279). Newbury Park, CA: Sage.

Douglas, A. (1975). The peaceful settlement of industrial and intergroup disputes. *Journal of Conflict Resolution, 1,* 69–81.

Downs, G., Rocke, D., & Siverson, R. (1986). Arms races and cooperation. In K. Oye (Ed.), *Cooperation under anarchy* (pp. 118–146). Princeton, NJ: Princeton University Press.

Dror, Y. (1986). *Policymaking under adversity.* New Brunswick, NJ: Transaction, Inc.

Druckman, D., Zechmeister, K., & Soloman, D. (1972). Determinants of bargaining behavior in a bilateral monopoly situation. *Behavioral Science, 17,* 514–531.

Easton, D. (1965). *A system analysis of political life.* New York: Wiley & Sons.

___. (1971). *The political system* (2nd ed.). New York: Knopf.

Ebbesen, E. B., & Konecni, V. J. (1980). On the external validity of decision making research: What do we know about decisions in the real world? In T. S. Wallsten (Ed.), *Cognitive process in choice and decision behavior.* Hillsdale, NJ: Erlbaum.

Eisenberg, E. M., & Witten, M. G. (1987). Reconsidering openness in organizational communication. *Academy of Management Review, 12,* 418–426.

Enthoven, A., & Smith, K. (1971). *How much is enough?* New York: Harper & Row.

Ervin-Tripp, S. (1976). Is Sybil there? The structure of some American English directives. *Language and Society, 5,* 25–66.

Etzion, D. (1984). Moderating effect of social support on the stress-burnout relationship. *Journal of Applied Psychology, 69,* 615–622.

Etzioni, A. (1969). Social-psychological aspects of international relations. In G. Linzey & E. Aronson (Eds.), *The handbook of social psychology: Vol. 5* (2nd ed.) (pp. 545–591). Reading, MA: Addison-Wesley.

Eulau, H., & Prewitt, K. (1973). *Labyrinths of democracy.* Indianapolis, IN: Bobbs-Merrill.

Everitt, B. S. (1977). *The analysis of contingency tables.* New York: John Wiley.

Faning, O. (1979). The world's newest profession. *Environment, 21,* 33–38.

Fischer, G. W. (1983). Conceptual models, judgment, and the treatment of uncertainty in nuclear threat assessment. *Journal of Social Issues, 39,* 87–116.

Fischhoff, B. (1983). Strategic policy preferences: A behavioral decision perspective. *Journal of Social Issues, 39,* 133–160.

Fisher, C. D. (1985). Social support and adjustment to work: A longitudinal study. *Journal of Management, 11,* 39–53.

Fisher, R., & Ury, W. (1981). *Getting to yes.* New York: Penguin.

Flanagan, J. C. (1954). The critical incident technique. *Psychological Bulletin, 54,* 327–358.

Folberg, J., & Taylor, A. (1984). *Mediation: A comprehensive guide to resolving conflict without litigation.* San Francisco: Jossey-Bass.

Frei, D. (1983). *Risks of unintentional nuclear war.* Totowa, NJ: Rowman & Allanheld.

____. (1986). *Perceived images: U.S. and Soviet assumptions and perceptions in disarmament.* Totowa, NJ: Rowman and Allanheld.

Freudenberger, H. J. (1974). Staff burn-out. *Journal of Social Issues, 30*(1), 159–165.

Funder, D. C., & Dobroth, K. M. (1987). Differences between traits: Properties associated with intergroup agreement. *Journal of Personality and Social Psychology, 52,* 409–418.

Funk, S. C., & Houston, B. K. (1987). A critical analysis of the hardiness scale's validity and utility. *Journal of Personality and Social Psychology, 53,* 572–578.

Fusilier, M. R., Ganster, D. C., & Mayes, B. T. (1987). Effects of social support, role stress, and locus of control on health. *Journal of Management, 13,* 517–528.

Ganellen, R. J., & Blaney, P. H. (1984). Hardiness and social support as moderators of the effects of life stress. *Journal of Personality and Social Psychology, 47,* 156–163.

Ganster, D., Mayes, B., & Fusilier, M. (1986). Role of social support in the experience of stress at work. *Journal of Applied Psychology, 71,* 102–110.

Garthoff, R. L. (1978). On estimating and inputing intentions. *International Security, 2*, 22–32.

George, A. L. (1980). *Presidential decision making and foreign policy*. Boulder, CO: Westview.

Gibson, D. L., Weiss, D. J., Davis, R. V., & Lofquist, L. H. (1970). *Manual for the Minnesota satisfactoriness scales*. Minneapolis, MN: University of Minnesota.

Glass, G., McGaw, B., & Smith, M. (1981). *Meta-analysis in social research*. Beverly Hills, CA: Sage.

Goodnow, F. (1900). *Politics and administration*. New York: Macmillan.

Gouldner, A. (1960). The norm of reciprocity: A preliminary statement. *American Sociological Review, 25*, 161–178.

Graham, J. G. (1978). *The analysis of cross-tabulated data*. New York: John Wiley.

Graham, J. L. (1983). Brazilian, Japanese, and American business negotiations. *Journal of International Business Studies, 14*, 47–61.

____. (1985). The influence of culture on the process of negotiations: An exploratory study. *Journal of International Business Studies, 16*, 81–96.

Greenberg, G., Miller, J. A., Mohr, L. B., & Valdeck, B. C. (1977). Developing public policy theory: Perspectives from empirical research. *American Political Science Review, 71*, 1532–1534.

Greenhalgh, L., Gilkey, R. W., & Pufahl, S. J. (1984). *Effects of sex-role differences on approach to business negotiations*. Paper presented at the annual convention of the Academy of Management, Boston.

Griffin, R. W. (1987). *Management* (2nd ed.). Boston, MA: Houghton-Mifflin.

Gruder, L. (1971). Relationships with opponent and partner in mixed-motive bargaining. *Journal of Conflict Resolution, 15*, 403–416.

Guetzkow, H., Ed. (1963). *Simulation in international relations: Developments for research and teaching*. Englewood Cliffs, NJ: Prentice-Hall.

Gulliver, P. H. (1979). *Disputes and negotiations*. New York: Academic Press.

Haberman, S. J. (1973). The analysis of residuals in cross-tabulated tables. *Biometrics, 29*, 205–219.

Hamner, W. (1974). Effects of bargaining strategy and pressure to reach agreement in a stalemated negotiation. *Journal of Personality and Social Psychology, 30*, 458–467.

Hanisch, K., & Carnevale, J. (1988, August). *Gender in negotiation and mediation and the perception of mediator bias.* Paper presented at the Academy of Management convention, Anaheim, CA.

Harter, P. (1983). Negotiating regulations: A cure for malaise. *Georgetown Law Journal, 71,* 1–118.

Haynes, J. M. (1981). *Divorce mediation: A practical guide for therapists and counselors.* New York: Springer.

Heclo, H. (1978). Issue networks and the executive establishment. In A. King (Ed.), *The new American political system* (pp. 87–124). Washington, D.C.: The Brookings Institution.

Hedges, L., & Olkin, I. (1985). *Statistical methods for meta-analysis.* Orlando, FL: Academic Press.

Hersey, P., and Blanchard, K. H. (1988). *Management of organizational behavior* (5th ed.). Englewood Cliffs, NJ: Prentice-Hall.

Hitch, C. J., & McKeen, R. N. (1960). *The economics of defense in the nuclear age.* Santa Monica, CA: The Rand Corporation.

Hoch, S. J. (1984). Availability and interference in predictive judgment. *Journal of Experimental Psychology: Learning, Memory, and Cognition, 10,* 649–662.

Hocker, J. C., & Wilmot, W. W. (1985). *Interpersonal conflict* (2nd ed.). Dubuque, IA: William C. Brown.

Hofstede, G. (1983). National cultures in four dimensions. *International Studies of Management and Organization, 12*(2), 52.

Horowitz, D. (1977). *The courts and social policy.* Washington, D.C.: The Brookings Institution.

House, J. S. (1981). *Work stress and social support.* Reading, MA: Addison-Wesley.

Hull, J. G., Van Treuren, R. R., & Virnelli, S. (1987). Hardiness and health: A critique and alternative approach. *Journal of Personality and Social Psychology, 53,* 518–530.

Hunter, J., Schmidt, F., & Jackson, G. (1982). *Meta-analysis.* Beverly Hills, CA: Sage.

Huser, V. (1982). The CREST dispute: A mediation success. *Environment, 24,* 18–36.

Ilter, S. A. (1983). *A longitudinal study of blue-collar worker attitudes in Turkey.* Unpublished doctoral dissertation, Georgia State University.

Jablin, F. M., & McComb, K. B. (1984). The employment screening interview: An organizational assimilation and communication perspective. In R. B. Bostrom (Ed.), *Communication yearbook 8* (pp. 137–163). Beverly Hills, CA: Sage.

Jamal, M. (1985). Relationship of job stress to job performance: A study of managers and blue-collar workers. *Human Relations, 38,* 409–429.

Janis, I. L. (1972). *Victims of groupthink.* Boston: Houghton-Mifflin.

Jervis, R. (1976). *Perception and misperception in international politics.* Princeton, NJ: Princeton University Press.

___. (1978). Cooperation under the security dilemma. *World Politics, 30,* 167–214.

___. (1982). Deterrence and perception. *International Security, 7,* 14–19.

___. (1985). Perceiving and coping with threat. In R. Jervis, R. N. Lebow, & J. G. Stein, (1985) *Psychology and deterrence* (pp. 13–33). Baltimore, MD: Johns Hopkins University Press.

___. (1986). Cognition and political behavior. In R. R. Lau & D. Sears (Eds.), *Political cognition* (pp. 319–336). Hillsdale, NJ: Lawrence Erlbaum.

Jervis, R., Lebow, R. N., & Stein, J. (1985). *Psychology and deterrence.* Baltimore, MD: Johns Hopkins University Press.

Johnson, D. W. (1971). Role reversal: A summary and review of the research. *International Journal of Group Tensions, 1,* 318–334.

Johnson, D. W., Johnson, R. T., & Maruyama, G. (1983). Interdependence and interpersonal attraction among heterogeneous and homogeneous individuals: A theoretical formulation and a meta-analysis of the research. *Review of Educational Research, 53,* 5–54.

Johnson, D. W., Maruyama, G., Johnson, R. T., Nelson, D., & Skon, S. (1981). Effects of cooperative, competitive, and individualistic goal structures on achievement: A meta-analysis. *Psychological Bulletin, 89,* 47–62.

Johnson, P. M., & Wells, R. S. (1986). Soviet military and civilian resource allocation, 1951–1980. *Journal of Conflict Resolution, 30,* 195–219.

Jones, C. O. (1984). *An introduction to the study of public policy* (3rd ed.). Monterey, CA: Brooks/Cole.

Jones, T. S. (1985). *'Breaking up is hard to do': An exploratory investigation of communication behaviors and phases in child-custody divorce mediation.* Unpublished doctoral dissertation, Ohio State University.

___. (1987, March). *An analysis of gender differences in mediator-disputant interaction for successful and unsuccessful divorce mediation.* Paper presented at the Temple Discourse Conference, Conflict Intervention: Perspectives on Process, Philadelphia, PA.

___. (1988). Phase structures in agreement and no-agreement mediation. *Communication Research, 15,* 470–495.

___. (1989). Lag sequential analyses of mediator-spouse and husband-wife interaction in successful and unsuccessful divorce mediation. In M. A. Rahim (Ed.), *Managing conflict: An interdisciplinary approach* (pp. 93–107). New York: Praeger.

Kagitcibasi, C. (1970). Social norms and authoritarianism: A Turkish-American comparison. *Journal of Personality and Social Psychology, 16,* 444–451.

Kahan, J. H. (1975). *Security in the nuclear age: Developing U.S. strategic arms policy.* Washington, D.C.: The Brookings Institution.

Kahn, H. (1984). *Thinking about the unthinkable in the 1980s.* New York: Simon and Schuster.

Kahn, R. L., Wolfe, D. M., Quinn, P. R., Snoak, J. D., & Rosenthal, R. A. (1964). *Organizational stress: Studies in role conflict and ambiguity.* New York: Wiley.

Kahneman, D., & Tversky, A. (1982). The psychology of preferences. *Scientific American, 246,* 160–173.

___. (1984a). Choices, values, and frames. *American Psychologist, 39,* 341–350.

___. (1984b). The simulation heuristic. In D. Kahneman, P. Slovic, & A. Tversky (Eds.), *Judgment under uncertainty: Heuristics and biases* (pp. 3–22). Cambridge: Cambridge University Press.

Kanner, A., Kafry, D., & Pines, A. (1978). Conspicuous in its absence: The lack of positive conditions as a source of stress. *Journal of Human Stress, 4,* 33–39.

Kaufmann, G. M., & Beer, T. A. (1986). Interactions between job stressors and social support: Some counterintuitive results. *Journal of Applied Psychology, 71,* 522–526.

Kearsley, G. P. (1976). Questions and question-asking in verbal discourse: A cross disciplinary review. *Journal of Psycholinguistic Research, 5*, 355–375.

Kelley, H. H. (1965). Experimental studies of threats in interpersonal negotiations. *Journal of Conflict Resolution, 9*, 80–107.

Kelman, H. C., Ed. (1966). *International behavior*. New York: Holt, Rinehart, & Winston.

Keltner, J. (1987). *Mediation: Toward a civilized system of dispute resolution*. Annandale, VA: SCA.

Kennedy, W., & Lansford, H. (1983). *The metropolitan water roundtable: Resource allocation through conflict management*. Boulder, CO: Accord Associates.

Kettl, D. F. (1988). *Government by proxy [Mis]managing federal programs*. Washington, D.C.: Congressional Quarterly Press.

Kienast, P. K., & Drexler, J. A., Jr. (1983). *Quality of work life and collective bargaining*. Working paper, Graduate School of Business Administration, University of Washington, Seattle.

Kiggundu, M. N., Jorgensen, J. J., & Hafsi, T. (1983). Administrative theory and practice in developing countries: A synthesis. *Administrative Science Quarterly, 28*, 66–84.

Kimmel, M. J., Pruitt, D. G., Magerau, J. M., Konar-Goldband, E., & Carnevale, P. J. (1980). Effects of trust, aspiration, and gender on negotiation tactics. *Journal of Personality and Social Psychology, 38*, 9–22.

Kirmeyer, S. L., & Dougherty, T. W. (1988). Work load, tension, and coping: Moderating effects of supervisor support. *Personnel Psychology, 41*, 124–139.

Kobasa, S. C. (1979). Stressful life events, personality, and health: An inquiry into hardiness. *Personality and Social Psychology, 37*, 1–11.

Kobasa, S. C., Maddi, S. R., & Courington, S. (1981). Personality and constitution as mediators in the stress-illness relationship. *Journal of Health and Social Behavior, 22*, 368–378.

Kobasa, S. C., Maddi, S. R., & Kahn, S. (1982). Hardiness and health: A prospective study. *Journal of Personality and Social Psychology, 42*, 168–177.

Kobasa, S. C., & Puccetti, M. C. (1983). Personality and social resources in stress resistance. *Journal of Personality and Social Psychology, 45*, 839–850.

Kochan, T. A., & Jick, T. (1978). The pubilc sector mediation process: A theory and empirical examination. *Journal of Conflict Resolution, 22,* 209–240.

Kochan, T. A., & Bazerman, M. H. (1986). Macro determinants of the future of the study of negotiations in organizations. In R. J. Lewicki (Ed.), *Research in Negotiations in Organizations, 1* (pp. 287–309). Greenwich, CT: JAI Press.

Kolb, D. M. (1983). *The mediators.* Cambridge, MA: MIT Press.

Kormorita, S., & Esser, J. (1975). Frequency of reciprocated concessions in bargaining. *Journal of Personality and Social Psychology, 32,* 699–705.

Kramer, R. M. (1989). Windows of vulnerability or cognitive illusions? Cognitive processes in the nuclear arms race. *Journal of Experimental Social Psychology, 25,* 79–100.

Krauss, R. M., & Deutsch, M. (1966). Communication in interpersonal bargaining. *Journal of Personality and Social Psychology, 4,* 572–577.

Kull, S. (1988). *Minds at war: Nuclear reality and the inner conflicts of defense policymakers.* New York: Basic Books.

LaFeber, W. (1976). *America, Russia, and the cold war 1945–1975* (3rd ed.). New York: John Wiley & Sons.

Lasswell, H. (1958). *Politics: Who gets what, when, how.* New York: Meridan Books.

Latourette, K. S. (1942). *The Chinese: Their history and culture.* New York: Barclay.

Lauter, G. P. (1968). *An investigation of the applicability of modern management processes by industrial managers in Turkey.* Unpublished doctoral dissertation, University of California, Los Angeles.

Lax, D. A., & Sebenius, J. K. (1986). *The manager as negotiator.* New York: Free Press.

Lebow, R. N. (1987). *Nuclear crisis management: A dangerous illusion.* Ithaca, NY: Cornell University Press.

Lee, K. (1982, Spring). Defining success in environmental dispute resolution. *Resolve,* 1–6.

Levenson, H. (1973). Multidimensional locus of control in psychiatric patients. *Journal of Consulting and Clinical Psychology, 41,* 397–404.

Levinger, G. (1987). Beyond deterrence. *Journal of Social Issues, 43,* whole issue.

Lewicki, R. J. (1983). Lying and deception: A behavioral model. In M. H. Bazerman & R. J. Lewicki (Eds.), *Negotiating in organizations* (pp. 68–90). Newbury Park, CA: Sage.

Lewicki, R. J., & Litterer, J. (1985). *Negotiation.* Homewood, IL: Irwin.

Lewicki, R. J., Weiss, S. E., & Lewin, D. (1988). *Models of conflict, negotiation, and third party intervention: A review and synthesis* (Working paper series 88–33). Columbus, OH: Ohio State University, College of Business.

Lewis, S. A., & Fry, W. R. (1977). Effects of visual access and orientation on the discovery of integrative bargaining alternatives. *Organizational Behavior and Human Performance, 20,* 75–92.

Lewis, S. A., & Pruitt, D. G. (1971). Orientation, aspiration level, and communication freedom in integrative bargaining. *Proceedings of the 79th Annual Convention of the American Psychological Association, 6,* 221–222.

Liebert, R., Smith, W., Hill, J., & Keiffer, M. (1968). The effects of information and magnitude of initial offer on interpersonal negotiation. *Journal of Experimental Social Psychology, 4,* 431–441.

Lord, R. G. (1985). An information processing approach to social perceptions, leadership, and behavioral measurement in organizations. In L. L. Cummings & B. M. Straw (Eds.), *Research in organizational behavior, Vol. 7* (pp. 87–128). Greenwich, CT: JAI Press.

Luce, R. D., & Raiffa, H. M. (1957). *Games and decisions: Introduction and critical survey.* New York: Wiley.

Maggilio, W. A. (1985). *Techniques of mediation.* Dobbs Ferry, NY: Ocean Publications.

Maslach, C., & Jackson, S. (1981a). *Maslach burnout inventory manual.* Palo Alto, CA: Consulting Psychologists Press.

_____. (1981b). *The cost of caring.* Englewood Cliffs, NJ: Prentice-Hall.

McCarthy, J. E. (1976). Resolving environmental conflicts. *Environmental Science and Technology, 10,* 40–43.

McCarthy, J., & Shorett, A. (1984). *Negotiating settlements: A guide to environmental mediation.* New York: American Arbitration Association.

McGillicuddy, N., Pruitt, D., & Syna, H. (1984). Perceptions of firmness and strength in negotiation. *Personality and Social Psychology Bulletin, 10,* 402–409.

McNamara, R. (1968). *The essence of security: Reflections in office.* New York: Harper & Row.

Miller, G., & Simons, H., Eds. (1974). *Perspectives on communication in conflict.* Englewood Cliffs, NJ: Prentice-Hall.

Miller, S. M. (1984). *Strategy and nuclear deterrence.* Princeton, NJ: Princeton University Press.

Minas, J., Scodel, A., Marlowe, D., & Rawson, H. (1960). Some descriptive aspects of two-person non-zero-sum games II. *Journal of Conflict Resolution, 4,* 192–197.

Miner, J. B. (1982). *Theories of organizational structure and process.* Chicago, IL: Dryden Press.

Mintzberg, H. (1986). The manager's job: Folklore and fact. In M. T. Matteson & J. M. Ivancevich (Eds.), *Management classics* (pp. 63–85). Plano, TX: Business Publications.

Mishler, E. G. (1975a). Studies in dialogue and discourse: II types of discourse initiated by and sustained through questioning. *Journal of Psycholinguistic Research, 4,* 99–121.

___. (1975b). Studies in dialogue and discourse: An exponential law of successive questioning. *Language and Society, 4,* 31–51.

Moore, C. W. (1986). *The mediation process: Practical strategies for resolving conflict.* San Francisco, CA: Jossey-Bass.

Morley, I., & Stephenson, G. (1977). *The social psychology of bargaining.* London: Allen & Unwin.

Motowidlo, S. J., Packard, J. S., & Manning, M. R. (1986). Occupational stress: Its causes and consequences for job performance. *Journal of Applied Psychology, 71,* 618–629.

Nadler, L. B., Broome, B. J., & Nadler, M. K. (1985). Culture and the management of conflict situations. In W. Gudykunst, L. Stewart, & S. Ting-Toomey (Eds.), *Communication, culture, and organizational processes* (pp. 87–113). Newbury Park, CA: Sage.

Nadler, M. K., & Nadler, L. B. (1987). The influence of gender on negotiation success in asymmetric power situations. In L. B. Nadler, M. K. Nadler, & W. R. Todd-Mancillas (Eds.), *Advances in gender and communication research* (pp. 189–218). Lanham, MD: University Press of America.

Namboodiri, N. K., Carter, L. F., & Blalock, H. M., Jr. (1975). *Applied multivariate analysis and experimental designs.* New York: McGraw-Hill.

Newhouse, J. (1983, February 13). Profiles, a sense of duty. *New Yorker,* pp. 417–82.

Nixon, R. M. (1980). *The real war.* New York: Warner Bros.

___. (1983). *Real peace.* Boston, MA: Little, Brown, & Co.

Nunnally, J. (1978). *Psychometric Theory* (2nd ed.). New York: McGraw-Hill.

Nye, J. (1987). The long-term future of deterrence. In R. Kolkowicz (Ed.), *The logic of nuclear terror* (pp. 233–250). Boston, MA: Allen & Unwin.

O'Toole, L. (1986). Policy recommendations for multi-actor implementation: An assessment of the field. *Journal of Public Policy, 6,* 181–210.

Osgood, C. (1962). *An alternative to war or surrender.* Urbana, IL: University of Illinois Press.

Oskamp, S. (1985). International conflict and national public policy issues. *Applied Social Psychology Annual, 6,* whole issue.

Peterson, R., Tracy, L., & Cabelly, A. (1981). Problem solving in labor negotiations, retest of a model. *Relations Industrielles, 36*(1), 87–104.

Phillips, E., & Cheston, R. (1979). Conflict resolution: What works? *California Management Review, 21,* 76–83.

Pitted against Pittston (1989, October 9). *Business Week,* 144–148.

Plous, S. (1987). Perceptual illusions and military realities: A social psychological analysis of the nuclear arms race. *Journal of Conflict Resolution, 29,* 5–33.

Podsakoff, P. M., & Organ, D. W. (1986). Self-reports in organizational research: Problems and prospects. *Journal of Management, 12,* 531–544.

Pruitt, D. G. (1981). *Negotiation behavior.* New York: Academic Press.

Pruitt, D. G., Fry, W. R., Castrianno, L., Zubek, J., Welton, G. L., McGillicuddy, N. B., & Ippolito, C. (1989). The process of mediation: Caucus, control, and problem solving. In M. A. Rahim (Ed.), *Managing conflict: An interdisciplinary approach* (pp. 201–208). New York: Praeger.

Pruitt, D. G., & Lewis, S. A. (1975). Development of integrative solutions in bilateral negotiation. *Journal of Personality and Social Psychology, 31,* 621–633.

Pruitt, D. G., & Syna, H. (1984). Successful problem solving. In D. Tjosvold & D. W. Johnson (Eds.), *Productive conflict management: Perspective for organizations* (pp. 69–90). Minneapolis, MN: Minneapolis Team Media.

Putnam, L. L. (1985). Bargaining as organizational communication. In R. D. McPhee & P. K. Tomkins (Eds.), *Organizational communication: Traditional themes and new directions* (pp. 129–148). Newbury Park, CA: Sage.

Putnam, L. L., & Bullis, C. (1984, May). *Intergroup relations and issue redefinition in teachers' bargaining.* Paper presented at the annual meeting of the International Communication Association, San Francisco.

Putnam, L. L., & Geist, P. (1985). Argument in bargaining: An analysis of the reasoning process. *Southern Speech Communication Journal, 50,* 225–245.

Putnam, L. L., & Jones, T. S. (1982a). Reciprocity in negotiation: An analysis of bargaining interaction. *Communication Monographs, 49,* 171–191.

____. (1982b). The role of communication in bargaining. *Human Communication Research, 8,* 262–280.

Putnam, L. L., & Pacanowsky (1983). *Communication and organizations: An interpretative approach.* Beverly Hills, CA: Sage.

Putnam, L. L., & Poole, M. S. (1987). Conflict and negotiation. In F. M. Jablin, L. L. Putnam, K. H. Roberts, & L. W. Porter (Eds.), *Handbook of organizational communication: An interdisciplinary perspective* (pp. 549–599). Newbury Park, CA: Sage.

Putnam, L. L., & VanHoeven, S. A. (1986, April). *Teacher bargaining as a cultural rite of conflict resolution.* Paper presented at the annual convention of the Central States Speech Association, Cincinnati, OH.

Putnam, L. L., & Wilson, C. E. (1982). Communicative strategies in organizational conflicts. In M. Burgoon (Ed.), *Communication yearbook 6* (pp. 629–652). Newbury Park, CA: Sage.

Putnam, L. L., & Wilson, S. (1989). Argumentation and bargaining strategies as discriminators of integrative and distributive outcomes. In M. A. Rahim (Ed.), *Managing conflict: An interdisciplinary approach* (pp. 121–141). New York: Praeger.

Putnam, L. L., Wilson, S. R., Waltman, M. S., & Turner, D. (1986). The evolution of case arguments in teachers' bargaining. *Journal of the American Forensic Association, 23,* 63–81.

Quirk, R., Greenbaum, S., Leech, G., & Svartvik, J. (1972). *A grammar of contemporary English.* London: Longman.

Rackham, N., & Carlisle, J. (1978a). The effective negotiator part 1: The behavior of successful negotiators. *Journal of European Industrial Training, 2*(6), 6–11.

___. (1978b). The effective negotiator part 2: Planning for negotiations. *Journal of European Industrial Training, 2*(7), 2–5.

Rahim, M. A. (1983a). A measure of styles of handling interpersonal conflicts. *Academy of Management Journal, 26,* 368–376.

___. (1983b). Measurement of organizational conflict. *Journal of General Psychology, 109,* 189–199.

___. (1983c). *Rahim organizational conflict inventories: Professional manual.* Palo Alto, CA: Consulting Psychologists Press.

___. (1986a). *Managing conflict in organizations.* New York: Praeger.

___. (1986b). Referent role and styles of handling interpersonal conflict. *Journal of Social Psychology, 125*(1), 79–86.

Raiffa, H. (1982). *The art and science of negotiation.* Cambridge, MA: Harvard University Press.

Rapoport, A., & Chammah, C. (1965). *Prisoner's dilemma: A study in conflict and cooperation.* Ann Arbor, MI: University of Michigan Press.

Reiches, N., & Harral, H. B. (1974). Argument in negotiation: A theoretical and empirical approach. *Communication Monographs, 41,* 36–48.

Renwick, P. A. (1975). Impact of topic and source of disagreement on conflict management. *Organizational Behavior and Human Performance, 16,* 416–425.

Riggs, C. J. (1983). Communication dimensions of conflict tactics in organizational settings: A functional analysis. In R. W. Bostrom (Ed.), *Communication yearbook 7* (pp. 516–531). Newbury Park, CA: Sage.

Rizzo, J. R., House, R. J., & Lirtzman, S. I. (1970). Role conflict and ambiguity in complex organizations. *Administrative Science Quarterly, 15,* 150–163.

Robinson, W. P., & Rackstraw, S. J. (1972). *A question of answers* (2 Vols.). London: Routledge & Kegan Paul.

Roloff, M. E., & Campion, D. E. (1987). On alleviating the debilitating effects of accountability on bargaining: Authority and self-monitoring. *Communication Monographs, 54,* 145–164.

Rosenbloom, D. (1983). *Public administration and law: Bench v. bureau in the United States.* New York: Marcel Dekker.

Rosenthal, R. (1984). *Meta-analytic procedures for social research.* Beverly Hills, CA: Sage.

Ross, L., Lepper, M., Strack, F., & Steinmetz, J. (1977). Social explanation and social expectation: Effects of real and hypothetical explanations on subjective likelihood. *Journal of Personality and Social Psychology, 37,* 817–829.

Ross, R. G., & DeWine, S. (1987, May). *Communication messages in interpersonal conflict: Reliability and validity of an assessment tool.* Paper presented at the annual meeting of the International Communication Association, Montreal.

_____. (1988). Assessing the Ross-DeWine Organizational Conflict Management Message Style (CMMS). *Management Communication Quarterly, 1,* 389–413.

Royal, R. F., & Schutt, S. R. (1976). *The gentle art of interviewing and interrogation: A professional manual and guide.* Englewood Cliffs, NJ: Prentice-Hall.

Rubin, J. Z. (1983). The use of third parties in organizations: A critical response. In M. Bazerman & R. J. Lewicki (Eds.), *Negotiating in organizations* (pp. 214–224). Beverly Hills, CA: Sage.

Rubin, J. Z., & Brockner, J. (1975). Factors affecting entrapment in waiting situations: The Rosencrantz and Guildenstern effect. *Personality and Social Psychology, 31,* 1054–1063.

Rubin, J. Z., & Brown, B. (1975). *The social psychology of bargaining and negotiation.* New York: Academic Press.

Russell, D. W., Altmaier, E., & Van Velzen, D. (1987). Job-related stress, social-support, and burnout among classroom teachers. *Journal of Applied Psychology, 72,* 269–274.

Russett, B. (1982). Defense expenditures and national well-being. *American Political Science Review, 76,* 767–777.

Sacarto, D. M. (1985, November). *Economic conflicts: Model program for dispute resolution.* National Conference of the State Legislature, Denver, CO. Whole issue.

Salem, P. J., & Berrios, N. L. (1987). *The communication differences of effective and ineffective negotiators: An analysis of U.S. and Latin American perceptions.* Paper presented at the annual meeting of the International Communication Association, Montreal.

Schelling, T. C. (1960). *The strategy of conflict.* Cambridge, MA: Harvard University Press.

Schilling, R. F., II (1987). Limitations of social support. *Social Service Review, 61,* 19–31.

Schuler, R. S. (1975). Role perceptions, satisfaction, and performance: A partial reconciliation. *Journal of Applied Psychology, 60,* 683–687.

Schurr, P., & Ozanne, J. (1985). Influences on exchange processes: Buyer's preconceptions of a seller's trustworthiness and bargaining toughness. *Journal of Consumer Research, 11,* 939–953.

Scodel, A., Minas, J., Ratoosh, P., & Lipetz, M. (1959). Some descriptive aspects of two-person non-zero-sum games. *Journal of Conflict Resolution, 3,* 114–119.

Seers, A., McGee, G. W., Serey, T. T., & Graen, G. B. (1983). The interaction of job stress and social support: A strong interference investigation. *Academy of Management Journal, 26,* 273–284.

Selby, P. (1979). The fine art of engineering an arbitration system to fit the needs of the parties: The United Mine Workers and the Bituminous Coal Operators. *Proceedings of the Thirty-Second Annual Meeting of the National Academy of Arbitrators.* (pp. 181–197). Washington, D.C.: The Bureau of National Affairs.

Sherman, S. J., Cialdini, R., Schwartzman, S., & Reynolds, P. (1985). Imagining can heighten or lower the perceived likelihood of contracting a disease: The mediating effect of ease of imagery. *Personality and Social Psychology Bulletin, 11,* 118–127.

Shirer, W. (1960). *The rise and fall of the third reich.* Greenwich, CT: Fawcett.

Shorett, A. J. (1980). The role of the mediator in environmental disputes. *Environmental Professional, 2,* 58–61.

Shrauger, J. S., & Osborne, T. M. (1981). The relative accuracy of self-predictions and judgments by others in psychological assessment. *Psychological Bulletin, 90,* 322–351.

Siegel, S., & Fouraker, L. E. (1960). *Bargaining and group decision making: Experiments in bilateral monopoly.* New York: McGraw-Hill.

Sillars, A. I. (1980). Attributions and interpersonal conflict resolution. *Communication Monographs, 47,* 180–200.

____. (1981). The sequential and distributional structure of conflict interactions as a function of attributions concerning the locus of responsibility and stability of conflicts. In D. Nimmo (Ed.), *Communication yearbook 4* (pp. 217–36). New Brunswick, NJ: Transaction Books.

Simon, H. (1959). Theories of decision-making in economic and behavioral science. *American Economic Review, 49,* 253–283.

Slovic, P. (1975). Choice between equally valued alternatives. *Journal of Experimental Psychology: Human Perception and Performance, 1,* 280–287.

Slovic, P., Fischhoff, B., & Lichtenstein, S. (1982). Response mode, framing, and information-processing effects in risk assessment. In R. Hogarth (Ed.), *New directions for methodology of social and behavioral science: Question framing and response consistency* (pp. 219–227). San Francisco, CA: Jossey-Bass.

Smith, M. J. (1988). *Contemporary communication research methods.* Belmont, CA: Wadsworth.

Smoke, G. H. (1984). *National security and the nuclear dilemma: An introduction to the American experience.* Menlo Park, CA: Addison-Wesley.

Snyder, G. H. (1961). *Deterrence and defense: Toward a theory of national security.* Princeton, NJ: Princeton University Press.

Spector, P. E. (1987). Method variance as an artifact in self-reported affect and perceptions at work: Myth or significant problem? *Journal of Applied Psychology, 72,* 438–443.

Spector, P. E., & Levine, E. (1987). Meta-analysis for integrating study outcomes: A Monte Carlo study of its susceptibility to Type I and Type II errors. *Journal of Applied Psychology, 72,* 3–9.

Staw, B. M., & Ross, J. (1987). Behavior in escalation situations: Antecedents, prototypes, and solutions. *Research in Organizational Behavior, 9,* 39–78.

Stein, J. (1988). Building politics in psychology. *Political Psychology, 9,* 245–271.

Steinbruner, J. D. (1974). *The cybernetic theory of decision: New dimensions of political analysis.* Princeton, NJ: Princeton University Press.

____. (1982). The doubtful presumption of rationality. In J. F. Reichart & S. R. Sturm (Eds.), *American defense policy* (5th ed.) (pp. 658–667). Princeton, NJ: Princeton University Press.

___. (1983). Beyond rational deterrence: The struggle for new conceptions. In K. Knorr (Ed.) *Power, strategy, and security* (pp. 118–131). Princeton, NJ: Princeton University Press.

Stewart, C. J., & Cash, W. B., Jr. (1988). *Interviewing: Principles and practices* (5th ed.). Dubuque, IA: William C. Brown.

Stiff, J. (1986). Cognitive processing of persuasive message cues: A meta-analytic review of the effects of supporting information on attitudes. *Communication Monographs, 53,* 75–89.

Street, R. L. (1986). Interaction processes and outcomes in interviews. In M. L. McLaughlin (Ed.), *Communication yearbook 9* (pp. 215–250). Beverly Hills, CA: Sage.

Susskind, L. (1981). Environmental mediation and the accountability problem. *Vermont Law Review, 6,* 1–47.

Susskind, L., & Weinstein, A. (1981). Towards a theory of environmental dispute resolution. *Boston College Environmental Affairs Law Review, 9,* 311–357.

Sutton, R., & Kramer, R. M. (in press). Transforming failure into success: Impression management, the Reagan administration, and the Iceland arms control talks. In R. Kahn, M. Zald, & R. Sutton (Eds.), *International conflict and cooperation: An organizational perspective.* San Francisco, CA: Jossey-Bass.

Talbot, A. R. (1983). *Settling things — six case studies in environmental mediation.* Washington, D.C.: The Conservation Foundation.

Tengler, C. D., & Jablin, F. M. (1983). Effects of question type, orientation, and sequencing in the employment interview. *Communication Monographs, 50,* 245–263.

Tetlock, P. E. (1986). Psychological advice on foreign policy: What do we have to contribute? *American Psychologist, 41,* 557–567.

___. (1988). Monitoring the integrative complexity of American and Soviet policy rhetoric: What can be learned? *Journal of Social Issues, 44,* 101–133.

Tetlock, P. E., & McGuire, C. E. (1986). Cognitive perspectives on foreign policy. In R. K. White (Ed.), *Psychology and the prevention of prevention of nuclear war* (pp. 255–273). New York: New York University Press.

Thaler, R. (1985). Mental accounting and consumer choice. *Marketing Science, 4,* 199–214.

Thayer, L. (1982). What would a theory of communication be for? *Journal of Applied Communication Research, 10*, 21–28.

Theye, L. D., & Seiler, W. J. (1979). Interaction analysis in collective bargaining: An alternative approach to the prediction of negotiated outcomes. In D. Nimmo (Ed.), *Communication yearbook 3* (pp. 375–394). Newbury Park, CA: Sage.

Thomas, K. W. (1976). Conflict and conflict management. In M. D. Dunette (Ed.), *Handbook of industrial and organizational psychology* (pp. 889–935). Chicago, IL: Rand-McNally.

____. (in press). Conflict and negotiation processes. In M. Dunette (Ed.), *Handbook of industrial and organizational psychology* (2nd ed.). Chicago, IL: Rand-McNally.

Thomas, K. W., & Schmidt, W. H. (1976). A survey of managerial interests with respect to conflict. *Academy of Management Journal, 19*, 315–318.

Tjosvold, D. (1974). Threat as a low-power person's strategy in bargaining: Social face and tangible outcomes. *International Journal of Group Tensions, 16*, 494–510.

____. (1977). The effects of constituent's affirmation and the opposing negotiator's self-presentation in bargaining between unequal status groups. *Organizational Behavior and Human Performance, 18*, 146–157.

____. (1982). Effects of the approach to controversy on superiors' incorporation of subordinates' information in decision making. *Journal of Applied Psychology, 67*, 189–193.

____. (1984). Cooperation theory and organizations. *Human Relations, 37*, 743–767.

____. (1985). Implications of controversy research for management. *Journal of Management, 11*, 221–238.

____. (1986a). Dynamics of interdependence in organizations. *Human Relations, 39*, 517–540.

____. (1986b). *Working together to get things done: Managing for organizational productivity.* Boston, MA: Lexington.

____. (1989). Interdependence approach to conflict management in organizations. In M. A. Rahim (Ed.), *Managing conflict: An interdisciplinary approach* (pp. 41–50). New York: Praeger.

Tjosvold, D., & Deemer, D. K. (1980). Effects of controversy within a cooperative or competitive context on organizational decision making. *Journal of Applied Psychology, 65*, 590–595.

Tjosvold, D., & Johnson, D. W. (1977). The effects of controversy on perspective-taking. *Journal of Educational Psychology, 69,* 679–685.

___. (1978). Controversy within a cooperative or competitive context and cognitive perspective taking. *Contemporary Educational Psychology, 3,* 376–386.

Touval, S. (1982). *The peace brokers: Mediators in the Arab-Israeli conflict 1948–1979.* Princeton, NJ: Princeton University Press.

Truman, D. (1951). *The governmental process.* New York: Knopf.

Turnbull, A. A., Strickland, L., & Shaver, K. G. (1976). Medium of communication, differential power, and phasing of concessions: Negotiating success and attributions to the opponent. *Human Communication Research, 2,* 262–270.

Tversky, A., & Kahneman, D. (1986). Rational choice and the framing of decisions. *Journal of Business, 59,* 251–279.

Valtin, R. (1978). The bituminous coal experiment. *Labor Law Journal, 29,* 469–476.

Van Zandt, H. F. (1970, November/December). How to negotiate in Japan. *Harvard Business Review,* 45–56.

Wagner, R., de Rivera, J., & Watkins, M. (1988). Psychology and the promotion of peace. *Journal of Social Issues, 44,* whole issue.

Waldo, D. (1948). *The administrative state.* New York: The Ronald Press.

Wall, J. (1977). Apparently conditioning a negotiator's concession making. *Journal of Experimental Social Psychology, 13,* 431–440.

___. (1981). An investigation of reciprocity and reinforcement theories of bargaining behavior. *Organizational Behavior and Human Performance, 27,* 267–385.

Wall, J., & Rude, D. E. (1985). Judicial mediation: Techniques, strategies, and situational effects. *Journal of Social Issues, 41,* 47–63.

___. (1987). Judges' mediation of settlement negotiations. *Journal of Applied Psychology, 72,* 234–239.

___. (1988, August). *The judge as a mediator.* Paper presented at the annual meeting of the Academy of Management, Anaheim, CA.

Wall, J., & Schiller, L. F. (1983). The judge off the bench: A mediator in civil settlement negotiations. In M. Bazerman & R. J. Lewicki (Eds.), *Negotiating in organizations* (pp. 117–192). Beverly Hills, CA: Sage.

Walton, R. E., & McKersie, R. B. (1965). *A behavioral theory of labor negotiations: An analysis of a social interaction system.* New York: McGraw-Hill.

Weber, R. P. (1985). *Basic content analysis.* Beverly Hills, CA: Sage.

Weingart, L. R., Thompson, L. L., Bazerman, M. H., & Carroll, J. S. (1988). *Tactics in integrative negotiations* (Working paper no. 22). Chicago: Northwestern University, Kellogg Graduate School of Management.

Weiss, C. H. (1972). *Evaluation research: Methods of assessing program effectiveness.* Englewood Cliffs, NJ: Prentice-Hall.

West, W. F. (1988, June/July). The growth of internal conflict in administrative regulation. *Public Administration Review,* 773–782.

White, R. K. (1986). *Psychology and the prevention of nuclear war.* New York: New York University Press.

Williams, G. R. (1983). *Legal negotiation and settlement.* St. Paul, MN: West.

Williams, S. (1901). *The middle kingdom.* New York: Scribner's Sons.

Wilson, W. (1987). The study of administration. *Political Science Quarterly, 102,* 197–222.

Wolf, F. (1986). *Meta-analysis.* Beverly Hills, CA: Sage.

Wright, P. (1981). Organizational behavior in Islamic firms. *Management International Review, 21,* 86–94.

Yeschke, C. L. (1987). *Interviewing: An introduction to interrogation.* Springfield, IL: Charles C. Thomas.

Young, O. R. (1972). Intermediaries: Additional thoughts on third parties. *Journal of Conflict Resolution, 16,* 51–65.

Zartman, W. I., Ed. (1978). *The negotiation process: Theories and applications.* Beverly Hills, CA: Sage.

Author Index

Subject Index

About the Editor and
Contributors

EDITOR-IN-CHIEF

M. AFZALUR RAHIM is Professor of Management at Western Kentucky University. He holds an M.Com. (Dacca, Bangladesh), M.B.A. (Miami, Ohio), and a Ph.D. (Graduate School of Business, University of Pittsburgh). Dr. Rahim teaches courses on strategic management, organizational behavior, and research methodology. He is the author of more than 65 articles and book chapters, 5 cases, and 3 instruments on power and conflict. He is the author of 5 books, including *Managing Conflict in Organizations* (Praeger, 1986), *Managing Conflict: An Interdisciplinary Approach* (Praeger, 1989) and *Rahim Organizational Conflict Inventories: Professional Manual* (1983), and is the founder and current president of the International Association for Conflict Management and editor of the *International Journal of Conflict Management*.

CONTRIBUTORS

MIKE ALLEN is currently Assistant Professor at the University of Wisconsin-Milwaukee. He received his Ph.D. in Communication from Michigan State University in 1987. His areas of research emphasis are methodology, argumentation, and theoretical modeling of communication processes. A special emphasis is placed on linking the theoretical with the practical to improve both thinking and practice. His current projects in conflict management involve the summarizing of the bargaining literature using meta-analysis. He has published articles in *Conciliation Courts Review, Communication Education, Mediation Quarterly, Communication Monographs, Argument and Advocacy,* and *Communication Research.*

ROBERT A. BARON is Professor and Chair of the Department of Psychology and Professor of Organizational Behavior in the School of Management at Rensselaer Polytechnic Institute. A University of Iowa Ph.D. (1968), he has held academic positions at Purdue University, Princeton University, the University of Minnesota, University of Texas, and University of South Carolina. He was a Visiting Fellow at the University of Oxford (1982), and served as a Program Director at the National Science Foundation (1979–1981). He is the author of more than 80 journal articles and the author or co-author of 18 books. Dr. Baron's current research interests focus on techniques for managing organizational conflict, self-presentation during employment interviews, and the impact of physical work settings on task performance and productivity.

J. WALTON BLACKBURN is Assistant to the President of Creighton University for Planning and Institutional Research. He holds a B.A. from Earlham College, a Master of City Planning from Ohio State, a Master of Professional Studies from Cornell, and a Ph.D. in Public Administration from Virginia Polytechnic Institute and State University. He has written a variety of planning, public administration, and applied research reports and articles, including "Environmental Mediation as an Alternative to Litigation" in the *Policy Studies Journal.*

G. STEVE BOURNE is Associate Professor of Management at Bluefield State College (W. Va.), with a teaching emphasis in Industrial Relations. He also serves as the Chair of the Division of Business. Dr. Bourne received his M.S. from Radford University and his Ph.D. from Virginia Tech. His research interests include collective bargaining, arbitration, compensation issues, and fair employment practices. Dr. Bourne is on the Board of Directors of the West Virginia Industrial Relations Research Association and is actively involved with the West Virginia Labor-Management Council's Southern Center for Labor-Management

Initiatives. He is also a member of the Academy of Management and Southern Management Association. Dr. Bourne has engaged in a variety of consulting activities for both management and labor.

GABRIEL F. BUNTZMAN (Ph.D. University of North Carolina) is Assistant Professor at Western Kentucky University. His publications include articles in *The International Journal of Conflict Management, The Journal of Psychology,* and *Psychological Reports* as well as pieces in two books in the conflict area, *Managing Conflict: An Interdisciplinary Approach* and *Theory and Research in Conflict Management.* His research interests are in the areas of conflict and organization performance, mediation, and arbitration.

NANCY A. BURRELL (Ph.D., Communication, Michigan State University) is Assistant Professor at the University of Wisconsin-Milwaukee. She has published in *Mediation Quarterly, Communication Monographs,* and *Communication Research.* Her research interests center on the role of language in discourse analysis in the contexts of mediation, relational development, and decision making. Currently, she is working with the Milwaukee Mediation Center, examining the training program for peer mediation using elementary, junior high, and high school students.

JOAN G. DAHL is Associate Professor of Management at the School of Business Administration and Economics, California State University, Northridge. She holds a Ph.D. in Business Administration from the University of Washington and an M.B.A. from the University of Oregon. She teaches courses in labor relations, collective bargaining and human resource management. Dr. Dahl's research interests focus primarily on productivity in negotiations.

GERALD DAVIS is a doctoral candidate in Organizational Behavior at the Stanford University Graduate School of Business. His research interests include the relation between ownership and control in large corporations, applications of organizational theory to international relations, and the organization of mental health and drug treatment services.

WILLIAM DONOHUE is Professor of Communication at Michigan State University. He received his Ph.D. in Communication from The from The Ohio State University in 1976. His conflict-related research interests focus on three areas: communication strategies in labor-management bargaining to discover the methods negotiators use to intermix relational and substantive information; communicative competence in divorce mediation settings, which seeks to describe how mediators increase cooperativeness among divorcing couples; and the management of hostage negotiation situations to describe the varieties of communication strategies negotiators use to gain control and ultimately resolve various terrorist activities.

JAMES B. DWORKIN is Associate Dean of the Krannert Graduate School of Management and Professor of Organizational Behavior and Human Resource Management at Purdue University. His research and teaching interests are in the areas of labor relations and collective bargaining. Dr. Dworkin is active as an arbitrator and mediator in a wide variety of labor-management disputes in the private and public sectors.

TRICIA S. JONES is Associate Professor of Speech Communication at the University of Denver. Dr. Jones earned her M.A. in Communication from Purdue University (1980) and her Ph.D. in Communication from Ohio State University (1985). She teaches courses in dispute resolution, negotiation, and mediation at the University of Denver and has published several articles examining the use and effect of communication strategies and tactics in negotiation and divorce mediation.

PHILIP K. KIENAST is Associate Professor of Management and Organization at the Graduate School of Business Administration at the University of Washington. He holds a Ph.D. in Social Science and an MLIR, both from Michigan State University. He is the former chair of Washington State's Public Employment Relations Commission. He is an arbitrator of labor disputes and a member of the National Academy of Arbitrators, having served on its research committee from 1981–1985. Dr. Kienast's current research and teaching focus on negotiations, dispute settlement, labor relations, and compensation.

M. KAMIL KOZAN received his Ph.D. in Organizational Studies from UCLA and taught for several years in Turkey and Jordan. He is currently Associate Professor of Management at St. John Fisher College in Rochester, New York. His research interests include organizational commitment and conflict management and cross-cultural issues in organizational conflict.

RODERICK KRAMER is Associate Professor of Organizational Behavior at the Stanford University Graduate School of Business. He received his Ph.D. in social psychology from the University of California, Los Angeles, in June, 1985. His current research interests include group decision making, social conflict and cooperation, social dilemmas, the arms race, and psychological aspects of negotiation. He has taught courses on conflict management and negotiation, group decision making and small group dynamics, and organizational behavior.

DEBRA MEYERSON is Assistant Professor of Organizational Behavior and Human Resources at the School of Business, University of Michigan. She received her Ph.D. in Organizational Behavior from the Graduate School of Business at Stanford University. Her research focuses on organizational culture, the experience of ambiguity, and decision making. She is also interested in how individuals assign meaning to various types of work experiences.

THOMAS J. PAVLAK is Professor of Public Administration and Director of the Public Administration Institute at Fairleigh Dickinson University. He received his Ph.D. in Political Science from the University of Illinois at Urbana-Champaign. Before assuming his current position, he was on the faculty of the Graduate School of Public and International Affairs at the University of Pittsburgh, where he had served in recent years as the Director of Doctoral Studies and Director of the MPA Program. Professor Pavlak's recent published work includes articles on AIDS in the workplace, administrative justice, and the grievance process and workplace justice.

GERALD M. POPS is Professor of Public Administration at West Virginia University in Morgantown. He holds a Ph.D. from Syracuse University's Maxwell School and a J.D. from the University of California at Berkeley School of Law. He is the author of *Emergence of the Public Sector Arbitrator* (1976), and co-author, with Max O. Stephenson, of *Conflict Resolution in the Policy Process* (1987). Dr. Pops has also published journal articles on such subjects as conflict management, administrative justice and administrative law judges, property tax dispute settlement, and administrative ethics.

JERALD F. ROBINSON is Professor of Employment Relations at Virginia Polytechnic Institute and State University. He received his undergraduate degree from Rhodes College, an M.A. from Duke University, and Ph.D. from the University of Illinois. Dr. Robinson has taught at Furman University and the University of Missouri, coming to Virginia Tech in 1970. He also worked as a research assistant at the Brookings Institution. Dr. Robinson is a practicing arbitrator, and his research interests include conflict management, grievance and arbitration issues, and employee rights.

MAX O. STEPHENSON, JR., serves as Assistant Professor of Urban Affairs and Planning at Virginia Polytechnic Institute and State University. He obtained his Ph.D. from the University of Virginia (1985) and has taught previously at West Virginia University. His current research focuses on the development of a more adequate theory of interorganizational policy making and conflict management.

BECKY STEWART is Assistant Professor of Communication Arts at Aquinas College in Grand Rapids, Michigan. She is a doctoral candidate at Michigan State University in the Department of Family and Child Ecology. She has conducted research in the areas of conflict management and divorce mediation. Her research has been presented at the International Communication Association and Speech Communication Association Conventions. Her current project involves the examination of ethical responsibilities involved in family communication.

DEAN TJOSVOLD (Ph.D., Minnesota, 1972) is Professor, Faculty of Business Administration, Simon Fraser University, Burnaby, BC. He has published more than 100 articles on managing conflict, cooperation, and competition, decision making, power, and other management issues. With David W. Johnson he edited *Productive Conflict Management: Perspectives for Organizations* (1983, 1989), and with Mary Tjosvold has written two books for health care professionals. He has published *Working Together to Get Things Done: Managing for Organizational Productivity* (1986) and *Managing Conflict: The Key to Making an Organization Work* (1989). He is presently writing *The Team*

Organization: Applying Group Research to the Workplace and *The Conflict-Positive Organization: Stimulate Diversity and Create Unity.* He is a partner in several health care businesses in Minnesota.

JAMES A. WALL, JR., is Professor and Chair of the Department of Management in the College of Business and Public Administration, University of Missouri, Columbia. He received an A.B. from Davidson College and an M.B.A. as well as a Ph.D. from the University of North Carolina. Before assuming his position at Missouri, he was Associate Professor at Indiana University. Professor Wall is the author of *Negotiation: Theory and Practice* (1985) and *Bosses* (1987). His research includes articles on negotiation and mediation in journals such as *American Journal of Trial Advocacy, Journal of Applied Psychology, Journal of Conflict Resolution, Journal of Dispute Resolution, Journal of Experimental Social Psychology, Journal of Personality and Social Psychology, Judicature,* and *Organizational Behavior and Human Decision Processes.*

DEANNA F. WOMACK (Ph.D., University of Kansas, 1982) is Lecturer in Management Communication, Harvard University Graduate School of Business Administration. Her primary research interest is communication theory concerning organizational conflict and negotiations. She has investigated orientations to conflict, male-female differences in negotiation, and argumentation and compliance-gaining strategies of negotiators and mediators. Her articles and chapters have appeared in *Management Communication Quarterly, Argumentation and Advocacy (JAFA), Rhetoric Society Quarterly,* the *Negotiation Sourcebook, Handbook of Applied Communication Research, Advances in Gender and Communication Research,* and *Oldspeak/Newspeak: Rhetorical Transformations.* With Dominic Infante and Andrew Rancer, she is co-author of *Building Communication Theory.*